The New York Times
ON THE WEB

Trivia

QUIZ BOOK

by

RAYMOND HAMEL

TIMES
T
BOOKS

Library of Congress Cataloging-in-Publication Data

Hamel, Raymond.
    The New York times trivia quiz book / by Raymond Hamel. — 1st
1999 ed.
        p.   cm.
    ISBN 0-8129-3057-6
    1. Questions and answers. 2. New York times—Miscellanea.
I. Times Books (New York, N.Y.) II. New York times. III. Title.
IV. Titile: Trivia quiz book.
AG195.H23 1999
301.02—dc21
                                                                99-20688

The New York Times on the Web World Internet Address:
www.nytimes.com
Random House Puzzles Website Address:
www.puzzlesatrandom.com

Test Design by H. Roberts
Typography by Mark Frnka
Manufactured in the United States of America
2 4 6 8 9 7 5 3
First Edition

Acknowledgments

I would like to extend the largest of all possible thank yous to Dale Jellings. He has been my friend, advisor, and collaborator on many projects over the past 20 years. His knowledge and encouragement helped make this book possible.

Big thanks to several people associated with The New York Times on the Web who have contributed to this effort: Will Shortz, Rich Meislin, William Stockton, Bill Doody, John Haskins, Hilda Cosmo, and Rob Fixmer. I thank my editor at Times Books, Stan Newman, and his assistant, Mark Gottlieb, for the vision and guidance that turned an idea into a reality.

My appreciation goes out to the many folks who have taken the time to say how much they enjoy the challenge of The New York Times on the Web Noodle Nudgers. Look for the new quizzes at http://www.nytimes.com/diversions/.

Finally, a big "I love you" to Mom and Dad, who never questioned the sanity of a son who amassed boxes of notecards filled with obscure little bits of trivia. Unbounding love goes to my wife and biggest supporter, Barb, and my son, Ryan. Their patience knows no limits as I scramble to find pen and paper to jot down that elusive bit of information that will surely find its way into a future quiz.

Quiz #1 — Starts with "O"

1. What creature is considered a good luck symbol for the Detroit Red Wings hockey team?
A. Otter
B. Octopus
C. Owl
D. Oriole
E. Ostrich

2. What was the name of the midget who assisted comic book hero Mister Miracle?
A. Orion
B. Ork
C. Oberon
D. Odysseus
E. Owl

3. "Who Will Buy?," "I'd Do Anything," and "As Long As He Needs Me" were songs featured in what stage and movie musical?
A. "Oklahoma!"
B. "Oliver!"
C. "On the Town"
D. "Once Upon a Mattress"
E. "On a Clear Day You Can See Forever"

4. What piece of music was used as the opening theme song for the popular radio show "The Shadow"?
A. "Outrageous Conflict"
B. "Orpheus Descending"
C. "Out of the Shadows"
D. "Omphale's Spinning Wheel"
E. "Orange Festival"

5. What mythological figure was the title character in a Jean Cocteau film, a George Balanchine ballet, and a Claudio Monteverdi opera?
A. Oedipus
B. Orpheus
C. Odysseus
D. Ossian
E. Odin

6. Two of the three Andrews Sisters rode the 1940s nostalgia boom to Broadway in 1974 in a production of what play?
A. "Our Lives"
B. "Once Is Never Enough"
C. "On the River"
D. "Over There"
E. "Old Enough to Know Better"

7. In the 12th-century French epic, "Chanson de Roland," what was the name of the wonderful horn of Roland that could be heard for 20 miles?
A. Olivant
B. Orzabal
C. Orestes
D. Orgolgio
E. Oberon

8. What was the name of the last living dusky sparrow that died in 1986?
A. Orange Band
B. Orville
C. Old Dusky
D. O'Hara
E. On the Hill

Answers to Quiz #1 — **Starts with "O"**

1. **(B) Octopus.** Someone threw an octopus onto the ice during the 1952 playoffs which was won by the Red Wings. Fans of the NHL team renew the tradition every year the team makes the playoffs.

2. **(C) Oberon.** Mister Miracle was a DC Comics hero from the planet of New Genesis, also featured in "The New Gods" comics. A master escape artist, his secret identity was, appropriately, Scott Free.

3. **(B) "Oliver!".** The Broadway production of "Oliver!" won Tony Awards in 1963 for Best Composer and Lyricist (Lionel Bart), Best Conductor and Musical Director (Donald Pippin), and Best Scenic Designer (Sean Kenny). The movie version won Oscars in 1968 for Best Picture, Best Director (Carol Reed), Best Musical Score (John Green), Best Art Direction, and Best Sound.

4. **(D) "Omphale's Spinning Wheel".** The symphonic poem "Le Rouet d'Omphale," Opus 31, was composed by the French composer Saint-Saëns in 1871.

5. **(B) Orpheus.** The titles are, respectively, "Orpheus" (1949), "Orpheus" (1948), and "La Favola d'Orfeo/The Fable of Orpheus" (1607). Orpheus was a mythological character who ventured to the underworld to rescue his love, Eurydice. Orpheus was allowed to return to life with Eurydice provided he did not look back at her until the journey was complete. Just before the journey was to end, Orpheus could no longer resist and looked back to see Eurydice sink back to Hades.

6. **(D) "Over There".** The Andrews Sisters (LaVerne, Maxene, and Patti) were a popular harmony group during World War II, often appearing on radio and in films. Maxene and Patti staged "Over There" with a "new" third sister. A young John Travolta also appeared in "Over There."

7. **(A) Olivant.** Roland was killed in a Saracen attack when he refused to surrender his pride and use his horn to summon help until it was too late.

8. **(A) Orange Band.** The last of the few living dusky sparrows were all male and therefore unable to reproduce. Orange Band was kept in Disney's Discovery Island at Disney World until his death.

Quiz #2 — **Seven Chances**

1. What city was the setting for Nathaniel Hawthorne's "House of the Seven Gables"?
A. Boston
B. Salem
C. New Haven
D. Concord
E. Lexington

2. What college football team once featured linemen nicknamed the 7 Mules?
A. Harvard
B. Wisconsin
C. Michigan State
D. Notre Dame
E. Florida

3. Which Shakespearean character said "All the world's a stage" and philosophized about the seven ages of man?
A. Romeo
B. Falstaff
C. King Lear
D. Olivia
E. Jaques

4. Gen. Robert E. Lee successfully defended what city during the U.S. Civil War's Seven Days' Battle?
A. Knoxville
B. Charleston
C. Richmond
D. Atlanta
E. Charlottesville

5. When Mickey Mantle's jersey #7 was retired at Yankee Stadium in 1969, what baseball great presented Mantle with the plaque?
A. Joe DiMaggio
B. Ty Cobb
C. Billy Martin
D. Babe Ruth
E. Roger Maris

6. While John Glenn made his historic orbit of the Earth in Friendship 7, what astronaut flew in Freedom 7?
A. Alan Shepard
B. Virgil "Gus" Grissom
C. John Crippen
D. John Young
E. Ed White

7. What actor provided the sneezes for Sneezy in Disney's "Snow White and the Seven Dwarves"?
A. Clarence "Ducky" Nash
B. Alan Reed
C. Billy Gilbert
D. Dean Stockwell
E. Donald Sutherland

8. Which of the Seven Against Thebes was the only survivor of the battle against Eteocles?
A. Adrastus
B. Polynices
C. Amphiarus
D. Capaneus
E. Tydeus

Answers to Quiz #2 — **Seven Chances**

1. **(B) Salem.** Hawthorne was born in Salem, Massachusetts on July 4, 1804.

2. **(D) Notre Dame.** The linemen fronted for the Four Horsemen of Notre Dame in 1924. Their names were: Ed Huntsinger (end), Charles Collins (end), Joe Bach (tackle), Edgar Miller (tackle), Noble Kizer (guard), John Weibel (guard), Adam Walsh (center).

3. **(E) Jaques.** The line was part of Shakespeare's "As You Like It."

4. **(C) Richmond.** The Seven Days' Battle was a series of skirmishes between June 25 and July 1, 1862 at the Confederate capital at Richmond.

5. **(A) Joe DiMaggio.** Mantle had replaced DiMaggio as center fielder for the Yankees in 1951.

6. **(A) Alan Shepard.** Shepard was the first American in space, riding the tiny Freedom 7 to an altitude of 185 miles on May 5, 1961. All of the original astronauts included the number 7 when naming their spacecrafts to honor the original seven astronauts.

7. **(C) Billy Gilbert.** Billy Gilbert (1893-1971) was a comedian said to have made the act of sneezing an artistic achievement. Gilbert phoned Disney after reading about the upcoming movie production in "Variety" and learning that one of the dwarves would be named Sneezy. After his impromptu audition for Disney, he was hired on the spot.

8. **(A) Adrastus**. In Greek mythology, this was an ill-fated expedition against the usurper Eteocles of Thebes to restore Polynices to the throne.

Quiz #3 — **Clowning Around**

1. What famous clown was originally created by Capitol Records in the 1940s as a character featured in a series of children's records?
A. Bozo
B. Bip
C. Koko
D. Clarabelle
E. Weepy Willie

2. "Cathy's Clown" was a #1 song for the Everly Brothers in 1960. What country singer's cover version hit #1 in 1989?
A. Vince Gill
B. Trisha Yearwood
C. Suzy Bogguss
D. Reba McEntire
E. Joe Diffie

3. What Stephen King novel featured a murderous clown figure called Pennywise?
A. "Gerald's Game"
B. "Insomnia"
C. "The Tommyknockers"
D. "The Dark Half"
E. "It"

4. What is the name of the hunchbacked clown in the opera "Pagliacci"?
A. Tonio
B. Silvio
C. Canio
D. Beppe
E. Calaban

5. In baseball's Negro Leagues, what city was the home of the Clowns from 1946 to 1950?
A. Lincoln
B. Philadelphia
C. Indianapolis
D. St. Paul
E. Columbus

6. What winner of a Best Actress Oscar co-wrote the title tune for the 1965 Best Picture nominee "A Thousand Clowns"?
A. Julie Andrews
B. Shirley Booth
C. Judy Holliday
D. Cher
E. Barbra Streisand

7. What rock singer ran for mayor of San Francisco in 1979 with a platform requiring all downtown businessmen to wear clown suits?
A. Neil Diamond
B. Ric Ocasek
C. Chuck Berry
D. David Lee Roth
E. Jello Biafra

8. What American circus clown legend was said to be a model for the original drawings of Uncle Sam done by Thomas Nast?
A. Dan Rice
B. Felix Adler
C. Joe Grimaldi
D. Lou Jacobs
E. Otto Griebling

Answers to Quiz #3 — **Clowning Around**

1. **(A) Bozo.** One of the men hired by Capitol Records to play Bozo the Clown at public appearances was Larry Harmon. Harmon obtained the rights to Bozo in 1956 and brought him to TV where he has enjoyed a long run in syndication.

2. **(D) Reba McEntire.** Reba's version was a mournful version of the upbeat number done by the Everlys. Dolly Parton recorded a demo of the song similar to Reba's, but never released it.

3. **(E) "It".** In the 1986 novel, "It," Pennywise was the fiend who lived in the sewers of Derry, Maine, using balloons to lure children to their deaths. Pennywise was played by Tim Curry in the 1990 TV mini-series adaptation of the novel.

4. **(A) Tonio.** The opera's plot: A theatrical troupe led by Canio arrives in the village of Calabria where the clown, Tonio, makes advances on Canio's wife, Nedda. Nedda drives him off with a whip, but not before Tonio overhears that she plans to leave Canio for her lover, a farmer named Silvio. After Tonio informs Canio, Canio demands Nedda tell him the name of her lover. When she refuses, he stabs her. Silvio rushes to her aid, only to also be stabbed by Canio.

5. **(C) Indianapolis.** In the Negro American Leagues, the Clowns represented Cincinnati in 1943 and 1945, Indianapolis in 1946-50, and both cities in 1944. Baseball Hall of Famer Oscar Charleston played for the Indianapolis Clowns.

6. **(C) Judy Holliday.** The title song was a collaboration between Judy Holliday and her saxophonist husband, Gerry Mulligan. Holliday died at the age of 43 before "A Thousand Clowns" was released.

7. **(E) Jello Biafra.** Jello Biafra, born Eric Boucher, was the leader of the San Francisco-based punk rock band, The Dead Kennedys.

8. **(A) Dan Rice.** The most familiar drawings of the lanky bearded Uncle Sam depicted him declaring "I Want You" in recruitment posters for WWI and WWII. The posters were drawn by James Montgomery Flagg who served as his own model.

Quiz #4 — **See Ya Later!**

1. What "Saturday Night Live" regular played a snippy flight attendant character who answered almost every request with "Bye bye"?
A. David Spade
B. Adam Sandler
C. Dennis Miller
D. Chris Rock
E. Chris Farley

2. What baseball player, nicknamed "Bye Bye," hit a season record 36 home runs in 1985 for the Kansas City Royals?
A. George Brett
B. Buddy Biancalana
C. Mike Brewer
D. Steve Balboni
E. Jim Sundberg

3. What U.S. state's motto translates into "By and by"?
A. Montana
B. Oregon
C. Idaho
D. Washington
E. Hawaii

4. Who ends his TV program every week by saying "Until next time...I bid you peace. Bye bye"?
A. Bob Barker
B. Geraldo Rivera
C. Robert Schuller
D. Conan O'Brien
E. Jeff Smith

5. What was the first name of the young girl who won a chance to be kissed by Conrad Birdie in the stage musical "Bye Bye Birdie"?
A. Linda
B. Chris
C. Jane
D. Kim
E. Nellie

6. Who wrote the music for the popular 1920s hit "Bye Bye Blackbird"?
A. Eddie Cantor
B. Hoagy Carmichael
C. Ray Henderson
D. George Gershwin
E. Harold Arlen

7. Who directed the 1968 movie "Bye Bye Braverman"?
A. Marlon Brando
B. George Roy Hill
C. Nicholas Roeg
D. Jerry Hopper
E. Sidney Lumet

8. What restaurant chain gets plenty of screen time in the 1995 film comedy "Bye Bye Love"?
A. McDonald's
B. Long John Silver's
C. Popeye's
D. Kentucky Fried Chicken
E. Applebee's

Answers to Quiz #4 — **See Ya Later!**

1. **(A) David Spade.** Spade was named the "Hot Stand-Up Comedian" of 1991 by "Rolling Stone" magazine. Spade also posed as a flight attendant in the movie "Tommy Boy."

2. **(D) Steve Balboni.** First baseman Balboni also set the Royals' club record with 166 strikeouts.

3. **(D) Washington.** Washington's state motto is "Alki" from the Chinook Indian language.

4. **(E) Jeff Smith.** Smith, the host of PBS' "The Frugal Gourmet," is also an ordained Methodist minister.

5. **(D) Kim.** The 1960 Tony-winning musical addressed the Generation Gap as Conrad Birdie (a clone of Elvis Presley) is about to leave to enter the Army. It was filmed in 1963 and brought to TV in 1996.

6. **(C) Ray Henderson.** "Bye Bye Blackbird" was popularized in 1926 by Eddie Cantor and the Duncan Sisters. It was also recorded by Russ Morgan and His Orchestra in 1948.

7. **(E) Sidney Lumet.** The plot revolves around four friends who get together to mourn the loss of "Braverman," the title character who is never seen.

8. **(A) McDonald's.** In "Bye Bye Love," not only do three pairs of divorced parents regularly exchange their kids by meeting at McDonald's, two of the film's characters are also employed by the hamburger palace franchise.

Quiz #5 — Odd Man Out

1. Which of the following tennis players did not win consecutive men's single's championships at the Wimbledon tennis tournament?
A. Rod Laver
B. Jimmy Connors
C. Boris Becker
D. John McEnroe
E. Bill Tilden

2. Which of the following was not an episode of the classic 1960s TV series "Star Trek"?
A. "Operation — Annihilate"
B. "Turnabout Intruder"
C. "Charlie X"
D. "Miri"
E. "Bem"

3. Which Speaker of the House did not belong to the majority party in the U.S. House of Representatives?
A. John Bell
B. Andrew Stevenson
C. James Orr
D. Thomas Reed
E. John Nance Garner

4. Which language does not belong to the Indo-European family?
A. Armenian
B. Greek
C. Yiddish
D. Finnish
E. Czech

5. Which of the following is not a species of whale?
A. Bryde's
B. Fin
C. Sei
D. Minke
E. Falkland Island

6. Which of the following was not a member of the Hollywood Ten?
A. Ring Lardner Jr.
B. Dalton Trumbo
C. Abraham Polonsky
D. Lester Cole
E. Edward Dmytryk

7. Which of the following is not a variety of sweet peas?
A. Rush Limbaugh
B. Brian Clough
C. Kiri Te Kanawa
D. Su Pollard
E. Alan Titchmarsh

8. Which one of the following popular TV shows did not run on CBS?
A. "Gunsmoke"
B. "The Lawrence Welk Show"
C. "The Millionaire"
D. "The Honeymooners"
E. "Alfred Hitchcock Presents"

Answers to Quiz #5 — Odd Man Out

1. (B) **Jimmy Connors.** Jimmy Connors was a two-time Wimbledon champ with victories in 1974 and 1982.

2. (E) **"Bem".** "Bem" was an episode of the animated "Star Trek" series that aired 1973-74 with voices provided by the original cast members.

3. (A) **John Bell.** Bell, a Whig from Tennessee, was elected Speaker during the 23rd Congress (1834-35) which had a Democratic majority.

4. (D) **Finnish.** The Finnish language, also called Suomi, is a member of the Finno-Ugric languages.

5. (E) **Falkland Island.** These whales are all members of the family Balaenopteridae, also known as rorquals — gigantic creatures which survive on tiny plankton. Also in this family is the blue whale. Weighing up to 150 tons, it is the largest animal ever to have lived on Earth.

6. (C) **Abraham Polonsky.** The Hollywood Ten was a group of producers, directors, and screenwriters singled out in 1947 by the House Committee on Un-American Activities (HUAC) as Communist-sympathizers when they refused to testify before Congress. The remaining members were Adrian Scott, Alvah Bessie, Sam Ornitz, Albert Maltz, John Howard Lawson, and Herbert Biberman. Abraham Polonsky was a screenwriter blackballed by the Hollywood community for nearly 20 years as an admitted Communist.

7. (A) **Rush Limbaugh.** Rush Limbaugh is a popular radio personality, but no one has named a plant after him yet.

8. (B) **"The Lawrence Welk Show".** All five shows debuted in 1955. "The Lawrence Welk Show" was a fixture on ABC's Saturday night lineup from 1955 to 1971, and continued as a syndicated show until 1982.

Quiz #6 — **Sweet Tooth**

1. Which of the following songs did not hit #1 on the Billboard pop charts?
A. "Sweet Dreams (Are Made of This)" by Eurhymthics
B. "Sweet Child o' Mine" by Guns N' Roses
C. "My Sweet Lord" by George Harrison
D. "One Sweet Day" by Mariah Carey and Boyz II Men
E. "Sweet Little Sixteen" by Chuck Berry

2. What movie musical was set in the fictional town of Sweethaven?
A. "Popeye"
B. "Bye Bye Birdie"
C. "Those Calloways"
D. "The Happiest Millionaire"
E. "Annie"

3. What TV western series was set in Sweetwater, Arizona?
A. "The Westerner"
B. "Cheyenne"
C. "Bret Maverick"
D. "Lancer"
E. "Nichols"

4. On the popular album, "Saturday Morning Cartoon's Greatest Hits," what cartoon theme song was performed by alternative rock guru Matthew Sweet?
A. "Scooby-Doo, Where Are You?"
B. "Josie and the Pussycats"
C. "Top Cat"
D. "Spider-Man"
E. "The Archies"

5. In what Shakespeare play would you encounter the character whom Slender calls "O sweet Anne Page"?
A. "Twelfth Night"
B. "Merry Wives of Windsor"
C. "Two Gentlemen of Verona"
D. "Hamlet"
E. "Richard III"

6. In what movie is the song "Sweet Georgia Brown" sung in Polish?
A. "Transylvania 6-5000"
B. "Midnight Run"
C. "Young Frankenstein"
D. "To Be or Not to Be"
E. "Man on a Tightrope"

7. What politician used the theme song "Sweet Adeline" in a successful campaign as mayor of Boston?
A. Warren G. Harding
B. Raymond Flynn
C. William Shields
D. John F. Fitzgerald
E. Thomas Calderan

8. "Sweet Leilani" won the Academy Award for Best Song of 1937. It was introduced in what movie starring Bing Crosby?
A. "Vogues of 1938"
B. "Shall We Dance"
C. "Waikiki Wedding"
D. "Make a Wish"
E. "Damsel in Distress"

Answers to Quiz #6 — **Sweet Tooth**

1. (E) **"Sweet Little Sixteen" by Chuck Berry.** "Sweet Little Sixteen" held the #2 spot for three weeks in 1958. It was kept out of the #1 spot by the Champs' hit "Tequila."

2. (A) **"Popeye".** Popeye's hometown in the comic strips was Sweetwater. "Bye Bye Birdie" was set in Sweet Apple, Ohio.

3. (C) **"Bret Maverick".** In 1981, James Garner returned to the character of Bret Maverick with this short-lived NBC series. Bret was no longer the gambling man from the 1960s series "Maverick," but a mature ranch owner and solid citizen. Garner also starred in the 1971-72 NBC western series "Nichols" as Nichols, the sheriff of Nichols, Arizona.

4. (A) **"Scooby-Doo, Where Are You?".** Sweet's albums include "Girlfriend," "Altered Beast," and "100 Percent Fun."

5. (B) **"Merry Wives of Windsor".** Anne is the daughter of Mistress Page, an associate of Falstaff.

6. (D) **"To Be or Not to Be".** Mel Brooks remade the 1942 Jack Benny-Carole Lombard comedy "To Be or Not to Be" in 1983. The plot of the film involves a troupe of theatrical actors who become involved with the Polish Underground during World War II. Anne Bancroft and Mel Brooks performed "Sweet Georgia Brown." The song is best recognized as the theme song of the Harlem Globetrotters.

7. (D) **John F. Fitzgerald.** John "Honey Fitz" Fitzgerald was the grandfather of Pres. John Fitzgerald Kennedy. Kennedy named his presidential yacht Honey Fitz to honor the man.

8. (C) **"Waikiki Wedding".** "Sweet Leilani" was composed by Harry Owens and sung by Bing Crosby. This movie also introduced the song "Blue Hawaii" later made popular in the 1960s by Elvis Presley.

Quiz #7 — **Straight As an Arrow**

1. What organization allows for the induction of members into the Order of the Arrow?
A. Sweet Adelines Inc.
B. Boy Scouts of America
C. Odd Fellows of America
D. The Kiwanis
E. The Elks

2. What TV special introduced the Nilsson song "Me and My Arrow"?
A. "The Prince and the Pauper"
B. "The Point"
C. "Our World"
D. "A Mouse, a Mystery and Me"
E. "Mr. Willowby's Christmas"

3. Two Americans won gold medals at both the 1976 and 1984 Summer Olympics. One was track star Edwin Moses. What archer was the other?
A. Jay Barrs
B. Richard McKinney
C. Darrell Pace
D. Kirk Ethridge
E. Butch Johnson

4. What NFL team once featured a helmet marked by a gold and white arrow on a burgundy background?
A. Seattle Seahawks
B. Kansas City Chiefs
C. San Diego Chargers
D. New England Patriots
E. Washington Redskins

5. Who wrote the lines: "I shot an arrow toward the sky/It hit a white cloud passing by/The cloud fell dying to the shore/I don't shoot arrows anymore"?
A. Edward Lear
B. Henry Wadsworth Longfellow
C. Shel Silverstein
D. Steve Allen
E. Henry Gibson

6. What TV talk show host kept a rubber chicken and a wooden arrow at his desk for good luck during tapings?
A. Johnny Carson
B. Merv Griffin
C. Jack Paar
D. David Frost
E. Dick Cavett

7. What was the name of the horse ridden by comic book cowboy Golden Arrow?
A. Hurricane
B. Lightning
C. Thunder
D. White Wind
E. Tornado

8. In what country was the Avro Arrow, a supersonic interceptor, developed?
A. Mexico
B. Brazil
C. India
D. China
E. Canada

Answers to Quiz #7 — **Straight As an Arrow**

1. **(B) Boy Scouts of America.** The Order of the Arrow is the Scouts' national honor camper association.

2. **(B) "The Point".** The 1971 TV special, "The Point," was based on a story written by Harry Nilsson. It is the tale of Oblio, a round-headed boy in a world of pointy-headed people, and his faithful dog, Arrow. The original TV version was narrated by Dustin Hoffman. When the program was released on videotape, Ringo Starr was the narrator.

3. **(C) Darrell Pace.** Darrell Pace first tried archery in 1970. Six years and three months later, he won his first Olympic gold medal in Montreal. Pace also won a silver medal in 1988. He has since become the most decorated archer in America.

4. **(E) Washington Redskins.** The Redskins have had four different helmet designs — a single white feather down the back of a burgundy helmet, a gold and white arrow on the sides of a burgundy helmet, a gold helmet with a white circle containing a burgundy "R," and the current design.

5. **(C) Shel Silverstein.** Shel Silverstein was the author of the popular poetry collections "A Light in the Attic" and "Where the Sidewalk Ends," adored by both adults and children. Silverstein was also an accomplished songwriter whose songs include "A Boy Named Sue," "Cover of the Rolling Stone," "Sylvia's Mother," and "The Unicorn."

6. **(A) Johnny Carson.** Johnny Carson started in TV as a game show host. He met Ed McMahon when the two worked together in 1958 on "Who Do You Trust?" Carson first hosted the "Tonight" show in 1958 as a guest host for Jack Paar. He took over the job full time in October 1962 until he relinquished his desk to Jay Leno in May 1992.

7. **(D) White Wind.** Whenever Golden Arrow mounted his steed, he would cry "Let's scratch gravel!" An unusual cowboy hero, he favored the bow and arrow over guns, shooting golden arrows. He appeared in Fawcett comics from 1942 to 1947.

8. **(E) Canada.** The Avro Arrow project was to be Canada's entry into the aerospace field, but it was killed in 1959 by Prime Minister John Diefenbaker as too ambitious and expensive. It was designed to be the world's highest flying and fastest jet interceptor fighter.

Quiz #8 — **It's the Berries**

1. What John Irving novel deals with the trials and tribulations of the Berry family?
A. "The Cider House Rules"
B. "The 158-Pound Marriage"
C. "A Prayer for Owen Meany"
D. "The World According to Garp"
E. "The Hotel New Hampshire"

2. To boost attendance, the Knott's Berry Farm added what mile-long roller coaster?
A. Rattler
B. Hercules
C. Jaguar
D. Excalibur
E. Viper

3. Which of the following was not a doll in the Strawberry Shortcake line?
A. Raspberry Tart
B. Apple Dumplin'
C. Lemon Meringue
D. Blueberry Pie
E. Lime Chiffon

4. Actress Halle Berry competed in the 1986 Miss U.S.A. pageant as the representative of what state?
A. Wisconsin
B. Washington
C. Ohio
D. California
E. South Carolina

5. In the 1979 Los Angeles City Section high school baseball championship game, the losing pitcher was future major leaguer Darryl Strawberry. The winning pitcher was what future NFL quarterback?
A. John Elway
B. Dan Marino
C. Steve Young
D. Randy Wright
E. Bernie Kosar

6. Bill Berry was the drummer for what rock band for 13 years before retiring in 1997 due to medical problems?
A. The Scorpions
B. Dexy's Midnight Runners
C. R.E.M.
D. Green Day
E. Strawberry Alarm Clock

7. T. Berry Brazelton is a noted author and national expert in what subject area?
A. Boxing
B. Quantum physics
C. Quilting
D. Mutual funds
E. Child care

8. NFL quarterback Bob Berry has suited up for the Super Bowl three times, but never played in any of the games. He was the backup quarterback for what team?
A. Green Bay Packers
B. Dallas Cowboys
C. San Francisco 49ers
D. Minnesota Vikings
E. Denver Broncos

Answers to Quiz #8 — It's the Berries

1. **(E) "The Hotel New Hampshire".** The eccentric Berry family set up house in three different locations, all of which they called "The Hotel New Hampshire" — one in Dairy, New Hampshire, one in Vienna, Austria, and one in Maine. John Irving was born in New Hampshire.

2. **(C) Jaguar.** Knott's Berry Farm is the oldest American theme park, established in 1920 at "the birthplace of the boysenberry." The Jaguar is a 2700'-long coaster with a Mayan/Aztec mythological theme. Other roller coasters at Knott's include Montezooma's Revenge, the Boomerang, and the Windjammer.

3. **(D) Blueberry Pie.** Strawberry Shortcake was a character created by American Greetings, first appearing as a TV character in the 1980. The doll line followed shortly in 1981, created by designer Annette Ruth Shelley.

4. **(C) Ohio.** Berry was the runner-up for the 1986 Miss U.S.A. spot. She has since gone onto a successful acting career in films like "Boomerang," "Jungle Fever," and "The Flintstones."

5. **(A) John Elway.** Elway played professional baseball in 1982 as an outfielder for Oneonta in the New York-Pennsylvania League. He was a second-round draft choice of the New York Yankees in 1981. Elway joined the Denver Broncos as QB in 1983.

6. **(C) R.E.M.** Fans of R. E. M. had quite a scare when Berry collapsed in Lausanne, Switzerland from a brain aneurysm in March 1995. After the band missed 40 tour dates, Berry recovered enough to rejoin his pals on the road.

7. **(E) Child care.** Brazelton is the host of the Lifetime cable TV series "What Every Baby Knows," and the author of many books on child rearing including "Touchpoints," "To Listen to a Child," "Infants and Mothers," and "What Every Baby Knows."

8. **(D) Minnesota Vikings.** Berry was a member of the Minnesota Vikings in their three losing Super Bowl efforts in 1974, 1975, and 1977.

Quiz #9 — **Jacks of All Trades**

1. Jack Boyle was the creator of what fictional detective of radio and TV?
A. Boston Blackie
B. Charlie Chan
C. Dan Fortune
D. The Falcon
E. Dr. Gideon Fell

2. In what sport is the Jack Adams Trophy awarded for Coach of the Year?
A. Soccer
B. Cricket
C. Polo
D. Tennis
E. Hockey

3. Which famous silent screen actress had a brother named Jack who was a noted actor in his own right?
A. Bessie Love
B. Theda Bara
C. Constance Talmadge
D. Mary Pickford
E. Clara Bow

4. What high school was attended by radio hero "Jack Armstrong, The All-American Boy"?
A. Bradley High
B. Hudson High
C. McConnell High
D. Franklin High
E. Valley High

5. In "Tim Burton's The Nightmare Before Christmas," what was the name of Jack Skellington's ghostly dog?
A. Nightmare
B. Streaky
C. Zero
D. Vincent
E. Max

6. Which "Beverly Hills 90210" character had an unscrupulous father named Jack?
A. Ray Pruit
B. Donna Martin
C. Andrea Zuckerman
D. Dylan McKay
E. Emily Valentine

7. Former game show host Jack Narz has a brother who was also a popular game show host. Name him.
A. Peter Tomarkin
B. Joe Garagiola
C. Art James
D. Tom Kennedy
E. Gene Rayburn

8. Who was the first batter to face Babe Ruth's pitching in the major leagues?
A. Jack Graney
B. Jack Willman
C. Jack Fisher
D. Jack Billingham
E. Jack Warhop

Answers to Quiz #9 — **Jacks of All Trades**

1. **(A) Boston Blackie.** Boston Blackie was the unscrupulous crime solver who appeared in short stories by Boyle in "Redbook" and "Cosmopolitan." Blackie's image was cleaned up a little for his radio show and movies starring Chester Morris, and his TV series starring Kent Taylor.

2. **(E) Hockey.** The first Jack Adams Trophy was awarded in 1974 to Fred Shero with the Philadelphia Phillies.

3. **(D) Mary Pickford.** When Mary Pickford signed her million-dollar contract with First National in 1917, she stipulated that her brother Jack also receive a lucrative contract. Jack became a romantic lead and also co-directed a couple of films.

4. **(B) Hudson High.** As the theme song for the radio series said: "Wave the flag for Hudson High, boys/Show them how we stand!/Ever shall our team be champion/Known throughout the land!" The radio series ran from 1933 to 1951 on CBS.

5. **(C) Zero.** Zero was created with an innovative technique that involved filming him with a mirrored device in the camera called a beam splitter. It made Zero appear translucent while still allowing him to interact directly with other "solid" characters.

6. **(D) Dylan McKay.** Jack McKay was killed in a car bombing. Luke Perry, the actor who played Dylan McKay, originally left the series after Dylan tried to unravel the murder plot, but later returned.

7. **(D) Tom Kennedy.** Jack Narz was caught up in the 1950s quiz show scandals while hosting "Dotto." He was innocent of any wrongdoing, and the "Dotto" sponsors, Colgate/Palmolive, quickly moved him into their next show, "Top Dollar." Tom Kennedy's real name is Jim Narz.

8. **(A) Jack Graney.** Graney hit a single off the Babe. Graney played 1402 games for the Cleveland Indians from 1908-20 and was later hired as a radio announcer for the team. Jack Warhop was the pitcher who gave up the first of Babe Ruth's 714 career home runs in May 1915.

Quiz #10 — Stormy Weather

1. In American folklore, what was the name of Capt. Stormalong's gigantic ship?
A. Courser
B. Lady of the Lake
C. Argo
D. Boston
E. Black Ball

2. "It was a dark and stormy night" is the familiar opening line used by would-be author Snoopy. What author originally used the trite line to open his 1830 novel "Paul Clifford"?
A. Karl von Knebel
B. Ferdinand Schiller
C. Edmund Stedman
D. Edward Bulwer-Lytton
E. Alfred Austin

3. What baseball player found himself in hot water after he verbally abused NBC sportscaster Hannah Storm at the 1995 World Series?
A. Carlos Baerga
B. Kenny Lofton
C. Alvaro Espinoza
D. Albert Belle
E. Charles Nagy

4. When a lightning storm threatens, what does Lee Trevino suggest you hold over your head for protection on the golf course?
A. One-iron
B. Umbrella
C. Glass of water
D. Your caddie
E. Golf glove

5. "In From the Storm" is an album featuring an all-star roster of musicians, including Sting, Stanley Clarke, Santana, Taj Mahal, and Steve Vai, performing cover versions of what musician's work?
A. Buddy Holly
B. Jim Morrison
C. Les Paul
D. Janis Joplin
E. Jimi Hendrix

6. What TV soap opera features a character named Storm Logan and a cast member named Jim Storm?
A. "One Life to Live"
B. "The City"
C. "The Bold and the Beautiful"
D. "The Young and the Restless"
E. "All My Children"

7. The only movie in which Doris Day was killed was the 1950 film "Storm Warning." What actor shot her?
A. Ronald Reagan
B. George Sanders
C. Lloyd Gough
D. Fred Astaire
E. Steve Cochran

8. Johnny and Sue Storm were charter members of what comic book superhero group?
A. The Avengers
B. Guardians of the Galaxy
C. Fantastic Four
D. Power Pack
E. Teen Titans

Answers to Quiz #10 — **Stormy Weather**

1. (A) **Courser.** Capt. Stormalong was to sailors what Paul Bunyan was to lumberjacks. His ship, the Courser, was too wide to fit through the English Channel. In order to squeeze through, sailors coated the sides of the Courser with soap. The fit was so tight at Dover that the soap scraped off leaving behind the white cliffs.

2. (D) **Edward Bulwer-Lytton.** The Bulwer-Lytton Fiction Contest is held as an annual tribute to lousy literature. Contestants vie for the honor of writing the worst opening line.

3. (D) **Albert Belle.** Storm was actually in the Indians' dugout to interview Kenny Lofton, but Belle took exception to her presence and unleashed a string of profanities at her. A Cleveland Indians official later made the understatement, "Albert's people skills leave something to be desired."

4. (A) **One-iron.** Trevino remarked "even the good Lord has trouble hitting a one-iron." Trevino, along with golfers Bobby Nichols and Jerry Heard, was struck by lightning on June 27, 1995 at the Western Open outside Chicago.

5. (E) **Jimi Hendrix.** Hendrix continues to be popular many years after his death at age 27. Reprise released the gold album "Monterey International Pop Festival" one day after Hendrix's death. In the years immediately following his death, Hendrix LPs "The Cry of Love," "Rainbow Bridge," and "Hendrix in the West" all went gold.

6. (C) **"The Bold and the Beautiful".** Storm Logan has been played on the CBS soap by Ethan Wayne (son of John Wayne) and Brian Patrick Clarke. Jim Storm plays William Spencer.

7. (E) **Steve Cochran.** "Storm Warning" featured Ronald Reagan vs. the Ku Klux Klan. The film was Day's first non-musical. Steve Cochran played the bigoted husband who accidentally shot and killed her.

8. (C) **Fantastic Four.** As members of the Marvel Comics' Fantastic Four, Sue Storm Richards is known as "Invisible Girl" and Johnny Storm is known as the "Human Torch." Reed "Mr. Fantastic" Richards and Ben "The Thing" Grimm complete the original quartet.

Quiz #11 — **Daddy's Home**

1. What popular TV series was a spinoff of Danny Thomas's "Make Room for Daddy"?
A. "Happy Days"
B. "The Dick Van Dyke Show"
C. "Private Secretary"
D. "The Andy Griffith Show"
E. "December Bride"

2. Which of these sports figures did not have the nickname "Big Daddy"?
A. Carl Hairston
B. Don Garlits
C. Dan Wilkinson
D. Jim Otto
E. Riddick Bowe

3. What movie featured a high school teacher nicknamed "Daddy-O" by his students?
A. "High School Confidential"
B. "Teachers"
C. "To Sir, with Love"
D. "Fast Times at Ridgemont High"
E. "Blackboard Jungle"

4. "Daddy longlegs" is the nickname of what insect?
A. Leatherjacket
B. Sniper fly
C. Hessian fly
D. Harvestman
E. Crane fly

5. In the Parker Brothers game "Don't Wake Daddy," the goal of the game is to reach what objective without waking Daddy?
A. Refrigerator
B. Alarm clock
C. Bathroom
D. Bedroom closet
E. Front door

6. What sports figure wore a famous t-shirt that read "2,130+ Hugs and Kisses for Daddy"?
A. Hulk Hogan
B. Cal Ripkin Jr.
C. Roger Clinton
D. Evel Knievel
E. Bobby Riggs

7. What was the real first name of "Daddy" Warbucks in the "Little Orphan Annie" comic strip?
A. Albert
B. Franklin
C. Theodore
D. Wilbur
E. Oliver

8. Elvis Presley hit the Billboard top 10 in 1969 with the single "Don't Cry, Daddy." Who wrote the song about his son, Scotty?
A. Mac Davis
B. Ronnie Milsap
C. Bobby Goldsboro
D. Bob Dylan
E. Otis Blackwell

Answers to Quiz #11 — **Daddy's Home**

1. (D) **"The Andy Griffith Show"**. Griffith appeared in the February 15, 1960 episode as the drawling mayor of a small town visited by Thomas called Mayberry. After seeing the ratings, Thomas ordered a spinoff. Upon seeing the "Make Room for Daddy" episode, Don Knotts asked to be added to the script and the character of Barney Fife was born.

2. (D) **Jim Otto.** Hairston and Wilkinson played football in the NFL. Garlits is a noted drag racer. Bowe was a heavyweight boxing champion in 1992.

3. (E) **"Blackboard Jungle"**. Glenn Ford played high school English teacher Richard Dadier. "Blackboard Jungle" was the first movie to use rock 'n' roll music featuring Bill Haley and the Comets' "Rock Around the Clock."

4. (E) **Crane fly.** The crane fly resembles a large mosquito with long legs. The harvestman is also nicknamed the "daddy longlegs." As a member of the arachnid family, it is not an insect.

5. (A) **Refrigerator.** Players encounter noisy objects during the game. Each encounter requires the player to hit a plunger on Daddy's alarm clock one or more times while hoping not to trigger the alarm that will spring the nightcap-clad Daddy out of his bed.

6. (B) **Cal Ripkin Jr.** Ripkin revealed the t-shirt during his record-breaking "iron man" stint of consecutive baseball games in 1995.

7. (E) **Oliver.** "Little Orphan Annie" was created by Harold Gray in 1924 capitalizing on the popularity of waiflike actress Mary Pickford. Two months into the strip, Annie was adopted by Daddy Warbucks, a self-made millionaire industrialist.

8. (A) **Mac Davis.** Mac Davis also wrote the Bobby Goldsboro hit "Watching Scotty Grow" about his son. Ronnie Milsap sang harmony with Elvis on "Don't Cry, Daddy."

Quiz #12 — **Name That State**

1. What is the only U.S. state with a state flag not in the usual rectangular shape?
A. Hawaii
B. Michigan
C. Ohio
D. Idaho
E. Florida

2. Which U.S. state is the only one to grow commercially produced tea?
A. Colorado
B. Michigan
C. South Carolina
D. Wyoming
E. Alaska

3. What state in the continental U.S. extends the farthest north?
A. Michigan
B. Maine
C. Montana
D. Minnesota
E. Washington

4. In what state would you find the Jefferson National Expansion Monument?
A. Virginia
B. Maryland
C. Missouri
D. Colorado
E. South Dakota

5. Mount Marcy is the highest peak in what state?
A. West Virginia
B. Montana
C. Arizona
D. Georgia
E. New York

6. In 1983, the Soviets shot down a South Korean airliner that strayed into air space over Soviet bases. Among the Americans killed was Larry P. McDonald, a Congressman from what state?
A. Rhode Island
B. Wisconsin
C. North Dakota
D. Georgia
E. South Carolina

7. In what state will you find counties named after Theodore Roosevelt, William McKinley, and Warren G. Harding?
A. New Mexico
B. Alaska
C. Wyoming
D. Hawaii
E. Arizona

8. In Ronald Reagan's landslide reelection of 1984, he lost only one state. Which state was it?
A. Maine
B. Vermont
C. New Hampshire
D. Minnesota
E. Oregon

Answers to Quiz #12 — Name That State

1. **(C) Ohio.** Ohio's somewhat triangular flag is its own version of the red, white, and blue with stars and stripes.

2. **(C) South Carolina.** American Classic Tea is produced from plants grown on Wadmalah Island near Charleston.

3. **(D) Minnesota.** A small tab of Minnesota extends north around several islands in the Lake of the Woods on the U.S.-Canada border.

4. **(C) Missouri.** Designed by Eero Saarinen, it is better known as the St. Louis Gateway Arch.

5. **(E) New York.** It is also the highest peak in the Adironacks.

6. **(D) Georgia.** 269 people were killed in the crash including 61 Americans. McDonald was also the leader of the John Birch Society.

7. **(A) New Mexico.** Harding is the most recent U.S. President to have a county named in his honor.

8. **(D) Minnesota.** Minnesota was the home state of Reagan's Democratic opponent, Walter Mondale. Mondale also won the District of Columbia.

Quiz #13 — **Word and Phrase Origins**

1. What island's name is said to have been derived from a corruption of "Go away" in a native language?
A. Hawaii
B. Samoa
C. Krakatoa
D. Sumatra
E. Bora Bora

2. What sports announcer introduced the baseball lingo "rhubarb" and "in the catbird seat"?
A. Mel Allen
B. Vin Scully
C. Ernie Harwell
D. Marty Brennaman
E. Red Barber

3. The Maxwell House coffee slogan "Good to the last drop" has been attributed to what famous person?
A. Babe Ruth
B. Hamlin Garland
C. Omar Bradley
D. Theodore Roosevelt
E. Mark Twain

4. What writer coined the phrases "radical chic" and "the Me Decade"?
A. Kurt Vonnegut Jr.
B. Tom Wolfe
C. Alvin Toffler
D. Aldous Huxley
E. James Joyce

5. What writer introduced the portmanteau word "chortle" to the English language?
A. Edward Lear
B. Mark Twain
C. Lewis Carroll
D. Charles Dickens
E. Dr. Seuss

6. The nonsense phrase "Notary Sojac" was associated with what long-running comic strip?
A. "Barney Google"
B. "Smokey Stover"
C. "Little Orphan Annie"
D. "Little Nemo"
E. "Li'l Abner"

7. What food item's name comes from words meaning to create gas in the bowels of the Devil?
A. Sauerbraten
B. Pumpernickel
C. Andouillette
D. Ratatouille
E. Frangipane

8. What ore derives its name from the ancient Greek for "blood" because it looks like clumps of dried blood?
A. Bauxite
B. Limonite
C. Hematite
D. Goethite
E. Malachite

Answers to Quiz #13 — **Word and Phrase Origins**

1. **(E) Bora Bora.** Legend has it that Captain Cook asked a native for the name of the island. The man replied "Apura! Apura!" which roughly translated as "Go away! Go away!" but was corrupted by Cook into Bora Bora.

2. **(E) Red Barber.** Walter "Red" Barber titled his autobiography "Rhubarb in the Catbird Seat." He started his career as an announcer for the Cincinnati Reds in 1934. He worked the booth for the Dodgers from 1939 to 1953, and then for the Yankees until his retirement in 1966. He was admitted into the Baseball Hall of Fame in 1978. Barber died October 22, 1992 at the age of 84.

3. **(D) Theodore Roosevelt.** In 1888, while visiting the Maxwell House Hotel in Nashville, Tennessee, Teddy Roosevelt was asked if he wanted another cup of coffee. He said yes, declaring their coffee was "good to the last drop."

4. **(B) Tom Wolfe.** Tom Wolfe introduced "radical chic" in the 1970 article "Radical Chic: That Party at Lenny's" which developed into the book "Radical Chic and Mau-Mauing the Flak Catchers." "The Me Decade" first appeared in Wolfe's 1976 book "Mauve Gloves & Madmen, Clutter & Vine."

5. **(C) Lewis Carroll.** Carroll created the word "chortle" by combining the words chuckle and snort. Carroll also created the term "portmanteau word" in a conversation between Humpty Dumpty and Alice, describing it as a word packing two meanings. Other portmanteau words include brunch (breakfast and lunch), smog (smoke and fog) and bodacious (bold and audacious).

6. **(B) "Smokey Stover".** "Smokey Stover" cartoonist Bill Holman regularly featured signs with unusual sayings such as "Foo" (which he claimed meant good luck) and "1506 Nix Nix." Holman said that "Notary Sojac" was his phonetic rendering of "Nodlaig Sodhach," meaning Merry Christmas in Gaelic.

7. **(B) Pumpernickel.** In Old German, "pumper" meant "to break wind" and "nickel" referred to "Old Nick," aka Satan.

8. **(C) Hematite.** Hematite is the principal ore of iron.

Quiz #14 — **Take My Wife, Please**

1. Who was the first of Henry VIII's six wives?
A. Catherine Parr
B. Catherine of Aragon
C. Anne Boleyn
D. Jane Seymour
E. Anne of Cleves

2. Who was the first Presidential wife dubbed the "First Lady"?
A. Dolly Madison
B. Mary Todd Lincoln
C. Julia Grant
D. Abigail Adams
E. Lucy Hayes

3. In the comic strip "Boner's Ark," what is the name of Boner's wife?
A. Pickles
B. Regina
C. Helga
D. Bubbles
E. Min

4. What musician was married to Dorothy Barton, Jane Mitcham, Myra Gale Brown, Jaren Elizabeth Pate, Shawn Stevens, and Kerrie McCarver?
A. Quincy Jones
B. James Brown
C. Rick James
D. Elvis Presley
E. Jerry Lee Lewis

5. What name was shared by the wife of Louis XVI and the second wife of Henry IV?
A. Anastasia
B. Marie
C. Sophia
D. Elizabeth
E. Catherine

6. How many times was Ivan the Terrible married?
A. 0
B. 3
C. 5
D. 7
E. 10

7. To which of her multiple husbands was Elizabeth Taylor married the longest?
A. Richard Burton
B. Larry Fortensky
C. John Warner
D. Nicky Hilton
E. Eddie Fisher

8. Margaret Ray is the name of the woman who has broken into what celebrity's house several times claiming to be his wife?
A. Tom Arnold
B. Tom Clancy
C. Stephen King
D. David Letterman
E. Kurt Russell

Answers to Quiz #14 — **Take My Wife, Please**

1. **(B) Catherine of Aragon.** Catherine of Aragon was his brother's widow, and Henry received a special papal dispensation in order to marry her. Her ran into trouble with the papacy later when he tried to divorce her.

2. **(E) Lucy Hayes.** It was newswoman Mary Clemmen Ames, who writing about Lucy Hayes, first referred to the President's wife as the "First Lady of the country." Lucy Hayes, wife of Rutherford B. Hayes was nicknamed "Lemonade Lucy" because lemonade was frequently served at White House functions. Both of the Hayes were teetotalers.

3. **(D) Bubbles.** In this comic strip created by Mort Walker (and later drawn by Frank Johnson), Boner is the blundering captain of an ark who collected only one animal of each species.

4. **(E) Jerry Lee Lewis.** Lewis was on the verge of greatness following the release of his 1957 hit "Whole Lot of Shakin' Goin' On." Lewis then submarined his musical career by marrying his 13-year-old cousin, Myra Gale Brown in 1958. Radio stations all over the country banned his records. Lewis managed to segue into a country music career. Lewis and Myra were divorced in 1971.

5. **(B) Marie.** Louis XVI was married to Marie Antoinette. Henry IV's second wife was Marie de Medicis.

6. **(D) 7.** Ivan IV's first wife was Anastasia Romanov. Though he was to marry six more times after her death in 1560, it was said he never loved another woman more.

7. **(A) Richard Burton.** Taylor married Burton two times. The first marriage followed their highly publicized affair during the filming of the movie "Cleopatra." They were married for a total of 10 years.

8. **(D) David Letterman.** Ray has also been arrested for stalking astronaut Stormy Musgrave.

Quiz #15 — **Hair Me Out**

1. What "Peanuts" character was proud of her "naturally curly hair"?
A. Violet
B. Patti
C. Sally
D. Marcie
E. Frieda

2. What TV comedian was the leader of a satirical rock 'n' roll band called "The Three Haircuts"?
A. Dick Van Dyke
B. Sid Caesar
C. Ernie Kovacs
D. George Burns
E. Jack Benny

3. What group released the highest ranking single on the pop charts with a song from the musical "Hair"?
A. Three Dog Night
B. The Fifth Dimension
C. Alvin and the Chipmunks
D. The Cowsills
E. America

4. What actress said that she and her college friends got stoned one afternoon and shaved off all the actress's hair because they thought she would look like Nefertiti?
A. Alfre Woodard
B. Lea Thompson
C. Sharon Stone
D. Halle Berry
E. Emma Thompson

5. What ancient breed of dog is known as the "Xolo" to its afficionados?
A. Wire-haired pointing griffon
B. Mexican hairless
C. German short-haired pointer
D. Long-haired Spitz
E. Wirehaired fox terrier

6. Shirley Temple's mother was also her hairstylist. She made sure that Shirley always had exactly how many ringlets of hair on her little moppet head?
A. 26
B. 38
C. 48
D. 56
E. 84

7. What actor kept his hair long because he felt that he derived his strength from long hair just as Samson did?
A. Michael Landon
B. Pete Deuel
C. Bruce Lee
D. Lorenzo Lamas
E. Bert Lahr

8. What Biblical character was born with "a body like a hairy mantle"?
A. Seth
B. Balaam
C. Esau
D. Methuselah
E. Samson

Answers to Quiz #15 — **Hair Me Out**

1. **(E) Frieda.** Frieda was named after Frieda Rich, an art-school colleague of Charles Schulz. Frieda has not appeared in the comic strip since the 1970s, although she can still be seen every year getting selected to play Pigpen's wife in the Christmas play on TV's "A Charlie Brown Christmas."

2. **(B) Sid Caesar.** Sid Caesar, Carl Reiner, and Howard Morris portrayed "The Three Haircuts" on TV's "Caesar's Hour."

3. **(B) The Fifth Dimension.** "Aquarius/Let the Sun Shine In" by the Fifth Dimension hit #1 on the pop charts in the week of April 12, 1969 and went on to be the second biggest single of 1969. Other "Hair" songs that hit the charts were "Hair" by the Cowsills (peaking at #2), "Good Morning, Starshine" by Oliver (#3), and "Easy to Be Hard" by Three Dog Night (#4).

4. **(E) Emma Thompson.** Thompson made the revelation in an interview in the February 1996 issue of "Vanity Fair." Never one to shy away from unusual roles, Thompson played a fictionalized version of herself as a lesbian on "Ellen" in 1997.

5. **(B) Mexican hairless.** The Mexican hairless is truly a hairless dog except for a fringe of hair on its nose and a brush of hair at the end of its tail.

6. **(D) 56.** Shirley Temple made her first million dollars at age 10. As an adult, Shirley Temple Black has pursued a political career. She served as the U.S. ambassador to Ghana from 1974-76 and has been U.S. ambassador to Czechoslovakia since 1989.

7. **(A) Michael Landon.** Landon finished 300th in a high school class of 301, but went to college on an athletic scholarship based on his prowess as a javelin hurler. He lost a tournament after his teammates shaved his head.

8. **(C) Esau.** In Genesis 25:25. "Esau" translates roughly as "hairy."

Quiz #16 — Bats in the Belfry

1. Who played "Bat Masterson" on the western TV series of the same name?
A. Vince Edwards
B. Gene Barry
C. William Shatner
D. James Drury
E. Peter Graves

2. In 1993-94, DC Comics ran a storyline in the Batman comics called "Knightfall" in which Bruce Wayne was replaced as Batman by Jean Paul Valley after Wayne's back was broken in a fight with what supervillain?
A. Clayface
B. The Joker
C. Bane
D. Solomon Grundy
E. Killer Croc

3. What rock star underwent a series of painful rabies shots after he bit the head off a bat during a 1982 perform- ance in Des Moines, Iowa?
A. Meat Loaf
B. Jello Biafra
C. Alice Cooper
D. Ozzy Ozbourne
E. Mark Mothersbaugh

4. Who became the first designated hitter to bat in the World Series in 1976?
A. Don Driessen
B. Lou Piniella
C. Carl Yastrzemski
D. Hal McRae
E. Rod Carew

5. What is the legal maximum length of a cricket bat?
A. 30 inches
B. 34 inches
C. 38 inches
D. 42 inches
E. 46 inches

6. What was the name of Grandpa's pet bat on "The Munsters"?
A. Spot
B. Vlad
C. Irving
D. Herman
E. Igor

7. What was the name of the handcrafted baseball bat used by Roy Hobbs for smacking his home runs in the 1984 movie "The Natural"?
A. Slugger
B. Lancelot
C. The Bump Bat
D. Little Roy
E. Wonderboy

8. Mexican mother bats all keep their pups together in one chamber of their cave residence. What name is given to the chamber?
A. Crash
B. Clutch
C. Crutch
D. Cache
E. Creche

Answers to Quiz #16 — Bats in the Belfry

1. (B) **Gene Barry.** From 1959-61, Barry played the dashing and daring Bat Masterson complete with "cane and derby hat." The real Masterson was a lawman and a professional gambler. In his later years, Masterson worked as a boxing referee.

2. (C) **Bane.** Jean Paul Valley took the batsuit and became an avenging assassin called Azrael. When Valley took a little too much pleasure in the job, he was replaced by the original Robin, Dick Grayson.

3. (D) **Ozzy Ozbourne.** Ozbourne said he thought the bat thrown on stage by a fan was made of rubber. Ozbourne was the former lead vocalist for Black Sabbath.

4. (B) **Lou Piniella.** Piniella batted for the New York Yankees vs. the Cincinnati Reds in 1976, going 3-for-9 in the series. Driessen, playing for the Reds in the same Series, was the National League's first DH.

5. (C) **38 inches.** The blade of the cricket bat may be no more than a shade over 4 inches wide.

6. (E) **Igor.** The Munsters' other family pet was Spot, the fire-breathing dragon who lived under the stairs.

7. (E) **Wonderboy.** When Wonderboy split during the climax of the film, young Bobby Savoy lent his "Savoy Special" to Roy who, in true movie fashion, launched the next pitch into the overhead lights.

8. (E) **Creche.** Mother bats can sort through millions of hungry bats to find their own offspring for nursing two times a day.

Quiz #17 — **Crazy Like a Fox**

1. Which of the following is not a real animal?
A. Fox sparrow
B. Fox spider
C. Fox squirrel
D. Fox snake
E. Flying fox

2. What religious group was organized in 1652 by George Fox?
A. Jehovah's Witnesses
B. Quakers
C. Pilgrims
D. Congregationalists
E. Baptists

3. What Native American tribe was constantly at war with the Fox over the possession of wild rice fields near Lake Superior?
A. Sioux
B. Ojibwa
C. Chipewyan
D. Otoe
E. Winnebago

4. What literary detective had a sidekick called Brer Teddy Fox?
A. Roderick Alleyn
B. Charlie Chan
C. Jim Chee
D. Inspector Wexford
E. Lord Peter Wimsey

5. What is the name of the mother of the Fox family in the comic strip "Fox Trot"?
A. Andy
B. Denise
C. Lois
D. Brenda
E. Fanny

6. What name did inventor William Fox Talbot give to his processes for making photographic negatives and positive prints?
A. Hypotypes
B. Collodotypes
C. Chromatypes
D. Daguerreotypes
E. Calotypes

7. What was the name of the "witch doctor," played by Bernard Fox, who tended to witches Samantha and Endora on the TV series "Bewitched"?
A. Dr. Delhi
B. Dr. Calcutta
C. Dr. Katmandu
D. Dr. Ganges
E. Dr. Bombay

8. In what century was the two-step dance, the fox trot, introduced?
A. 16th
B. 17th
C. 18th
D. 19th
E. 20th

Answers to Quiz #17 — **Crazy Like a Fox**

1. **(B) Fox spider.** The flying fox is the largest species of bat with a wingspan of over five feet.

2. **(B) Quakers.** George Fox founded the Society of Friends, aka the Quakers, in England in the 1652.

3. **(B) Ojibwa.** The Fox and the Sac went to war with the United States in 1832 in the Black Hawk War over a treaty forcing the tribes out of Wisconsin territory.

4. **(A) Roderick Alleyn.** Alleyn was the 1930s-40s Scotland Yard Inspector featured in mysteries by New Zealand author Ngaio Marsh.

5. **(A) Andy.** Andy's husband is Roger. Their kids are Peter, Paige, and Jason. Bill Amend is the artist behind the "Fox Trot" strip.

6. **(E) Calotypes.** The calotype negative was produced through a cheap process using a paper base, but the coarseness of the paper prevented the detail made possible through Daguerre's process involving metallic plates. The calotype made possible "contact printing," creating multiple copies of an image from a single negative.

7. **(E) Dr. Bombay.** The doctor was summoned with the call "Calling Dr. Bombay! Come right away!"

8. **(E) 20th.** The jerky fox trot, created by Ziegfeld performer Harry Fox, caught on with the dance-hungry American public late in 1913. American soldiers of WWI introduced the dance worldwide.

Quiz #18 — **Dollars and Cents**

1. On what piece of U.S. currency will you find the picture of a 1927 Hupmobile?
A. $5 bill
B. $10 bill
C. $50 bill
D. $100 bill
E. $1000 bill

2. On coins minted in the U.S., a mint mark of "D" means the coin was minted in Denver and "S" stands for San Francisco. What city was represented by the obsolete mint mark "O"?
A. Oakland, CA
B. Oklahoma City, OK
C. Norfolk, VA
D. New Orleans, LA
E. Omaha, NE

3. In 1873, a U.S. law was passed stating that what symbol must appear on the reverse of all American coins larger than ten cents?
A. "U.S.A."
B. Statue of Liberty
C. Eagle
D. Liberty Bell
E. Pyramid

4. More $1 bills are printed annually in the U.S. than any other denomination. What size bill ranks second?
A. $5
B. $10
C. $20
D. $50
E. $100

5. What animal appears on the reverse side of the Canadian dollar coin first issued in 1988?
A. Loon
B. Moose
C. Beaver
D. Wolverine
E. Wolf

6. How many arrows are clutched in the talon of the bald eagle pictured on the $1 bill?
A. 1
B. 3
C. 10
D. 12
E. 13

7. To money collectors, what is a "shinplaster"?
A. A bill of little value
B. Aluminum coin
C. Triangular coin
D. $10,000 bill
E. $2 silver certificate

8. In 1917, what manufacturing magnate printed his own penny, inscribed with "Help The Other Fellow"?
A. Andrew Carnegie
B. Howard Hughes
C. John D. Rockefeller
D. Henry Ford
E. Charles Nash

Answers to Quiz #18 — **Dollars and Cents**

1. **(B) $10 bill.** It is the little automobile parked outside the U.S. Treasury building on the reverse side of the $10 bill.

2. **(D) New Orleans, LA.** Other cities and their mint marks included Charlotte, NC (C — gold coins only); Dahlonega, GA (D — gold coins only); Carson City, NV (CC), and West Point, NY (W).

3. **(C) Eagle.** On the Franklin half-dollar, the eagle appears on the reverse as a tiny little symbol above the much larger Liberty Bell.

4. **(C) $20.** The $20 bill has become a popular currency due to the proliferation of automated teller machines.

5. **(A) Loon.** The dollar coins have been nicknamed "Loonies." The nickname does not sit well with the Canadian government which has threatened to replace the loon with the image of the Parliament buildings.

6. **(E) 13.** In the other talon, the eagle holds an olive branch with 13 leaves. Thirteen stars appear above the eagle's head, and there are 13 stripes on the shield in front of the eagle.

7. **(A) A bill of little value.** The term originated during the American Revolution when soldiers used worthless bills to bandage leg wounds.

8. **(D) Henry Ford.** Ford planned to offer a million Ford pennies to friends and customers as a goodwill gesture. The project was aborted by World War I.

Quiz #19 — **All in the Family**

1. Actress Lauren Bacall is the first cousin of a former Prime Minister of what country?
A. Canada
B. Denmark
C. Israel
D. Great Britain
E. The Bahamas

2. What singer is the maternal granddaughter of Nobel Prize-winning physicist Max Born?
A. Sheena Easton
B. Belinda Carlisle
C. Patti Page
D. Olivia Newton-John
E. Shania Twain

3. What TV and film actor is the third cousin of President Calvin Coolidge?
A. Ernest Borgnine
B. E.G. Marshall
C. John Mahoney
D. Orson Bean
E. Lane Smith

4. Actor Glenn Ford and singer Nelson Eddy were both descendants of which president?
A. Rutherford B. Hayes
B. Ulysses S. Grant
C. Thomas Jefferson
D. John Quincy Adams
E. Martin Van Buren

5. Who are the only father-son team to win Academy Awards for the same movie?
A. Henry and Peter Fonda
B. Walter and David Matthau
C. Walter and John Huston
D. Jack and Chris Lemmon
E. Kirk and Michael Douglas

6. Which of these actor pairs were not brothers?
A. Barry Fitzgerald and Arthur Shields
B. Steve Forrest and Dana Andrews
C. Peter Graves and James Arness
D. Tom Conway and George Sanders
E. Frank Morgan and Ralph Byrd

7. What father and son won Rookie of the Year Awards in different professional sports leagues?
A. Calvin and Grant Hill
B. Yogi and Tim Berra
C. Dick and B.J. Surhoff
D. Kyle Rote Sr. and Jr.
E. Jack and J.T. Snow

8. What actress is the maternal granddaughter of behaviorial psychologist John B. Watson?
A. Susan Saint James
B. Christine Belford
C. Mariette Hartley
D. Winona Ryder
E. Lea Thompson

Answers to Quiz #19 — **All in the Family**

1. **(C) Israel.** Bacall, born Betty Perske, is the first cousin of Shimon Peres, born Shimon Perske.

2. **(D) Olivia Newton-John.** Max Born shared the Nobel Prize for Physics in 1954 with Walther Bothe for providing a link between wave mechanics and quantum theory.

3. **(D) Orson Bean.** Orson Bean's great-grandmother and Coolidge's mother were sisters. Bean played shopkeeper Loren Bray on the CBS TV series "Dr. Quinn, Medicine Woman."

4. **(E) Martin Van Buren.** Van Buren was the first President born as a citizen of the United States on December 5, 1872. There was no First Lady during Van Buren's administration. His wife, Hannah, died 19 years before he was elected. Van Buren's daughter-in-law served as the hostess of White House functions.

5. **(C) Walter and John Huston.** Walter Huston won the 1948 Best Supporting Actor Oscar for "The Treasure of the Sierra Madre." The film was directed by his son, John, who won Best Director and Best Screenplay for the same picture.

6. **(E) Frank Morgan and Ralph Byrd.** Frank Morgan does have an actor-brother named Ralph Morgan. Ralph Byrd starred in the "Dick Tracy" films. Barry Fitzgerald and Arthur Shields both appeared in "The Quiet Man." When George Sanders tired of doing "The Falcon" movies in 1942, his brother, Tom Conway, took over in the movie "The Falcon's Brother."

7. **(A) Calvin and Grant Hill.** Calvin Hill won Rookie of the Year in the NFL in 1969 while playing for the Dallas Cowboys. Grant Hill won Rookie of the Year in the NBA in 1995.

8. **(C) Mariette Hartley.** John Broadus Watson founded the school of behaviorism which strongly influenced psychology from the 1920s to the 1940s. Mariette Hartley has appeared on numerous TV programs, starring in "Goodnight, Beantown" with Bill Bixby. She also appeared in a series of popular TV commercials for Polaroid cameras with James Garner.

Quiz #20 — **Kiddie Lit**

1. Who was the traveling companion of aspiring young naturalist Tommy Stubbins?
A. Dr. Dolittle
B. Pippi Longstocking
C. Ralph S. Mouse
D. Homer Price
E. Uncle Jeptha

2. Who was the Assistant Pig-Keeper of Caer Dallben?
A. Clay
B. Fog
C. Ribsy
D. Taran
E. Soup

3. What small town was the home of boy detective Encyclopedia Brown?
A. Popperville
B. Drakeville
C. Smallville
D. Toadville
E. Idaville

4. Who was the original illustrator of A.A. Milne's Winnie-the-Pooh books?
A. A.A. Milne
B. L. Leslie Brooke
C. Marguerite de Angeli
D. John R. Neill
E. Ernest H. Shepard

5. What writer's creations include The Woozy, Professor Woggle-Bug, and the Fuddles of Fuddlecumjig?
A. C.S. Lewis
B. Lewis Carroll
C. Joel Chandler Harris
D. Maurice Sendak
E. L. Frank Baum

6. In "Mike Mulligan and His Steam Shovel," what was the name of Mike's steam shovel?
A. Ramona
B. Mary Anne
C. Beatrice
D. Sophie
E. Rebecca

7. In "Make Way for Ducklings," a mother duck and her eight ducklings stop traffic as they wend their way through what city?
A. San Francisco
B. Washington, D.C.
C. Duluth
D. Boston
E. Seattle

8. In which Dr. Seuss book would you encounter the Key-Slapping Slippard, the Quilligan quail, and Dr. Sam Snell?
A. "The 500 Hats of Bartholomew Cubbins"
B. "Yertle the Turtle"
C. "I Had Trouble in Getting to Solla Sellew"
D. "And to Think That I Saw It on Mulberry Street"
E. "McElligot's Pool"

Answers to Quiz #20 — **Kiddie Lit**

1. **(A) Dr. Dolittle.** Tommy was a supporting human character in "The Voyages of Dr. Dolittle" by Hugh Lofting.

2. **(D) Taran.** Taran was the hero of Lloyd Alexander's "Chronicles of Prydain."

3. **(E) Idaville.** In a series of books by Donald J. Sobol, Leroy "Encyclopedia" Brown ran The Brown Detective Agency out of his garage at 13 Rover Avenue, charging 25 cents (plus expenses) per case. He was also frequently enlisted in helping his father, the chief of police, solve larger crimes.

4. **(E) Ernest H. Shepard.** John R. Neill was the original illustrator for the "Oz" books.

5. **(E) L. Frank Baum.** The Woozy was a one-of-a-kind "square" beast in "The Patchwork Girl of Oz." Professor Woggle-Bug was a highly educated insect in "The Land of Oz." The Fuddles of Fuddlecumjig were characters in "The Emerald City of Oz" who break apart like living jigsaw puzzles.

6. **(B) Mary Anne.** In a single day, Mike and Mary Anne dig a cellar for the new town hall in Popperville, but dig the hole so deep they are unable to get out.

7. **(D) Boston.** A statue of the mother duck and her youngsters featured in the Robert McCloskey book appears in the Boston Common where the family of ducks elected to make their home.

8. **(C) "I Had Trouble in Getting to Solla Sellew".** Nearly all of Dr. Seuss's 50+ titles are still in print. His "Green Eggs and Ham" is the third largest-selling book in the English language. Dr. Seuss was awarded an honorary Pulitzer Prize in 1984 citing his half-century contribution to "the education and enjoyment of America's children and their parents."

Quiz #21 — Elvis Lives

1. Elvis Cole is a fictional Los Angeles private detective in a series of novels, including "The Monkey's Raincoat" and "Voodoo River," by what author?
A. Michael Connelly
B. Robert Crais
C. Bill Pronzini
D. Marcia Muller
E. Les Roberts

2. On the TV series, "Miami Vice," Don Johnson's character, Sonny Crockett, had an unusual pet named Elvis. What kind of animal was it?
A. Ostrich
B. Ferret
C. Cockatoo
D. Alligator
E. Turtle

3. Elvis Costello first recorded with an American band named Clover. Since then, he has been backed by an amalgam of musicians going by what other name?
A. The Attractions
B. The Blue Moon Boys
C. Rockpile
D. Quiet Desperation
E. The Abbotts

4. Hollywood phenom Quentin Tarantino claims he wrote the screenplays for "Reservoir Dogs" and "Pulp Fiction" while living off the residual payments from his appearance as a member of a chorus of Elvis impersonators singing at the wedding of one of the characters on what TV series?
A. "The Golden Girls"
B. "Who's the Boss"
C. "Night Court"
D. "Amen"
E. "Moonlighting"

5. Elvis Grbac was the backup quarterback during the 1995 and 1996 seasons to the most efficient passer in NFL history. Name this all-pro quarterback.
A. Jeff Hostetler
B. Dan Marino
C. Steve Young
D. Warren Moon
E. Troy Aikman

6. What TV show featured a character who had an obsession with Elvis Presley, and often exclaimed "Great shades of Elvis!"?
A. "Lois and Clark: The New Adventures of Superman"
B. "Eek the Cat"
C. "The Nanny"
D. "Home Improvement"
E. "Cleghorne"

7. What former NFL coach left tickets to his games at the will-call window for the late Elvis Presley?
A. Joe Gibbs
B. Mike Ditka
C. George Allen
D. Buddy Ryan
E. Jerry Glanville

8. Which Elvis Presley movie featured the songs "Adam and Evil," "Am I Ready," "All That I Am," and "Beach Shack"?
A. "Spinout"
B. "Speedway"
C. "Live a Little, Love a Little"
D. "Paradise, Hawaiian Style"
E. "Double Trouble"

Answers to Quiz #21 — **Elvis Lives**

1. **(B) Robert Crais.** Elvis is a Tinseltown detective whose office features directors' chairs for prospective clients and whose desk is adorned with statues of cartoon characters like Mickey Mouse, Jiminy Cricket, and a Pinocchio clock. He is forever describing bad guys as Boris Badanov types or Wile E. Coyotes.

2. **(D) Alligator.** Elvis was the "watchdog" aboard Crockett's boat, the St. Vitus' Dance.

3. **(A) The Attractions.** Costello's real name is Declan Patrick McManus. One member of Clover was Huey Lewis, later the leader of Huey Lewis and the News.

4. **(A) "The Golden Girls".** Tarantino was one of about a dozen Elvis impersonators who sang at the wedding of Dorothy (Bea Arthur) to Blanche's uncle Lucas (Leslie Nielsen) in the final episode of "The Golden Girls."

5. **(C) Steve Young.** Under the NFL's complicated system of ranking quarterbacks using percentages of completion, touchdowns, interceptions, and yards per pass, San Francisco's Steve Young is now the career leader in passing efficiency eclipsing such legends as Joe Montana, Bart Starr, and Sonny Jurgensen.

6. **(A) "Lois and Clark: The New Adventures of Superman."** The producers of "Lois and Clark" tried to update editor Perry White a bit. White had an Elvis Presley story for every situation and shouted "Great shades of Elvis" instead of his comic book predecessor's "Great Caesar's ghost!"

7. **(E) Jerry Glanville.** The always outrageous Glanville began leaving tickets for Elvis in 1988. He stopped the practice after Lisa Marie Presley married Michael Jackson. "I think it killed [Elvis]," Glanville declared.

8. **(A) "Spinout".** "Spinout" was Elvis's 22nd movie, released in November 1966. During preproduction the film was titled "Never Say No," then changed to "Never Say Yes" and finally to "Spinout." Carl Betz played the father of Shelley Fabares in "Spinout" as he did on the TV series "The Donna Reed Show."

Quiz #22 — **Treasure Islands**

1. When Tom Sawyer and Huck Finn ran away to become pirates, they stayed on what island?
A. Jackson's Island
B. Island No. 10
C. Harper Island
D. Brown Island
E. Blackjack Island

2. Jaluit, Wotho, Eniwetok, and Kwajalein are atolls in what island group?
A. Shetland Islands
B. Mariana Islands
C. Marshall Islands
D. Aleutian Islands
E. Kuril Islands

3. Napoleon I was banished to the island of Elba in 1814. The island of Elba lies off the coast of Italy in what sea?
A. Adriatic
B. Ligurian
C. Baltic
D. Tyrrhenian
E. Ionian

4. Easter Island, famous for the unusual carved statues called "moai" by the natives, belongs to what country?
A. Chile
B. Spain
C. Portugal
D. The Netherlands
E. Great Britain

5. What large island is connected to the nearest mainland by a chain of shoals called Adam's Bridge?
A. Baffin
B. Corsica
C. Ceylon
D. Madagascar
E. Tasmania

6. What island was aviatrix Amelia Earhart's destination when she disappeared in 1937?
A. New Guinea
B. Nikumaroro
C. Prince Edward Island
D. Howland Island
E. Phoenix Island

7. What world capital's name translates literally into "island of poles"?
A. Reykjavík
B. Stockholm
C. Ulan Bator
D. Mogadishu
E. Bujumbura

8. Channel Islands National Park lies off the coast of what U.S. state?
A. Texas
B. California
C. Washington
D. New York
E. South Carolina

Answers to Quiz #22 — **Treasure Islands**

1. **(A) Jackson's Island.** They returned home only after learning that they were thought dead, and Tom learned how saddened his Aunt Polly was. The boys interrupted their own funeral service.

2. **(C) Marshall Islands.** The Marshall Islands were the scene of heavy fighting between the Americans and Japanese in 1944. The Americans took over the island of Majuro, the first Japanese possession captured during WWII. The atolls of Eniwetok and Bikini became American nuclear testing grounds. Kwajalein is the largest island in the group.

3. **(D) Tyrrhenian.** While exiled on Elba in 1814-15, Napoleon I ruled the island as a principality with the title of Emperor.

4. **(A) Chile.** The island is called Rapa Nui by the natives. It was dubbed Easter Island by the Dutch explorer Roggeveen who discovered the island on Easter Sunday in 1722. The island was annexed by Chile in 1888.

5. **(C) Ceylon.** Legend holds that the chain is the remains of a causeway built by Rama, the hero of the "Ramayana," to allow his armies passage from India to Ceylon while rescuing his wife, Sita.

6. **(D) Howland Island.** Howland was meant to be a brief refueling stop in July 1937 after a flight from New Guinea during Earhart's attempt to circumnavigate the globe by air. Instead, she and her navigator Fred Noonan disappeared from the face of the earth. Howland Island no longer has a runway.

7. **(B) Stockholm.** The capital of Sweden is built on several islands and the adjacent mainland. The city has been nicknamed "The Venice of the North," where canals are navigated by ferries rather than gondolas.

8. **(B) California.** The best known of the islands is Santa Catalina, a popular resort spot and subject of the 1963 hit song "26 Miles (Santa Catalina)" by the Four Preps.

Quiz #23 — Hats All, Folks

1. Which Disney character wore a Tyrolean hat?
A. Dopey
B. Pinocchio
C. Goofy
D. Dumbo
E. Aladdin

2. What last name was shared as Rock Hudson's alias in the movie "Pillow Talk" and Scarecrow's real name on the TV series "Scarecrow and Mrs. King"?
A. Fedora
B. Boater
C. Derby
D. Stetson
E. Havelock

3. Who designed the pillbox hat frequently worn by Jackie Kennedy?
A. Lilly Dache
B. Yves St. Laurent
C. Anne Klein
D. Halston
E. Helen Kaminski

4. What runner came back from last place to win Olympic gold in the men's 800-meter race in 1972 wearing his favorite golf cap?
A. Dave Wottle
B. Glenn Cunningham
C. Jim Ryun
D. Dick Wilmarth
E. Sebastian Coe

5. What is the name of the monocled dandy who appears in cover art for "The New Yorker"?
A. Robert Dudley
B. Eustace Tilley
C. Sidney Webb
D. Patrick Asquith
E. Arthur Jerome

6. What James Bond movie featured a large Oriental gentleman named Oddjob who could fling his bowler hat boomerang-style with deadly force?
A. "Dr. No"
B. "Moonraker"
C. "For Your Eyes Only"
D. "The Living Daylights"
E. "Goldfinger"

7. What hat shares its name with a top 40 song by the British rock group Procol Harum?
A. Green Beret
B. Homburg
C. Tam O'Shanter
D. Panama Hat
E. Sombrero

8. What hat was invented by William Coke in 1849, but named after the firm that first produced them?
A. Derby
B. Stetson
C. Homburg
D. Dolly Varden
E. Bowler

Answers to Quiz #23 — Hats All, Folks

1. **(B) Pinocchio.** A Tyrolean hat is soft-brimmed, usually made of green felt, with a peaked crown and a feather or brush ornament on the hatband.

2. **(D) Stetson.** In "Pillow Talk," Rock Hudson starred as playboy Brad Allen who tried to pass himself off to Doris Day as Texan "Rex Stetson." Scarecrow, a government agent played by Bruce Boxleitner on "Scarecrow and Mrs. King," was named Lee Stetson.

3. **(D) Halston.** The pillbox had its detractors, including Bob Dylan who lampooned the style in the song "Leopard Skin Pillbox Hat." Designer Halston's real name was Roy Frowick.

4. **(A) Dave Wottle.** In the excitement following the race, Wottle forgot to remove his cap during the medal ceremony. Afraid he might have offended people, he apologized for his action on national television.

5. **(B) Eustace Tilley.** Eustace Tilley was created by Rea Irvin, the magazine's original art director. The February 21, 1994 cover of "The New Yorker" featured a youngster named "Elvis Tilley," drawn by underground comic artist R. Crumb.

6. **(E) "Goldfinger".** Oddjob, played by Harold Sakata, was an assassin working for Auric Goldfinger in the 1964 film "Goldfinger."

7. **(B) Homburg.** "Homburg" was the 1967 follow-up hit to "Whiter Shade of Pale." Procol Harum, Latin for "far from these things," was actually named for the cat of a friend of songwriter Keith Reid, a non-performing member of the group.

8. **(E) Bowler.** The hats were first manufactured in London by Thomas Bowler and Sons.

Quiz #24 — The Old West

1. What western heroine was born in Ohio as Phoebe Ann Moses?
A. Belle Starr
B. Annie Oakley
C. Calamity Jane
D. Hannie Caulder
E. Etta Place

2. What western outlaw has been played on film by Paul Newman, Nick Adams, Anthony Dexter, and Robert Taylor?
A. Billy the Kid
B. Cole Younger
C. Jesse James
D. John Wesley Hardin
E. Doc Holliday

3. The Anaconda Copper Mining Company was based in what western U.S. state?
A. Montana
B. Wyoming
C. Colorado
D. Arizona
E. Nevada

4. Which of the following was not a brother of lawman Wyatt Earp?
A. Warren
B. James
C. Billy
D. Virgil
E. Morgan

5. The Pony Express had way stations for its riders every 10 miles between St. Joseph, Missouri and what western city?
A. Sacramento
B. San Diego
C. Carson City
D. San Francisco
E. Tombstone

6. The Cherokee Strip was a part of what U.S. state?
A. Texas
B. Kansas
C. Arizona
D. Oklahoma
E. New Mexico

7. Wild Bill Hickok served as a U.S. marshal in what city?
A. Deadwood
B. Santa Fe
C. Abilene
D. Dodge City
E. Tombstone

8. Who invented the pistol nicknamed the "hide-away gun"?
A. Samuel Colt
B. Ned Buntline
C. Bat Masterson
D. Richard Gatling
E. Henry Derringer

Answers to Quiz #24 — **The Old West**

1. **(B) Annie Oakley.** As the trick-shooting sensation of Buffalo Bill's Wild West Show, Annie Oakley could shoot the cigarette out a man's mouth, fire backwards using mirrors, and once broke 943 out of 1000 glass balls thrown into the air using a .22 caliber rifle.

2. **(A) Billy the Kid.** In "The Left-Handed Gun" (1957), "Strange Lady In Town" (1955), "The Parson and the Outlaw" (1957), and "Billy the Kid" (1940), respectively.

3. **(A) Montana.** The open-pit copper mine operation run by Marcus Daly and his mining company in Butte, Montana was so large it forced sections of the town to relocate.

4. **(C) Billy.** Wyatt was deputy sheriff of Pima County, and his brother, Virgil, was the town marshal in Tombstone when the gunfight at the OK Corral occurred on October 26, 1881. Two months later, Virgil was shot and wounded in an ambush. In March 1882, Morgan was killed.

5. **(A) Sacramento.** The transcontinental telegraph was completed on October 24, 1881. The Pony Express was abandoned two days later, after a short lifespan of 18 months.

6. **(D) Oklahoma.** The Cherokee Strip was Indian territory until the U.S. government opened it to settlers as a part of the Oklahoma land rush at the end of the 19th century. Settlers who jumped the gun during the rush races were nicknamed "Sooners."

7. **(C) Abilene.** After the U.S. Civil War, James Butler Hickok became a marshal in Hays City, Kansas. In April 1871, he moved to a post in Abilene. Hickok was killed on August 2, 1876 — shot in the back by Jack McCall while playing cards in Tombstone, Arizona.

8. **(E) Henry Derringer.** The Derringer was a compact, single-shot pistol, easily tucked away in a sleeve or boot. The Derringer achieved notoriety after John Wilkes Booth used one to assassinate Abraham Lincoln.

Quiz #25 — Lucky Charms

1. In what movie does Clint Eastwood taunt a criminal with: "You've got to ask yourself one question: 'Do I feel lucky?' Well, do ya, punk?"
A. "The Dead Pool"
B. "Dirty Harry"
C. "The Enforcer"
D. "The Gauntlet"
E. "Magnum Force"

2. During World War II, what U.S. general referred to his advance headquarters as "Lucky Forward"?
A. Dwight D. Eisenhower
B. John J. Pershing
C. Joseph Stilwell
D. George S. Patton
E. Douglas MacArthur

3. What was the first name of mobster "Lucky" Luciano?
A. Alvin
B. Frank
C. Charles
D. Louis
E. Alfonso

4. What former news anchor formed his or her own production company called Lucky Duck Productions?
A. Linda Ellerbee
B. Edwin Newman
C. Deborah Norville
D. Jessica Savitch
E. Tom Snyder

5. What was the name of the magician on the children's TV series "Lucky Pup"?
A. Uncle Croc
B. Hoodoo
C. Chisholm
D. Foodini
E. Rosebud

6. On the 1959-60 TV series, "Mr. Lucky," Mr. Lucky was a professional gambler who used what floating casino ship as his base of operations?
A. Fortuna
B. Midas
C. Happenstance
D. Opportunity
E. Blessed Lady

7. What movie cowboy helped keep young hothead Lucky Jenkins out of trouble?
A. Hopalong Cassidy
B. Roy Rogers
C. Sunset Carson
D. Gene Autry
E. Hoot Gibson

8. What R&B group scored consecutive #1 hits in 1989 with "Dial My Heart" and "Lucky Charm"?
A. New Edition
B. The Boys
C. Today
D. Surface
E. Bell Biv DeVoe

Answers to Quiz #25 — **Lucky Charms**

1. (B) "Dirty Harry". At the time, Eastwood, playing police officer Harry Callahan, has his vaunted .44 Magnum handgun pointed at the cringing Andrew Robinson, trying to recall how many bullets he has fired.

2. (D) George S. Patton. Patton used the nickname "Lucky" to refer to his Third Army troops in Europe.

3. (C) Charles. The ruthless Luciano looked the part of the mobster with a scarred face and a droopy right eye — the result of a deep knife slash through the muscles of his right cheek by either gangland rivals or rogue cops.

4. (A) Linda Ellerbee. Ellerbee, a former NBC news anchorperson, went on to produce news programs for kids on Nickelodeon.

5. (D) Foodini. Lucky was a dog with a $5-million inheritance that the villain, Foodini, hoped to steal. Foodini proved popular enough to warrant his own spinoff series titled "Foodini the Great."

6. (A) Fortuna. The TV series, starring John Vivyan, was based on the 1943 Cary Grant film with the same name. The music from the TV series was made available on two successful albums for Henry Mancini titled "Music from Mr. Lucky" and "Mr. Lucky Goes Latin."

7. (A) Hopalong Cassidy. Hoppy's young sidekick was played by Russell Hayden in about two dozen film westerns between 1937 and 1941.

8. (B) The Boys. The members of The Boys are all brothers — Tajh, Khiry, Hakeem, and Bilal Abdul-Samad. The songs came from their debut album "Message from The Boys."

Quiz #26 — **Ring a Bell?**

1. The Liberty Bell cracked in 1835 while tolling in mourning the death of what former government official?
A. John Marshall
B. Alexander Hamilton
C. Benjamin Franklin
D. John Quincy Adams
E. John Jay

2. Who became the first human to break the sound barrier while piloting the Bell X-1 experimental plane?
A. Steve Austin
B. Chuck Yeager
C. Jacqueline Cochrane
D. Alan Shepard
E. John Glenn

3. According to the introduction of their hit song "Tighten Up," Archie Bell and the Drells hailed from what city?
A. Houston
B. Philadelphia
C. Denver
D. Seattle
E. Honolulu

4. The winner of what college football rivalry earns the right to keep the Victory Bell?
A. Michigan-Minnesota
B. Brigham Young-Utah
C. Michigan State-Indiana
D. Mississippi-Mississippi State
E. USC-UCLA

5. "Bella Notte" is a love serenade from what Disney classic film?
A. "Cinderella"
B. "Lady and the Tramp"
C. "The Little Mermaid"
D. "Sleeping Beauty"
E. "Beauty and the Beast"

6. What was the name of the assistant summoned by Alexander Graham Bell in the first working demonstration of his telephone?
A. Thomas Watson
B. David Whitewater
C. Henry Stanley
D. Joseph Walton
E. George Gottlieb

7. From what movie is the line: "Every time a bell rings, an angel gets its wings"?
A. "Chances Are"
B. "The Bishop's Wife"
C. "Blithe Spirit"
D. "Angel on My Shoulder"
E. "It's a Wonderful Life"

8. What author won a Pulitzer Prize in 1945 for his novel "A Bell for Adano"?
A. Ernest Hemingway
B. William Faulkner
C. Harold Robbins
D. Booth Tarkington
E. John Hersey

Answers to Quiz #26 — Ring a Bell?

1. (A) **John Marshall.** The Liberty Bell was created in 1751 to celebrate Pennsylvania's 50th anniversary as a British colony. It cracked while being tested, and was recast twice by brass founders John Stow and John Pass. John Marshall was a former Chief Justice of the U.S. Supreme Court.

2. (B) **Chuck Yeager.** Famed test pilot Chuck Yeager flew the X-1 34 times. On the plane's 50th flight, on October 14, 1947, Yeager exceeded Mach 1 for the first time flying over Murac Dry Lake Air Field (now Edwards Air Force Base) in California. Yeager reenacted the flight for his 75th birthday in 1997.

3. (A) **Houston.** The song is introduced with "We're Archie Bell and the Drells from Houston, Texas, and we not only sing but we dance as good as we walk." Bell felt the introduction was necessary. "When Kennedy was assassinated, I heard a disk jockey say "nothing good ever came from Texas," so I wanted people to know we were from Texas and we were good." "Tighten Up" went to #1 in 1968.

4. (E) **USC-UCLA.** The Victory Bell was first awarded in 1942. Another Victory Bell is awarded in games between Duke and North Carolina. Other college football trophies include the Bee Hive Boot in Brigham Young-Utah football games, the Little Brown Jug in Michigan vs. Minnesota, the Brass Spittoon in Michigan State vs. Indiana, and the Golden Egg in Mississippi-Mississippi State football games.

5. (B) **"Lady and the Tramp".** Lady and the Tramp are serenaded during their spaghetti dinner by the benevolent Italian chef, Tony, who feeds them in the alley next to his restaurant.

6. (A) **Thomas Watson.** Bell cried "Mr. Watson, come here, I want you" into his telephone after spilling battery acid on himself on March 10, 1876.

7. (E) **"It's a Wonderful Life".** Good guy George Bailey, played by Jimmy Stewart, is informed about this phenomenon by his guardian angel, Clarence, and later by his young daughter, Zuzu.

8. (E) **John Hersey.** A reporter for both "Time" and the "New Yorker," Hersey also gained notoriety for his non-fiction works "Hiroshima," "Into the Valley" and "The Wall." Hersey died in 1993 at age 78.

Quiz #27 — I, Robot

1. The term "robot" first appeared in the 1921 play "R.U.R." This play was written by what Czech playwright?
A. Thomas Masaryk
B. Karel Čapek
C. Václav Havel
D. Emil Synek
E. Josef Kodicek

2. What is the name of the robot who assists the Mighty Morphin Power Rangers?
A. Zordon
B. Andy
C. Alpha
D. Robert
E. Quark

3. What was the name of the woman that the mad scientist Rotwang replaced with an evil robot in the 1926 silent film classic "Metropolis"?
A. Maria
B. Hel
C. Brigitte
D. Leni
E. Eliza

4. What 8-legged robot was designed with the help of NASA for the exploration of active volcanos?
A. Nettie
B. Yoshi 5
C. Dante II
D. Alvin
E. Knowbot

5. What robot was marketed exclusively through Neiman-Marcus catalogs?
A. Cromer Jr.
B. Rossum
C. Buddha
D. Comro 1
E. Chadwick

6. What was the name of the popular cigarette-smoking robot built by Westinghouse as an exhibit at the 1939-40 World's Fair?
A. Hero
B. King Grey
C. Mego Man
D. Oliver
E. Electro

7. What was the name of the robot maid owned by "The Jetsons"?
A. Irona
B. Brenda
C. Wilma
D. Roberta
E. Rosie

8. In the Jim Meddick comic strip "Robotman," what is the name of Robotman's roommate?
A. Spot
B. Thomas
C. Monty
D. Rimshot
E. Fluffy

Answers to Quiz #27 — I, Robot

1. **(B) Karel Čapek.** In Čapek's native language of Czech, "robot" was related to the word for slave in this story of artificial workers and their revolt against humanity. "R.U.R." stood for Rossum's Universal Robots.

2. **(C) Alpha.** Comic relief is provided by Alpha whose favorite saying is "Aye-aye-aye!"

3. **(A) Maria.** The evil Maria robot incites a riot among the human work force leading revolting workers to a watery grave in this futuristic Fritz Lang film.

4. **(C) Dante II.** Dante II went into Alaska's Mount Shurr in 1994 in a test of the robot that might explore planets in the future.

5. **(D) Comro 1.** According to Neiman-Marcus, Comro 1 would "uncomplainingly open doors, serve guests, take out trash, bring in the paper, sweep, fetch, do light hauling, water the plants, pick up after children and pets, caddy at the putting green, [and] walk the dog." The company also offered WIRES, a robotic pet to keep Comro 1 company.

6. **(E) Electro.** Electronic pets must be the rage. Electro had his own robotic dog companion named Sparky.

7. **(E) Rosie.** Rosie's voice was supplied by Jean Vanderpyl, who is also the voice of Wilma and Pebbles Flintstone.

8. **(C) Monty.** Monty thinks he is an alien, and that his mother was a lava lamp.

Quiz #28 — Library Card

1. "Marian the Librarian" is a song from what Broadway and movie musical?
A. "The Harvey Girls"
B. "Singin' in the Rain"
C. "How to Succeed in Business Without Really Trying"
D. "The Music Man"
E. "A Chorus Line"

2. In the 1945 book, "Black Boy," author Richard Wright was determined to get books from the Memphis Public Library which did not serve blacks. What author did Wright want to read?
A. Laura Ingalls Wilder
B. H.L. Mencken
C. Sinclair Lewis
D. Frederick Douglass
E. Mark Twain

3. The lions guarding the steps of the New York Public Library are known by what names?
A. Patience and Fortitude
B. Cleo and Leo
C. Wisdom and Knowledge
D. Castor and Pollux
E. Donny and Marie

4. In which Sinclair Lewis novel does the heroine, Carol Milford, attend library school?
A. "Arrowsmith"
B. "Babbitt"
C. "Main Street"
D. "Dodsworth"
E. "Elmer Gantry"

5. The Carnegie Corporation of New York funded almost 2000 libraries in towns in the United States. In what state will you find the most Carnegie libraries?
A. New York
B. Minnesota
C. Texas
D. California
E. Indiana

6. What adventurer/author spent his later years as Count Waldstein's librarian at the Chateau of Dux?
A. Christopher Columbus
B. Marco Polo
C. Mark Twain
D. Casanova
E. Meriwether Lewis

7. What Umberto Eco novel was a medieval murder mystery connected to a monastery library?
A. "The Brotherhood"
B. "The Incident at Santa Lucia"
C. "The Name of the Rose"
D. "The Enchanters"
E. "Foucault's Pendulum"

8. What author appeared on "Celebrity Jeopardy!" and won $11,400 for the Bangor Public Library?
A. Stephen King
B. Tom Clancy
C. Leo Buscaglia
D. Scott Turow
E. Kurt Vonnegut Jr.

Answers to Quiz #28 — **Library Card**

1. (D) "The Music Man". Marian Paroo, town librarian and piano teacher, is among the residents of River City, Iowa, who fall under the spell of con man Prof. Harold Hill in "The Music Man." Composer Meredith Willson's classic musical set records on Broadway and was a hit film for Warner Brothers starring Robert Preston, Shirley Jones, and a young Ronny Howard.

2. (B) H.L. Mencken. In 1926, Wright read a denunciation of Mencken in his local newspaper, and wanted to know what Mencken had said that caused such an outburst of rage. Wright said Mencken was the first writer to affect him greatly, showing him that "My words are my weapons."

3. (A) Patience and Fortitude. The lions were also known, at one time, as Lady Astor and Lord Lenox.

4. (C) "Main Street". Carol is about to drop out of library school until she discovers the wonders of the "Cumulative Index."

5. (E) Indiana. Andrew Carnegie established the Carnegie Corporation of New York in 1911 to administer the distribution of his personal fortune for philanthropic purposes. Directing the Corporation himself until his death in 1919, he gave a large number of grants for public libraries and church organs. Indiana has 146 Carnegie libraries.

6. (D) Casanova. In the 18th century, Casanova worked as a spy, a chemist, a philosopher, an author, a critic, and the director of the French lottery, but for the last 13 years of his life, "the idol of all women" was a librarian.

7. (C) "The Name of the Rose". The film version starred Sean Connery and Christian Slater, and left many with a dry mouth and even drier fingers.

8. (A) Stephen King. Stephen King edged out David Duchovny, of "X-Files" fame, to take the cash on a Final Jeopardy! question about Truman Capote and "Breakfast at Tiffany's."

1. What toy was invented by the son of noted architect Frank Lloyd Wright?
A. Lincoln Logs
B. Tinkertoys
C. Etch A Sketch
D. Whizzer
E. Silly Putty

2. The name of what toy company translates as "I assemble" in Latin, though the name is actually an abbreviation of "play well"?
A. Mattel
B. Tonka
C. Lego
D. Kusan
E. Cadaco

3. What is the most popular Matchbox car model?
A. Station wagon
B. Squad car
C. Doubledecker bus
D. Ambulance
E. Ice cream truck

4. Which of the following board games is the oldest?
A. Candy Land
B. Chutes and Ladders
C. Stratego
D. Go to the Head of the Class
E. Mouse Trap

5. A.C. Gilbert, the inventor of the Erector set, won an Olympic gold medal in 1908 in what event?
A. High jump
B. Shot put
C. Decathlon
D. Pole vault
E. Marathon

6. What toy was supposedly invented by Lisa Loopner's father in the Lisa and Todd skits, featuring Gilda Radner and Bill Murray, on "Saturday Night Live"?
A. Yo-yo
B. Magic 8-Ball
C. Slinky
D. Super Ball
E. Pogo stick

7. What was the first toy advertised on TV?
A. Silly Putty
B. Play-Doh
C. Easy Bake Oven
D. Betsy Wetsy
E. Mr. Potato Head

8. What was the name of the first black doll to join Barbie's group of Mattel friends?
A. Tutti
B. P.J.
C. Julia
D. Christie
E. Tammy

Answers to Quiz #29 — Toy Box

1. (A) **Lincoln Logs.** John Lloyd Wright developed the building blocks in 1916 based on a design of Japanese wood-joint techniques he observed on a bridge built without the use of nails or steel.

2. (C) **Lego.** Lego was shortened from the Danish "leg godt." The first Lego product was a baby rattle sold in 1947. The first Lego blocks were introduced in 1949, called Automatic Binding Bricks.

3. (C) **Doubledecker bus.** Matchbox sells an average of a million vehicles per week.

4. (D) **Go to the Head of the Class.** Go to the Head of the Class was first issued in 1938, followed by Chutes and Ladders in 1943, Candy Land in 1949, and Mouse Trap and Stratego in the 1960s.

5. (D) **Pole vault.** Alfred Gilbert tied with fellow American Edward Cooke with a vault of 12'2". Gilbert worked his way through Yale University as a magician, and was the owner of the Mysto Manufacturing Co. which sold professional magic equipment. In 1913, while watching the placement of steel girders in the construction of his company's headquarters, he came up with the idea of the Erector set. With the release of the toy, he changed the name of the company to the A.C. Gilbert Company.

6. (C) **Slinky.** The Slinky was actually invented in 1943 by a civilian naval engineer by Richard James.

7. (E) **Mr. Potato Head.** Mr. Potato Head experienced a resurgence with his popularity among viewers of the 1995 movie "Toy Story."

8. (D) **Christie.** Talking Brad was the first black male doll in Barbieland.

Quiz #30 — Kissing Cousins

1. What was the name of Samantha Stephens' identical cousin on the TV series "Bewitched"?
A. Sabrina
B. Serena
C. Jeannie
D. Drina
E. Hagatha

2. What is the last name of long-time New York disc jockey "Cousin Brucie"?
A. Adams
B. Lennon
C. Morrow
D. Carter
E. Turner

3. What operatic character had aristocratic cousins named Maximilian and Cunegonde?
A. Idamante
B. Candide
C. Fredda
D. Carmen
E. Rienzi

4. What humorist developed a cult following after the publication of his first two books "I Smell Esther Williams" and "My Cousin, the Gastroenterologist"?
A. Mark Leyner
B. Garrison Keillor
C. Art Buchwald
D. Dave Barry
E. P.J. O'Rourke

5. What actor, who once played a villain in a James Bond movie, is a cousin of Ian Fleming, the creator of James Bond?
A. Richard Kiel
B. Christopher Walken
C. Donald Pleasence
D. Telly Savalas
E. Christopher Lee

6. Which U.S. president married his own fifth cousin?
A. Jimmy Carter
B. John Quincy Adams
C. Rutherford B. Hayes
D. Franklin Roosevelt
E. Ulysses S. Grant

7. What was the name of Bambi's male cousin in the book "Bambi" by Felix Salten?
A. Brennan
B. Owl
C. Rufus
D. Gobo
E. Knobby

8. What is the name of the young heroine in Louisa May Alcott's "Eight Cousins"?
A. Rose
B. Amy
C. May
D. June
E. Daisy

1. **(B) Serena.** Elizabeth Montgomery played both roles using the alias "Pandora Sparks" for Serena in the show's credits.

2. **(C) Morrow.** Bruce Morrow helped publicize the Beatles' first American tour in 1964. Still with WCBS in New York, he hosts "Saturday Night's Oldie Party." Morrow was inducted into the Broadcasting and Cable Hall of Fame in 1993.

3. **(B) Candide.** The trio of cousins have a tutor named Dr. Pangloss who teaches them that this is "the best of all possible worlds," but they soon experience the atrocities of life, including rape and war, learning they must make the best of their world that they can. The operetta, "Candide," was composed by Leonard Bernstein, with the libretto based on the novel by Voltaire.

4. **(A) Mark Leyner.** His success broadened with the 1992 novel "Et Tu, Babe" about a successful, self-obsessed novelist named Mark Leyner.

5. **(E) Christopher Lee.** Lee played Scaramanga, a high-priced assassin, in "The Man with the Golden Gun."

6. **(D) Franklin Roosevelt.** Genealogists assert that FDR was also related to 11 prior U.S. presidents, either by blood or through marriage. Eleanor Roosevelt's maiden name was Roosevelt.

7. **(D) Gobo.** Bambi grew up with his cousins Faline and Gobo. Gobo disappeared, later to return as a pitiful stranger wearing a horsehair halter, indicating he had been used by man.

8. **(A) Rose.** Rose is an orphaned teenager who lives with her maiden aunts, Peace and Plenty. Rose is adored by seven male cousins, all of whom live nearby.

Quiz #31 — Go Ask Alice

1. In the comic strip, "Dennis the Menace," Dennis's mother is named Alice. What is his father's first name?
A. Peter
B. Harold
C. George
D. Henry
E. Roger

2. On the TV series "Alice," starring Linda Lavin, what was Alice's last name?
A. Cooper
B. Krieger
C. Walker
D. Nelson
E. Hyatt

3. Alice Rosenbaum is the real name of what noted author?
A. Joyce Carol Oates
B. Ayn Rand
C. Alice Walker
D. Barbara Vine
E. Toni Morrison

4. Alice Coachman was the first black female athlete to win a gold medal in the Summer Olympics. What event did she win in 1948?
A. Heptathlon
B. 100-yard dash
C. High jump
D. 100-meter breaststroke
E. Pole vault

5. In 1939, comedienne Fanny Brice threatened to sue 20th-Century Fox claiming that what Alice Faye movie followed too closely to Brice's real-life story?
A. "Poor Little Rich Girl"
B. "You Can't Have Everything"
C. "Wake Up and Live"
D. "Little Old New York"
E. "Rose of Washington Square"

6. What was the title of the debut album from the Seattle-based band, Alice in Chains?
A. "Jar of Flies"
B. "Dirt"
C. "Facelift"
D. "Alice in Chains"
E. "Sap"

7. In the animated Disney film, "Alice in Wonderland," who provided the voice of the Cheshire Cat?
A. John Fiedler
B. Sterling Holloway
C. Paul Winchell
D. Sebastian Cabot
E. Walt Disney

8. On the TV series "The Honeymooners," what was Alice Kramden's maiden name?
A. Gibson
B. Hart
C. MacGillicuddy
D. Adams
E. Roosevelt

Answers to Quiz #31 — **Go Ask Alice**

1. (D) **Henry.** "Dennis the Menace," created by Hank Ketcham, first appeared on March 12, 1951. It now appears in nearly 800 U.S. newspapers daily.

2. (E) **Hyatt.** The series was based on the 1974 movie "Alice Doesn't Live Here Anymore," starring Ellen Burstyn as Alice. Diane Ladd appeared in both the film, as Flo, and the TV series, as Flo's replacement, Belle.

3. (B) **Ayn Rand.** Born and raised in Russia, Ayn Rand's philosophical fiction includes the novels "We, the Living," "Anthem," "The Fountainhead," and "Atlas Shrugged."

4. (C) **High jump.** Coachman, a native of the state of Georgia, cleared 5'6" on her first attempt to win the gold.

5. (E) **"Rose of Washington Square".** Nearly 30 years later, Barbra Streisand would win an Oscar for playing Fanny Brice in the movie "Funny Girl."

6. (C) **"Facelift".** Alice in Chains is a hard rock guitar band from the Pacific Northwest hotbed that gave birth to Nirvana, Pearl Jam, and Soundgarden in the 1980s. Band members are Mike Starr, Layne Staley, Sean Kinney, and Jerry Cantrell. Their fifth album is called "Grind."

7. (B) **Sterling Holloway.** The slow-speaking Holloway may be most familiar to Disney fans as the voice of Winnie-the-Pooh. Holloway also appeared in the 1933 live-action film production of "Alice in Wonderland" as The Frog.

8. (A) **Gibson.** Pert Kelton originated the role of Alice Kramden, but did not enter into "The Honeymooners" series due to a heart condition. Kelton did appear in one episode of the series as Mrs. Gibson, the mother of her successor Alice, Audrey Meadows.

Quiz #32 — **Quiz Kids**

1. The Cisco Kid was a popular western TV character played by Duncan Renaldo in the 1950s. He first appeared in the writings of what author?
A. James Fennimore Cooper
B. O. Henry
C. Louis L'Amour
D. Bat Masterson
E. Erich Maria Remarquez

2. What TV personality's autobiography was titled after his catchphrase, "I Kid You Not"?
A. Tommy Smothers
B. Don Adams
C. Jack Paar
D. Hugh Downs
E. Jonathan Winters

3. The hard rock band Ugly Kid Joe and country artist Ricky Skaggs both released cover versions of what Harry Chapin song?
A. "Cats in the Cradle"
B. "Taxi"
C. "Six-String Orchestra"
D. "Sequel"
E. "Tangled-Up Puppet"

4. What actor starred in the movies "Frisco Kid," "The St. Louis Kid," and "The Oklahoma Kid"?
A. James Cagney
B. Jack Benny
C. Brian Dennehy
D. Harrison Ford
E. Richard Starrett

5. Which of the following was not an original member of the Dead End Kids?
A. Huntz Hall
B. Leo Gorcey
C. Stanley Clements
D. Bernard Punsley
E. Bobby Jordan

6. Jason Kidd, the 1994-95 NBA Rookie of the Year, was drafted by the Dallas Mavericks after Kidd declared his eligibility during his sophomore year of college. What university did Kidd attend?
A. Marquette
B. UNLV
C. Michigan State
D. UC-Berkeley
E. Georgetown

7. What was the title of choreographer Michael Kidd's first, and so far, only, ballet?
A. "The Bald Prima Donna"
B. "The Maids"
C. "The Entertainer"
D. "The Count of Monte Cristo"
E. "On Stage"

8. What Edgar Allan Poe story is about William Legrand's search for the buried treasure of Captain Kidd?
A. "The Telltale Heart"
B. "Ligeia"
C. "The Narrative of Arthur Gordon Pym"
D. "The Purloined Letter"
E. "The Gold Bug"

*Answers to Quiz #32 — **Quiz Kids***

1. (B) O. Henry. The Cisco Kid was known as "The Robin Hood of the West." The "Cisco Kid" TV series was the first TV western filmed in color.

2. (C) Jack Paar. Paar was Johnny Carson's predecessor as the host of "The Tonight Show" from July 1957 until March 1962. Paar's sidekick during the entire run was Hugh Downs, and his former Army buddy, Jose Melis, served as his "Tonight Show" bandleader.

3. (A) "Cats in the Cradle". Ugly Kid Joe reached the top 10 in 1993 with their pop/metal version of the song. Skaggs's version was on the Billboard country charts in the spring of 1996.

4. (A) James Cagney. Cagney played a truck driver accused of murder in "The St. Louis Kid" (1934), a waterfront sailor who rises to a position of power on the Barbary Coast in "Frisco Kid" (1935), and a gunfighter called "The Oklahoma Kid" (1939).

5. (C) Stanley Clements. When "Dead End" moved from the Broadway stage to the silver screen in 1939, producer Samuel Goldwyn brought along the group of young actors who played the streetwise punks idolizing Baby Face Martin, played by Humphrey Bogart in the movie. Although the youths weren't exactly idol material, they proved to be popular, and starred in a string of films as the "Dead End Kids," "East Side Kids," and "Bowery Boys." Stanley Clements didn't join the cast until 1958 when Leo Gorcey departed from the film series after his father's death.

6. (D) UC-Berkeley. Jason Kidd shared NBA Rookie of the Year honors in 1994-95 with Grant Hill.

7. (E) "On Stage". Created for the American Ballet Theatre, "On Stage" is a fantasy tale about a janitor who helps a timid young dancer at an audition.

8. (E) "The Gold Bug". Legrand is an impovished Southern gentleman who discovers a gold scarab and a piece of parchment that leads him to Kidd's treasure. Afraid to let others know what he is up to, he feigns an increasing insanity until locating the treasure with the aid of his servant, Jupiter, and the story's narrator.

Quiz #33 — **Baby Animals**

1. "Pony Time" was one song in a string of #1 dance hits for what 1960s rock star?
A. Chubby Checker
B. James Brown
C. Little Eva
D. Jackie Wilson
E. Wilson Pickett

2. What major league baseball franchise began as the Colt .45s?
A. Texas Rangers
B. Kansas City Royals
C. Houston Astros
D. California Angels
E. Colorado Rockies

3. Dan'l Baboon, Pauley Cracker, Roger Ranger, and Tadpole were the friends of what cartoon animal?
A. Odie Cologne
B. Lippy the Lion
C. Top Cat
D. Magilla Gorilla
E. Kimba the White Lion

4. "Hot Smoke and Sasafrass" reached #14 on the Billboard pop charts in 1969. The song was recorded by what one-hit wonder group?
A. Bubble Puppy
B. Alvin and the Chipmunks
C. The Peachicks
D. The Small Frye
E. Chick Corea's Elektric Orchestra

5. Joey Maxim, Joey Girardello, Joey Archibald, and Joey Gamache all won championships in what sport?
A. Boxing
B. Billiards
C. Bowling
D. Badminton
E. Auto Racing

6. On the TV series, "Gomer Pyle, USMC," Sgt. Carter had a rarely seen, but often referred to, girlfriend by what name?
A. Kitten
B. Lambkins
C. Chick
D. Duckling
E. Bunny

7. Which of the following animals does not have a baby called a calf?
A. Camel
B. Beaver
C. Hippopotamus
D. Whale
E. Elephant

8. What was the nickname of major league baseball pitcher Harvey Haddix?
A. Tadpole
B. Fawn
C. Spat
D. Cub
E. Kitten

Answers to Quiz #33 — **Baby Animals**

1. (A) **Chubby Checker.** Chubby Checker, born Ernest Evans, is the only artist to take the same record to #1 in different years. "The Twist" first reached #1 in September 1960. After Chubby appeared on "The Ed Sullivan Show" on October 22, 1961 doing "The Twist," the song returned to the charts reaching #1 again in January 1962.

2. (C) **Houston Astros.** The .45s played their home games in Houston's Colt Stadium until the Harris County Domed Stadium was built. With the stadium name changed to the Astrodome, with the playing surface of Astro-turf, the team name change was imminent.

3. (E) **Kimba the White Lion.** Kimba and his friends patrolled the ancient jungles of Africa in this Japanese series. The show was distributed in the U.S. in 1966 by NBC's syndicated division. There has been a lot of speculation about how much "Kimba" inspired the Disney film "The Lion King."

4. (A) **Bubble Puppy.** The group name Bubble Puppy came from a phrase in Aldous Huxley's "Brave New World." The Texas-based group disbanded shortly after their single hit, but reunited in 1986 and released their second album, distributed only in Europe.

5. (A) **Boxing.** Maxim was a light heavyweight champion (1950-52); Giardello, a middleweight champ (1963-65); Archibald, a featherweight crown holder (1938-40); and Gamache, a 1992 WBA lightweight champion.

6. (E) **Bunny.** Barbara Stuart made occasional appearances as the beloved "Bunny." Sometimes Carter and Bunny would double-date with Gomer (Jim Nabors) and his girl, Lu Ann Poovie (Elizabeth MacRae), with the expected disastrous results.

7. (B) **Beaver.** Baby beavers are called kittens or kits.

8. (E) **Kitten.** Haddix is the only pitcher to carry a perfect game beyond nine innings, retiring 36 batters in a row for the Pittsburgh Pirates against the Milwaukee Braves in 1959. The Braves finally scored in the 13th inning when Joe Adcock hit a home run off of Haddix, winning 1-0.

Quiz #34 — **Killer Quiz**

1. A womanizer named Killer is a recurring character in what popular comic strip?
A. "Beetle Bailey"
B. "Funky Winkerbean"
C. "Hi and Lois"
D. "Dilbert"
E. "Zippy the Pinhead"

2. In 1985, author Jack Early's "A Creative Kind of Killer" won the first award for best novel from the Private Eye Writers of America. What name is given to this award?
A. Shamus Award
B. Marlowe Award
C. Gumshoe Award
D. Hammett Award
E. The Gat

3. "Cop Killer" was a controversial song released in 1992 by what rap artist?
A. Ice Cube
B. Vanilla Ice
C. Ice-T
D. Ice Cold
E. Icee Ice

4. What comic strip hero faced a mortal enemy named Killer Kane?
A. Prince Valiant
B. Tarzan
C. Flash Gordon
D. Green Ghost
E. Buck Rogers

5. What musical brother group released the one-hit wonder "Killer Joe" in 1963?
A. Tavares
B. Rocky Fellers
C. The Cascades
D. The Ran-Dells
E. The Tams

6. The 1964 movie, "The Killers," was the last film for what actor?
A. Tom Tryon
B. Ronald Reagan
C. Cary Grant
D. William Conrad
E. Alan Ladd

7. Geraldine Jones was a hussy with a boyfriend named Killer in the comedy routines of what comedian?
A. Flip Wilson
B. Johnny Brown
C. Bill Dana
D. Redd Foxx
E. Eddie Murphy

8. What TV soap opera featured a plot involving a serial killer called "The Carnation Killer"?
A. "One Life to Live"
B. "All My Children"
C. "Santa Barbara"
D. "Another World"
E. "The Doctors and the Nurses"

Answers to Quiz #34 — **Killer Quiz**

1. **(A) "Beetle Bailey".** Killer's hat wiggles whenever he encounters an attractive woman.

2. **(A) Shamus Award.** Sue Grafton has three Shamus Awards to her credit with her A-B-C mystery series featuring detective Kinsey Milhone. Grafton had her own "Killer" novel with "K Is for Killer."

3. **(C) Ice-T.** Ice-T, born Tracey Morrow, featured the song on his 1992 album "Body Count."

4. **(E) Buck Rogers.** In the Asian-dominated world of the 25th century, Kane was a Major in the resistance forces. He was also the lover of soldier Wilma Deering, until she jilted him for Buck Rogers. In Buck's words, Kane has "a criminal career of such utter daring and magnificent proportions as to be unequalled in the annals of two centuries."

5. **(B) Rocky Fellers.** The Rocky Fellers — the Feller brothers, Eddie, Albert, Tony, and Junior — were all born in raised in Manila. Their only hit was this novelty tribute to society dancer Frank "Killer Joe" Piro.

6. **(B) Ronald Reagan.** "The Killers" was the only film in which Reagan played the heavy, the head of a criminal gang. Reagan only took the role as a favor to the head of Universal, who was Reagan's former agent. It was a decision Reagan would forever regret. "The Killers" was originally made for NBC, but was deemed too violent for television and was given theatrical release.

7. **(A) Flip Wilson.** Flip Wilson dressed in drag to play Geraldine whose catchphrase was "The devil made me do it!"

8. **(C) "Santa Barbara".** Peter Flint, played by Stephen Meadows, turned out to be "The Carnation Killer." His most unusual murder was dropping the neon letter "C" from the Capwell Hotel sign onto the head of Mary Duvall (Harley Jane Kozak).

Quiz #35 — Science and Nature

1. Dating from 12-14 million years ago, the fossil of what apelike creature is the earliest fossil distinguishing the hominid family of man from the pongid family of the apes on the basis of dental characteristics?
A. Australopithecus
B. Ramapithecus
C. Java Man
D. Neanderthal
E. Peking Man

2. Snackjack is a hybrid variety of what plant grown for commercial production of its peanut-sized seeds that may be used as a high-protein snack?
A. Pomegranate
B. Radish
C. Pea
D. Sunflower
E. Pumpkin

3. The long-tailed hopping mouse, the pig-footed bandicoot, and the Toolache wallaby are mammal species that have become extinct in the past century from what continent?
A. Australia
B. North America
C. South America
D. Africa
E. Asia

4. Although it has little impact in the West, what disease killed an estimated 90% of Ethiopia's cattle in 1889?
A. African swine fever
B. Bovine pneumonia
C. Rinderpest
D. Cowpox
E. Anthrax

5. Cementum is a bone-like tissue that grows in bands in the human body, not unlike tree rings, and has been used as an indicator of age. In what specific area of the body does cementum develop?
A. Liver
B. Mouth
C. Fingers and toes
D. Heart
E. Ears

6. What effect occurs when a single spectral line is split into a group of closely spaced lines by subjecting the substance producing the single line to a uniform magnetic field?
A. Compass effect
B. ILO effect
C. Temag effect
D. Funnel effect
E. Zeeman effect

7. How many tentacles does a cuttlefish have?
A. 6
B. 8
C. 10
D. 12
E. 16

8. Which element boils at the lowest temperature?
A. Hydrogen
B. Helium
C. Neon
D. Fluoride
E. Mercury

Answers to Quiz #35 — **Science and Nature**

1. **(B) Ramapithecus.** Ramapithecus was first discovered in the Siwalik Hills of India by G.E. Lewis in 1934. It is classified as hominid because its relatively small front teeth and reduced canines suggest the use of the forelimbs in food gathering.

2. **(E) Pumpkin.** The hull-less snackjack seeds are about 40% protein and almost free of saturated fat.

3. **(A) Australia.** The long-tailed hopping mouse disappeared in 1901, followed by the pig-footed bandicoot in 1926 and the Toolache wallaby in 1927.

4. **(C) Rinderpest.** Rinderpest, aka cattle plague, was introduced into Africa in the late 19th century when the Italian army sought to conquer Ethiopia. The year 1889 is remembered in Ethiopia as "Yekebit Elkit" — the Year of the Annihilation of Cattle. A reliable vaccine for rinderpest was created in 1993.

5. **(B) Mouth.** Cementum anchors the teeth in the mouth. As the tooth crown wears down, new cementum is deposited on the roots so that the tooth gradually rises in the socket, keeping the bite even.

6. **(E) Zeeman effect.** The effect was discovered in 1896 by Dutch physicist Pieter Zeeman and successfully explained by H. A. Lorentz. Zeeman and Lorentz shared the 1902 Nobel Prize in Physics.

7. **(C) 10.** Eight of the cuttlefish's tentacles have muscular suction cups on the inner surface. The other two are longer arms used for grasping prey.

8. **(B) Helium.** Helium has a boiling point of -268.6 degrees Centigrade at 1 atmosphere pressure.

Quiz #36 — **Tough TV Trivia**

1. What TV detective lived at the King Edward Hotel and drove a car nicknamed "The Blue Ghost"?
A. Matt Helm
B. Richie Brockelman
C. Richard Diamond
D. Tony Baretta
E. B.L. Stryker

2. What was Laverne Todd's hometown on "Empty Nest"?
A. Cicely, Alaska
B. Rock Throw, West Virginia
C. Hickory, Arkansas
D. Madison, Wisconsin
E. Snailville, Georgia

3. What artist appeared on the 200th episode of "The Love Boat" and was the 999th guest on the show?
A. Peter Max
B. Andy Warhol
C. Leroy Neiman
D. Norman Rockwell
E. Paloma Picasso

4. On the TV series "Friends," what holiday was boycotted by Chandler because that was the day his parents told him about their divorce?
A. Halloween
B. Thanksgiving
C. Christmas
D. New Year's Day
E. Valentine's Day

5. On the TV series "Seinfeld," what was Jerry and Kramer's favorite brand of cereal?
A. Chocolate Bombs
B. Double Crunch
C. Sugar Smacks
D. Ka-boom
E. King Vitamin

6. On the TV series "Quantum Leap," what was the name of Sam Beckett's younger sister?
A. Katie
B. Donna
C. Tina
D. Terri
E. Beth

7. The star of what TV series was seen reading the book "Tissue Decomposition: A Homicide Primer" in the show's opening credits?
A. "Barnaby Jones"
B. "Quincy, M.E."
C. "The Rockford Files"
D. "The Commish"
E. "Longstreet"

8. On the TV series "The X-Files," what was the name of Agent Dana Scully's dog?
A. Ishmael
B. Ahab
C. Starbuck
D. Melville
E. Queequeg

Answers to Quiz #36 — **Tough TV Trivia**

1. **(D) Tony Baretta.** Tony Baretta, played by Robert Blake from 1975-78, lived in apartment 2-C of the King Edward Hotel with his cockatoo, Fred. "The Blue Ghost" was a 1966 Chevy with license plate 532 BEN.

2. **(C) Hickory, Arkansas.** Cicely, Alaska was the setting for "Northern Exposure." Rock Throw, Virginia is the hometown of Jennifer Marlowe on "WKRP in Cincinnati." Larry Appleton of "Perfect Strangers" hailed from Madison, WI. While auditioning for "The Dukes of Hazzard," John Schneider tried to pass himself off as an authentic Southern boy with the fictional hometown of Snailville, GA. His real hometown is Mt. Kisco, NY.

3. **(B) Andy Warhol.** Most of the "Love Boat" episodes were filmed aboard the cruise ships "Pacific Princess" and "Island Princess." Paying passengers were invited to participate as extras, and cruises on which filming was planned were always booked solid long in advance.

4. **(B) Thanksgiving.** Chandler's (Matthew Perry) traditional Thanksgiving meal consisted of tomato soup, grilled cheese, and Funyuns. His mother was played by Morgan Fairchild.

5. **(B) Double Crunch.** Other "Seinfeld" food trivia: Jerry's favorite snack food was Drake's Coffee Cake. The gang regularly ate at a diner called Monk's. Jerry was a devoted Snapple drinker. Kramer's acting part in a Woody Allen film was the single line "These pretzels are making me thirsty," but his part wound up on the cutting room floor. Kramer was banned from Joe's Fruit Market after complaining about a bad peach.

6. **(A) Katie.** Katie Beckett married naval officer Lt. Jim Bonnick, and lived in Hawaii. Bonnick was also a character on "Magnum, P.I." "Magnum" and "Quantum Leap" were both produced by Don Bellisario.

7. **(D) "The Commish".** "The Commish," starring Michael Chiklis as Police Commissioner Tony Scali, was based on the real life story of police commissioner Tony Schembri of Rye, NY.

8. **(E) Queequeg.** Scully's father nicknamed her "Starbuck" and she called him "Ahab." She continued the "Moby Dick" link naming her dog "Queequeg." Queequeg disappeared from the series after he was eaten by an alligator.

Quiz #37 — **The Name's the Same**

1. The last NFL runningback to lead the league in pass receptions shares his name with what major league skipper who led his team to the 1989 World Series, where his team lost four straight games?
A. Rick Young
B. Tom Moore
C. Paul Owens
D. Dick Williams
E. Roger Craig

2. The author of such books as "Bad Habits" and "Claw Your Way to the Top" shares his name with what referee who has shouldered the blame for the infamous 14-second "long count" in the first Jack Dempsey-Gene Tunney fight?
A. Art Donovan
B. Steve Covey
C. Howard Fast
D. Mills Lane
E. Dave Barry

3. "Tossin' and Turnin' " was a number one Billboard hit for what artist who shared his name with the man who was the head baseball coach for the University of Pittsburgh for 36 years?
A. Bobby Lewis
B. Frank Marino
C. Johnny Brown
D. Lee Paterno
E. Robert Darin

4. What S.E. Hinton novel shares its title with the Monkees' first top 20 hit after reuniting in 1986, nearly 20 years after their last charted song in 1968?
A. "Valleri"
B. "The Outsiders"
C. "Tex"
D. "Take the Long Way Home"
E. "That Was Then, This Is Now"

5. Norm Snead's favorite receiver with the Minnesota Vikings and New York Giants; the last major league rookie pitcher to win 20 games in a season; and the 1959 Indianapolis 500 Rookie of the Year all shared what same name?
A. Roger Clemens
B. Jim Clark
C. Jack McDowell
D. Bob Grim
E. Paul Flatley

6. An important 1859 painting by Jean-Francois Millet; the family name and dynasty of three Byzantine emperors; and a prayer of the Roman Catholic Church traditionally announced three times daily by a bell all share what name?
A. Maria
B. Lerins
C. Angelus
D. Light
E. Sixtus

7. The golfer who set the PGA U.S. Open record of 203 for 54 holes and the actor who wore a golf cap throughout the movie "Oh, God!" share what name?
A. David Stiers
B. Arnold Palmer
C. John Denver
D. George Burns
E. Ted Wass

8. The first episode of the TV shows "Have Gun, Will Travel" and "Quantum Leap" shared what title?
A. "Leap into the Fray"
B. "Genesis"
C. "Paladin"
D. "Wired"
E. "San Francisco"

Answers to Quiz #37 — **The Name's the Same**

1. (E) **Roger Craig.** Roger Craig, San Francisco 49ers runningback, led the NFL with 92 catches in 1985. Roger Craig, the manager, took the San Francisco Giants into the 1989 World Series, only to lose four straight to the Oakland A's, and have his world rocked by an earthquake just before Game 3 that year.

2. (E) **Dave Barry.** Barry, the Pulitzer Prize-winning humorist and syndicated columnist, sold his life story as the basis of the TV sitcom "Dave's World." Barry, the referee, earned his infamy honestly. Shortly before the 1927 Dempsey-Tunney fight, boxing rules were changed to protect a downed fighter by requiring the standing boxer to retreat to a neutral corner and wait while the referee counts over the fallen opponent. Before this rule, an aggressor could hover over his opponent, poised to deliver another blow as soon as the groggy fighter regained his feet. After Dempsey leveled Tunney, he attempted this tactic despite referee Barry's repeated attempts to direct him to a neutral corner. Unaccustomed to the new rule, Dempsey had inadvertently allowed Tunney the extra seconds necessary to clear his head and win the fight.

3. (A) **Bobby Lewis.** Singer Bobby Lewis also hit the top 10 with "One Track Mind." Lewis, the coach, was an icon in college baseball coaching the Pitt Panthers from 1955 to 1990.

4. (E) **"That Was Then, This Is Now".** The Monkees reunited following a revival of their TV series on MTV. Sans Michael "Wool Hat" Nesmith, they returned to the recording studio and went on tour.

5. (D) **Bob Grim.** Grim, the receiver, led the Vikings in receptions in 1971 before accompanying Snead to the Giants. Grim, the Yankee pitcher, won rookie of the year in 1954 for his 20-win season and also went on to be an excellent relief pitcher becoming one of only a handful of hurlers to post a 20-win season and later a 20-save season. Grim, the Indy car driver, won few races after his shining 1959 Indy performance.

6. (C) **Angelus.** Millet's "The Angelus" was painted in 1859 and sold in 1860 by the artist for $100. It was purchased by the Louvre in 1890 for $150,000. The Angelus Bell rang at sunrise, noon, and sunset to invite the faithful to the recitation of "Ave Maria."

7. (D) **George Burns.** Actor George Burns was an avid golfer in his own right, often playing with his friends Jack Benny and Bob Hope.

8. (B) **"Genesis".** Richard Boone starred in "Have Gun, Will Travel" as Paladin, a refined gentleman who hired himself out as a gunfighter dressing in black. The successful western series ran for 156 episodes between 1957-63. Scott Bakula starred in "Quantum Leap" as Dr. Sam Beckett, a scientist who discovered a means of time travel that caused him into "leap" into the bodies of others. The cult series ran on NBC from 1989 to 1993.

Quiz #38 — **Washington Pie**

1. Dinah Washington had two top 10 duets: "Baby (You've Got What It Takes)" and "A Rockin' Good Way (To Mess Around and Fall in Love)." Who was her male duet partner on these 1960 hits?
A. Ben E. King
B. Marvin Gaye
C. Al Green
D. Lionel Hampton
E. Brook Benton

2. Harold Washington was the mayor of what large American city in the 1980s?
A. Dallas, TX
B. Chicago, IL
C. San Diego, CA
D. Washington, DC
E. Columbus, OH

3. Which of the following stories was not included in the original collection of George Washington Cable stories titled "Old Creole Days"?
A. "Jean Ah Poquelin"
B. "Tite Poulette"
C. "Cafe des Exiles"
D. "Belles Demoiselles"
E. "Madame Delphine"

4. The Henry James novel, "Washington Square," served as the basis of what movie starring Olivia de Havilland?
A. "The Well-Groomed Bride"
B. "The Ambassador's Daughter"
C. "My Love Came Back"
D. "My Cousin Rachel"
E. "The Heiress"

5. The 555-foot tall Washington Monument was the tallest man-made structure in the world at the time of its construction in 1884. Its record was surpassed by what structure?
A. Eiffel Tower
B. John Hancock Tower
C. Sears Tower
D. Golden Gate Bridge
E. Empire State Building

6. What was the collective name given to George Fox, Alexander Goode, Clark Poling, and John Washington, who perished aboard the troopship Dorchester during WWII?
A. The Sea Vanguards
B. The Sons of Oklahoma
C. The Four Chaplains
D. The Fighting Sullivans
E. The Horsemen

7. Where did George Washington bid farewell to his officers in 1783?
A. Admiral Benbow Inn
B. Mount Vernon
C. Holmesdale
D. Fraunces Tavern
E. Chartwell

8. Who holds the career scoring record for the Washington Redskins with 1206 points?
A. Chip Lohmiller
B. Sammy Baugh
C. Mark Moseley
D. Charley Taylor
E. Eddie Murray

Answers to Quiz #38 — **Washington Pie**

1. **(E) Brook Benton.** Blues singer Dinah Washington was born Ruth Jones in 1924. In 1942, she changed her name and got a job singing with Lionel Hampton's band. Four years later, she began her career as a solo singer. Her biggest solo hit was "What a Difference a Day Makes" in 1959. On December 14, 1963, she was found dead due to an accidental overdose of sleeping pills.

2. **(B) Chicago, IL.** Washington was elected the first black mayor of Chicago in 1983, defeating incumbent Jane Byrne in the Democratic primary. He held the office until his death in November 1987.

3. **(E) "Madame Delphine".** "Madame Delphine" was a long short-story, published as a book in 1881, and was included in later editions of "Old Creole Days."

4. **(E) "The Heiress".** The 1949 film followed the successful Broadway play of 1946-47 by Ruth and Augustus Goetz. Olivia de Havilland won her second Best Actress Oscar for this film.

5. **(A) Eiffel Tower.** Only five years after the Washington Monument was completed, the Eiffel Towel, at 986', easily set the height record. With the addition of a TV antenna in 1957, the Eiffel Tower now stands at 1,052' in height.

6. **(C) The Four Chaplains.** A priest, a rabbi, and two ministers — these men died when their troop transport ship, the Dorchester, was torpedoed and sank on February 3, 1943. They gave up their life jackets to soldiers who had none. Linking arms, they prayed together, going down with the ship. They were commemorated on a U.S. postage stamp in 1948.

7. **(D) Fraunces Tavern.** Located at the corner of Pearl and Broad Streets in Manhattan, the Fraunces Tavern was originally constructed as a residence for Stephen De Lancey. The tavern became famous for its Long Room, where Washington delivered his Farewell Address in 1783. The building still stands, containing a George Washington museum, though the building was bombed in 1975 by the Puerto Rican terrorist group, FALN.

8. **(C) Mark Moseley.** Moseley spent his first season with the Philadelphia Eagles in 1971, and the following season with the Houston Oilers. Cut by the Oilers, Moseley was installing septic systems in 1973, trying to hook back up with an NFL team. In 1974, he was signed as a free agent by the Washington Redskins, where he went on to lead the NFL in field goals in 1976, 1977, 1979, and 1982. In 1982, he was the first kicker ever selected as the NFL's Most Valuable Player. His career total of 1382 points places him at #11 on the NFL's all-time scorer's list.

Quiz #39 — Oh Oh!

1. Who was the tailor appointed Lord High Executioner in Gilbert and Sullivan's "The Mikado"?
A. Bo-Bo
B. Ko-Ko
C. Lo-Lo
D. Mo-Mo
E. Po-Po

2. "Tiny Toons Adventures" character Gogo Dodo lives in what part of Acme Acres?
A. Wackyland
B. Gogoland
C. Dodoland
D. Toonland
E. Tinyland

3. Who is the champion pairs skating partner of JoJo Starbuck?
A. Todd Sand
B. Ronald Kauffman
C. Ronald Ludington
D. Ronald Joseph
E. Ken Shelley

4. Rei Momo was the 14-piece Latin-influenced Pan American band that joined the solo tour of what rock band leader in 1990?
A. David Lee Roth
B. David Byrne
C. Sammy Hagar
D. Daryl Hall
E. Paul Simon

5. In what state would you find Lolo National Forest, Lewis and Clark National Forest, and Kootenai National Forest?
A. Michigan
B. Mississippi
C. Montana
D. New Mexico
E. North Dakopta

6. In what sport would you be participating if you used the slang terms "hoho plant," "shred betty," and "stale fish"?
A. Snowboarding
B. Racquetball
C. Polo
D. Frisbee golf
E. Parasailing

7. What country singer could balance a fiddle on his forehead while spinning his trademark yo-yo?
A. Carl Perkins
B. Roy Acuff
C. Grandpa Jones
D. Little Jimmy Dickens
E. Porter Wagoner

8. What does the Cowardly Lion call Toto when he first spots the dog in the 1939 movie "The Wizard of Oz"?
A. Squirt
B. Munchkin
C. Toto
D. Peewee
E. Runt

Answers to Quiz #39 — Oh Oh!

1. **(B) Ko-Ko.** Perhaps the most unusual actor to play Ko-Ko was Groucho Marx who fulfilled his ambition to play the part in a 1960 TV production of "The Mikado" for "The Bell Telephone Hour."

2. **(A) Wackyland.** The character Gogo Dodo was based on the Dodo in the 1938 surreal cartoon "Porky in Wackyland," and its 1949 sequel "Dough for the Do-Do," where Porky hunts for the Dodo through a Daliesque landscape. Voice master Frank Welker provided the voice for Gogo Dodo on "Tiny Toons Adventures."

3. **(E) Ken Shelley.** Starbuck and Shelley were the U.S. pairs champions three times, 1970-72. Starbuck was married to former Pittsburgh Steelers quarterback Terry Bradshaw.

4. **(B) David Byrne.** The tour was Byrne's first without his usual band, Talking Heads. Byrne has also released a solo album with a title similar to this quiz — "Uh Oh!"

5. **(C) Montana.** The isolated Montana home of Unabomber suspect Ted Kaczynski was located just on the edge of the Lolo National Forest.

6. **(A) Snowboarding.** A "hoho plant" is a handstand on the apex of a halfpipe. A "shred betty" is a female snowboarder. The "stale fish" is a jump in which the rider grabs the backside edge on the board between the bindings with the rear hand.

7. **(B) Roy Acuff.** Acuff was a man of multiple talents. He almost became a professional baseball player, but was sidelined for a long period with sunstroke. He ran for governor of Tennessee in a losing 1948 campaign. He achieved 55 years of success as a top attraction at the Grand Ole Opry with his band, the Smoky Mountain Boys.

8. **(D) Peewee.** Toto was played by a terrier named Terry. Terry missed a few days of filming when one of the Wicked Witch's guards accidentally stepped on him.

Quiz #40 — Lost Cause

1. Who told Ernest Hemingway that he represented young writers that were "all a lost generation"?
A. Malcolm Cowley
B. Emilie Loring
C. John Steinbeck
D. Ambrose Bierce
E. Gertrude Stein

2. What group hit #1 in 1987 with the song "Lost in Emotion"?
A. Vanity 6
B. Morris Day and the Time
C. Atlantic Starr
D. Whitesnake
E. Lisa Lisa and Cult Jam

3. What was the name of the spaceship on the TV series "Lost in Space"?
A. Spindrift
B. Endeavor
C. Columbia
D. Jupiter II
E. Searcher

4. Whose 1949 musical, "Lost in the Stars," was based on the Alan Paton novel "Cry, the Beloved Country"?
A. Tommy Overstreet
B. Kurt Weill
C. Alan Jay Lerner
D. Robert Palmer
E. Bobby Short

5. What movie critic's first book was titled "I Lost It at the Movies"?
A. Roger Ebert
B. Gene Shalit
C. Gene Siskel
D. Michael Medved
E. Pauline Kael

6. In the movies, what comedy team was "Lost in a Harem" and "Lost in Alaska"?
A. Olsen and Johnson
B. Laurel and Hardy
C. Burns and Allen
D. Martin and Lewis
E. Abbott and Costello

7. In what state would you supposedly find the Lost Dutchman mine?
A. California
B. Nevada
C. Alaska
D. Idaho
E. Arizona

8. "Rage Over a Lost Penny" was a musical composition by what classical composer?
A. J.S. Bach
B. Beethoven
C. Rossini
D. Liszt
E. Bartók

Answers to Quiz #40 — **Lost Cause**

1. **(E) Gertrude Stein.** Others categorized as "Lost Generation" writers of post-WWI include F. Scott Fitzgerald, e.e. cummings, John Dos Passos, Morley Callaghan, Malcolm Cowley, Samuel Putnam, and Robert McAlmon.

2. **(E) Lisa Lisa and Cult Jam.** Songwriter Lou George says he was inspired while listening to the greatest hits of Mary Wells. "Lost in Emotion" is a combination of "Two Lovers" and "You Beat Me to the Punch." Lisa Lisa's real name is Lisa Velez.

3. **(D) Jupiter II.** The Jupiter II, carrying the Robinson family, was "Lost in Space" after it was sabotaged by the sniveling Dr. Zachary Smith (played by Jonathan Harris).

4. **(B) Kurt Weill.** It was Weill's last major work. At the end of 1949, he began to collaborate with Maxwell Anderson on a musical based on "Huckleberry Finn," but he was taken ill and died in 1950 before completing it.

5. **(E) Pauline Kael.** Kael was a philosophy major at the University of California, Berkeley and working in the Bay Area when "I Lost It at the Movies" was published in 1965. Three years later, she was the regular film critic for "The New Yorker," where she stayed until her retirement in 1991. Her second book, "Kiss Kiss, Bang Bang," published in 1968, was also very successful.

6. **(E) Abbott and Costello.** Both of these films were considered pretty routine for Abbott and Costello. "Lost in a Harem" was released in 1944; "Lost in Alaska" hit theaters in 1952.

7. **(E) Arizona.** Jake Walzer, the Dutchman for whom the mine was named, claimed the mine was worth $100 million. Since his death, hundreds of searchers have combed the Superstition Mountains outside of Phoenix, AZ in hopes of finding their fortune.

8. **(B) Beethoven.** Beethoven gave the title "Rage Over a Lost Penny" to his Opus 129, a whimsical rondo.

Quiz #41 — **Magic Tricks**

1. What basketball team warms up in "the Magic Circle"?
A. L.A. Lakers
B. Harlem Globetrotters
C. Utah Jazz
D. Orlando Magic
E. Milwaukee Bucks

2. Which of the following songs hit #1 on the Billboard pop charts?
A. "Magic" by Pilot
B. "Magic Man" by Heart
C. "Hocus Pocus" by Focus
D. "Abracadabra" by Steve Miller Band
E. "Witchcraft" by Frank Sinatra

3. Whose short story collections include "Rembrandt's Hat," "Idiots First," and "The Magic Barrel"?
A. John Irving
B. Philip Roth
C. John Updike
D. Saul Bellow
E. Bernard Malamud

4. "Operation Magic Carpet" in 1949-50 involved airlifting 50,000 Jews to Israel from what country?
A. Yemen
B. USSR
C. Cambodia
D. United States
E. Romania

5. Max Factor created the perfume "Magic Beat," a celebrity fragrance marketed using what celebrity?
A. Elizabeth Taylor
B. Daryl Hannah
C. Michael Jackson
D. Tom Selleck
E. Bruce Springsteen

6. "Magic Moments," a 1958 hit for singer Perry Como, was the first hit song for what songwriting team?
A. Paul Simon and Art Garfunkel
B. Carly Simon and James Taylor
C. John Lennon and Paul McCartney
D. Burt Bacharach and Hal David
E. Ellie Greenwich and Jeff Barry

7. In what year did the Magic 8-Ball make its debut on toy store shelves?
A. 1930
B. 1947
C. 1959
D. 1971
E. 1980

8. Who played a crimefighting magician named Tony Blake on the TV series "The Magician"?
A. Hal Linden
B. Bill Bixby
C. Alan Thicke
D. Lee Horsley
E. Tom Selleck

Answers to Quiz #41 — **Magic Tricks**

1. **(B) Harlem Globetrotters.** The Globetrotters form a circle to show off their ballhandling skills to the strains of "Sweet Georgia Brown." Befitting this quiz category, the Globetrotters are nicknamed "The Magicians of Basketball" and "The Houdinis of the Hardcourt."

2. **(D) "Abracadabra" by Steve Miller Band.** The Steve Miller Band hit #1 with "Abracadabra" in 1982. Pilot peaked at #5 in 1975 with "Magic." "Magic Man" and "Hocus Pocus" got no higher than #9. Ol' Blue Eyes made it to #6 with "Witchcraft."

3. **(E) Bernard Malamud.** Malamud is also the author of the novels "The Natural," made into a movie starring Robert Redford, and "The Fixer," for which he won a Pulitzer Prize.

4. **(A) Yemen.** The Yemenite Jews were housed in crude barracks called ma'abarot, and many were separated from their children. Told the children were being sent to hospitals or nurseries, several hundred of the children disappeared. The controversy over these lost children plagued Israel for many years.

5. **(C) Michael Jackson.** The fragrance came in moon-shaped and star-shaped packaging, and included such novelty items as a scented ink pen.

6. **(D) Burt Bacharach and Hal David.** "Magic Moments" peaked at #4. It was the flip side to the #1 song "Catch a Falling Star." Another Bacharach-David composition on the charts at the same time was "The Story of My Life," a top 20 song recorded by Marty Robbins. Bacharach and David wrote a slew of hit songs for Dionne Warwick including "Alfie," "I Say a Little Prayer," "Make It Easy on Yourself," "Let Me Go to Him," "Promises, Promises," and "This Girl's in Love with You."

7. **(B) 1947.** The Magic 8-Ball is manufactured by Tyco Toys, the nation's third-largest toy company and maker of Matchbox cars and View Master.

8. **(B) Bill Bixby.** On "The Magician," Tony Blake lived at the Magic Castle and flew in a private jet called the Spirit. Bill Bixby performed many of his own magic tricks for the series under the tutelage of Mark Wilson.

Quiz #42 — **Mystery Date**

1. Who was the original host of the PBS anthology series "Mystery!"?
A. Vincent Price
B. Diana Rigg
C. Gene Shalit
D. Alistair Cooke
E. Nigel Bruce

2. What is the name of the award given annually by the British Crime Writer's Association for best mystery novel?
A. Scarab
B. Gold Dagger
C. Edgar
D. Poe
E. Ramsey

3. Who was the first mystery guest on the TV game show "What's My Line"?
A. John Daly
B. Phyllis Diller
C. Al Smith
D. Alfred Hitchcock
E. Phil Rizzuto

4. The literary detective, Nigel Strangeways, created by Nicholas Blake, was based on what real-life poet?
A. W.B. Yeats
B. W.H. Auden
C. Joyce Kilmer
D. Carl Sandburg
E. William Carlos Williams

5. What was the title of the last published Hercule Poirot novel written by Agatha Christie?
A. "The Murder of Roger Ackroyd"
B. "Murder on the Links"
C. "Curtain"
D. "The Big Four"
E. "The Mysterious Affair at Styles"

6. Who turned an unfinished Charles Dickens novel into the Broadway musical "The Mystery of Edwin Drood"?
A. Rupert Holmes
B. Neil Diamond
C. Lee Ritenour
D. Wendy Wasserman
E. Fred Knobloch

7. In the movie "Meatballs," camper Jeffrey Corbin wins the Mystery Meat Contest by identifying veal as "some kind of beef." According to the announcement in the movie, what was Jeffrey's prize?
A. Julia Child's autograph
B. 2-week trip to Guadalupe, Mexico
C. Bus pass home
D. Chrysler Cordoba
E. Week of KP

8. Which of the following was not a character on the radio show "I Love a Mystery"?
A. Jack Packard
B. Doc Long
C. Reggie Yorke
D. Gerry Booker
E. Linda Dale

Answers to Quiz #42 — **Mystery Date**

1. **(C) Gene Shalit.** Shalit hosted the series for its first season in 1980. He was replaced by Vincent Price in 1981. Diana Rigg assumed hosting duties in 1989.

2. **(B) Gold Dagger.** The Gold Dagger has been awarded since 1960, making it the oldest literary prize awarded in England. Winners include "Black and Blue" by Ian Rankin (1997), "Dead of Night" by Paula Gosling (1996), "The Mermaids Singing" by Van McDiarmid (1995), and "The Scold's Bride" by Minette Walters (1994).

3. **(E) Phil Rizzuto.** Rizzuto was a shortstop for the NY Yankees. The premiere show on February 2, 1950 also featured a hatcheck girl from the Stork Club, a veterinarian from Greenwich Village, and a delivery man from the Cascade Diaper Service.

4. **(B) W.H. Auden.** Blake was the pen name of poet Cecil Day Lewis. In the 1930s, Lewis was an associate of Auden. Lewis was named Poet Laureate in 1968.

5. **(C) "Curtain".** "Curtain" was written in the 1930s, long before Christie's death, but kept locked away and published posthumously in 1975. Christie's debut novel in 1920, "The Mysterious Affair at Styles" featured Poirot. Poirot appeared in 33 novels and 56 short stories before being put to rest in "Curtain."

6. **(A) Rupert Holmes.** Holmes won Tony Awards in 1986 for Best Book and Best Score. Holmes is also remembered as the singer-songwriter of the pop hit "Escape (The Pina Colada Song)." More recently, he created the TV show "Remember WENN" that aired on American Movie Classics.

7. **(D) Chrysler Cordoba.** The 1979 film comedy starring Bill Murray spawned several sequels: "Meatballs, Part II" starring Richard Mulligan, "Meatballs III" starring Sally Kellerman and Patrick Dempsey, and "Meatballs IV" with Corey Feldman.

8. **(E) Linda Dale.** Jack, Doc, and Reggie met in an Oriental prison. They survived the experience to join forces as crime solvers. Jack was the brains of the operation, Doc was an expert lock picker, and Reggie was a strongman. They teamed up with a beautiful secretary named Gerry Booker, forming the A-1 Detective Agency where "No job too tough, no mystery too baffling" was their motto.

Quiz #43 — **Have Some Moore**

1. What was the nickname of heavyweight boxer Archie Moore?
A. The Brown Bomber
B. The Human Punching Bag
C. The Walking Whimper
D. The Old Mongoose
E. The Michigan Assassin

2. What is the pen name used by novelist David John Moore Cornwall?
A. Graham Greene
B. Tom Clancy
C. John le Carré
D. Jonathan Kellerman
E. Joseph Heller

3. What former pro athlete turned sportcaster was originally named Bobby Moore?
A. Kareem Abdul-Jabbar
B. Hulk Hogan
C. Ping Bodie
D. Ahmad Rashad
E. Mahmoud Abdul-Rauf

4. Hugh Moore was the entrepreneur behind what company originally concerned about sanitary conditions?
A. Dixie Cups
B. Tupperware
C. Corning Glass
D. Thermos
E. Johnson Wax

5. Sara Jara Moore and Lynette Fromm both tried to shoot what U.S. President?
A. Harry Truman
B. Theodore Roosevelt
C. Ronald Reagan
D. Lyndon Johnson
E. Gerald Ford

6. Considered by many to be the first rockabilly artist, who hit the Billboard top 40 country charts in 1961 with "Drunk Again"?
A. Michael Moore
B. Tiny Moore
C. Scottie Moore
D. Dickie Moore
E. Lattie Moore

7. Who was the first player to score 20 touchdowns in a single NFL season?
A. Lenny Moore
B. Artie Moore
C. George Moore
D. Ernie Moore
E. Johnson Moore

8. In the 1990 Heisman Trophy balloting, quarterback Shawn Moore finished 4th and wide receiver Herman Moore finished 6th. Both played at what school?
A. Notre Dame
B. Navy
C. Michigan
D. Virginia
E. Stanford

Answers to Quiz #43 — **Have Some Moore**

1. **(D) The Old Mongoose.** Archie Moore holds the record of most career TKOs at 145.

2. **(C) John le Carré.** Le Carré's espionage novels include "The Spy Who Came in from the Cold," "The Looking-Glass War," "The Little Drummer Girl," and "A Perfect Spy." Le Carré is the creator of secret service agent George Smiley.

3. **(D) Ahmad Rashad.** Rashad set 14 school football records while playing for the Oregon Ducks, 1968-72. In the NFL, he once teamed up with quarterback Jim Hart for a 98-yard pass play that failed to produce a touchdown.

4. **(A) Dixie Cups.** Moore invented a porcelain dispenser for chilled drinking water, but discovered a more profitable niche in the creation of a disposable paper cup for such dispensers. Originally called Health Kups, Moore borrowed the name of his neighbor's business, the Dixie Doll Company, to become the Dixie Cup Company.

5. **(E) Gerald Ford.** The assassination attempts were made on Ford's life in California in the span of three weeks in September 1975. Both Moore and Fromm also escaped from the Alderson Federal Correctional Institute in West Virginia — Moore in 1979, Fromm in 1987.

6. **(E) Lattie Moore.** Lattie Moore toured with movie western star Lash LaRue in the 1940s, and hosted his own radio show in Indianapolis in the 1950s called "Midwest Jamboree."

7. **(A) Lenny Moore.** Lenny Moore scored 20 TDs in 1964 with the Baltimore Colts. Moore also set an NFL record by scoring touchdowns in 18 consecutive regular season games for the Colts in 1963-65.

8. **(D) Virginia.** In 1964, Notre Dame also had two players finish in the top 10 of Heisman balloting — quarterback John Huarte and wide receiver Jack Snow.

Quiz #44 — **Street Smart**

1. What Presidential candidate was nicknamed "The Barefoot Boy from Wall Street"?
A. Walter Mondale
B. Thomas E. Dewey
C. Adlai Stevenson
D. Al E. Smith
E. Wendell Willkie

2. Bank Street Grounds, the Palace of the Fans, and Crosley Field were various homes of what major league baseball team?
A. Cincinnati Reds
B. Philadelphia Phillies
C. San Francisco Giants
D. Oakland A's
E. Chicago Cubs

3. On what London street would you find Madame Tussaud's Wax Museum and the Abbey National Building Society?
A. Fleet
B. Downing
C. Walpole
D. Reynolds
E. Baker

4. Who originated the role of Blanche DuBois in the 1947 stage production of "A Streetcar Named Desire"?
A. Katharine Hepburn
B. Elizabeth Taylor
C. Kim Hunter
D. Vivien Leigh
E. Jessica Tandy

5. "Vanya on 42nd St." was the last film of what director?
A. Elia Kazan
B. Louis Malle
C. Krzysztof Kieslowski
D. Ed Wood Jr.
E. Martin Ritt

6. "South Street," "Don't Hang Up," and "Wah-Wahtusi" were top 40 songs for what '60s group?
A. Dovells
B. Passions
C. Orlons
D. Orioles
E. Pastels

7. What poet's volumes of verse include "The Happy Marriage," "The Pot of Earth," "Land of the Free," "Act Five," and "Streets in the Moon"?
A. Marianne Moore
B. Carl Sandberg
C. Conrad Aiken
D. Archibald MacLeish
E. John Greenleaf Whittier

8. What is the name of the Muppet magician who appears on "Sesame Street" uttering the magic phrase "À la peanut butter sandwiches"?
A. Muppetini
B. Bruno
C. Mumford
D. Zelmo
E. Buster

Answers to Quiz #44 — **Street Smart**

1. (E) **Wendell Willkie.** Willkie was the president of a large utility company and had never been elected to public office when he ran for President. A Democrat for many years, he switched to the Republican Party to oppose FDR and the New Deal in 1940.

2. (A) **Cincinnati Reds.** The Reds moved to their present home field, Riverfront Stadium, after playing at Crosley Field from 1912 to 1970.

3. (E) **Baker.** The Abbey National Building Society, aka Abbey House, is located at 221-B Baker Street, the fictional home address of Sherlock Holmes. Madame Tussaud's Wax Museum has been on Baker Street since 1833.

4. (E) **Jessica Tandy.** The 1947 Broadway production was directed by Elia Kazan and featured a young Marlon Brando as Stanley Kowalski. Vivien Leigh won an Oscar for playing Blanche in the 1951 film version, also directed by Elia Kazan.

5. (B) **Louis Malle.** Louis Malle, the husband of actress Candice Bergen, died of brain cancer in 1995. The French film director's most acclaimed works were French films like "Au Revoir Les Enfants." Some of his American films were also well received including "Atlantic City," "Pretty Baby," and "My Dinner with Andre."

6. (C) **Orlons.** The song "South Street" is about locations in Philadelphia, the hometown of the Orlons. "Wah-Wahtusi" was the group's first and biggest hit, released in 1962.

7. (D) **Archibald MacLeish.** MacLeish was awarded the Pulitzer Prize for Poetry in 1933 for "Conquistador" and in 1953 for "Collected Poems," and for Drama in 1959 for "J.B.," a play based on the book of Job.

8. (C) **Mumford.** Muppets appearing on "Sesame Street" have included roommates Bert and Ernie, Oscar the Grouch, Big Bird, the Cookie Monster, Grover, Elmo, and Kermit the Frog. The series premiered on November 10, 1969.

Quiz #45 — On the Fly

1. Which member of "Monty Python's Flying Circus" was an American?
A. Terry Gilliam
B. Michael Palin
C. Graham Chapman
D. Eric Idle
E. John Cleese

2. What area is said to be haunted by Capt. Vanderdecken and his ghost ship, the Flying Dutchman?
A. Sargasso Sea
B. St. Lawrence Seaway
C. Bering Strait
D. Strait of Gibraltar
E. Cape of Good Hope

3. Karl Wallenda, patriarch of the Flying Wallendas, fell to his death while attempting to cross the highwire between two hotels in what city?
A. Chicago
B. London
C. Cairo
D. San Juan
E. Milwaukee

4. What WWII aircraft was nicknamed the "Flying Pencil"?
A. Junkers Ju-52
B. Dormier Do-17
C. Douglas A-1
D. Lockheed U-2
E. Fairchild C-119

5. How many gold medals were won in the Summer and Winter Olympic Games between the two athletes nicknamed "The Flying Finn"?
A. 5
B. 7
C. 9
D. 11
E. 13

6. What radio and TV character was the owner of the Flying Crown Ranch?
A. Sky King
B. The Lone Ranger
C. Matt Dillon
D. Bret Maverick
E. Wild Bill Hickok

7. In the movie, "The Man on the Flying Trapeze," Ambrose Wolfinger (W. C. Fields) asked his boss for a personal day from work to attend his mother-in-law's funeral. Where did Wolfinger really go?
A. Monopoly tournament
B. Horse race
C. White House
D. Wrestling match
E. Flagpole sitting

8. The "flying toaster" is familiar to computer owners as a motif used in the "After Dark" screen saver by Berkeley Systems Inc. The "flying toaster" was originally on the cover of a 1973 album by what rock group?
A. Styx
B. The Who
C. Jefferson Airplane
D. Jethro Tull
E. Big Brother and the Holding Company

Answers to Quiz #45 — On the Fly

1. **(A) Terry Gilliam.** Gilliam was the resident animator on "Monty Python." He made his solo film directing debut with the 1976 film "Jabberwocky" and has since directed the successful films "Time Bandits," "Brazil," and "12 Monkeys."

2. **(E) Cape of Good Hope.** In old American and English sea tales, Vanderdecken gambled his salvation on a pledge to outrun a storm around the Cape of Good Hope. Failing, he is condemned to sail the cape forever. The tale of the Flying Dutchman was the subject of the Wagner opera "Der Fliegende Hollander."

3. **(D) San Juan.** Wallenda was 73 years old at the time of his death. Two other Wallenda family members were killed in 1962 when a 7-member pyramid collapsed in Detroit.

4. **(B) Dormier Do-17.** The Dormier Do-17 bomber was developed by German aircraft designer Claude Dormier. The twin engine plane had a top speed of 255 MPH and a bomb payload of 2200 lbs.

5. **(E) 13.** Paavo Nurmi won nine gold medals in distance running in the 1920, '24, and '28 Olympics. Matti Nykanen won four gold medals in ski jumping during the 1984 and '88 Olympics.

6. **(A) Sky King.** "Sky King" began as a radio series in 1947, moving to television in 1951. Kirby Grant starred in the children's TV series as the ranch owner who used his small plane, the Songbird, to enact heroic rescues and capture dangerous criminals.

7. **(D) Wrestling match.** The 1935 film is the only Fields' movie not yet available on video.

8. **(C) Jefferson Airplane.** A group of flying toasters appeared on the cover of the 1973 Jefferson Airplane album "Thirty Seconds over Winterland."

Quiz #46 — **Outstanding Female Olympians**

1. Who was the first female track athlete to successfully defend her Olympic title in a sprint event?
A. Wyomia Tyus
B. Evelyn Ashford
C. Florence Griffith Joyner
D. Wilma Rudolph
E. Jackie Joyner-Kersee

2. What diver broke her arm during the 1968 Olympics when she hit the board during an inward reverse 1½ layout?
A. Gertrude Ederle
B. Florence Chadwick
C. Pat McCormick
D. Donna De Varona
E. Micki King

3. Who won the first women's Olympic marathon in 1984?
A. Greta Waitz
B. Joan Benoit
C. Kathrine Switzer
D. Nina Kuscsik
E. Roberta Gibb Bingay

4. Controversy raged in the 1984 women's 3000-meter race when American runner Mary Decker bumped into barefoot South African wonder girl, Zola Budd, and fell with two laps left to run in the race. Who won that race?
A. Candace Cable-Brooks
B. Zola Budd
C. Maricica Puica
D. Tatiana Samolenko
E. Lynn Williams

5. What was the only new sport for women added to the Olympic slate in 1992?
A. Judo
B. Yachting
C. Heptathlon
D. Softball
E. Fencing

6. What gymnast performed the first backward somersault on the uneven bars in Olympics competition, a "loop" that would be named after her?
A. Mary Lou Retton
B. Cathy Rigby
C. Olga Korbut
D. Nelli Kim
E. Nadia Comaneci

7. Who set world records in the 80-meter hurdles, javelin, and high jump at the 1932 Olympics?
A. Fanny Blankers-Koen
B. Joan Joyce
C. Babe Didrikson
D. Ulrike Meyfarth
E. Alice Coachman

8. What defending American backstroke champion was removed from the Olympic team in 1936 for her public drinking and discipline problems aboard the passenger ship to Germany?
A. Eleanor Holm
B. Suzanne Zimmerman
C. Lynn Burke
D. Alice Bridges
E. Bonny Mealing

1. (A) **Wyomia Tyus.** Wyomia Tyus won back-to-back 100-meter dashes in 1964 and 1968.

2. (E) **Micki King.** The accident dropped Maxine "Micki" King from 1st to 4th in the 1968 springboard diving event. She quickly announced her retirement, but recanted to train for the 1972 Olympics. In Munich, she handily won the gold medal in the springboard event.

3. (B) **Joan Benoit.** Benoit won the Boston Marathon in 1979 in only her second marathon race ever, setting a new American record at the same time. In 1984, she won the Sullivan Trophy as the best American amateur athlete of the year.

4. (C) **Maricica Puica.** Puica represented Romania. Zola Budd finished in 7th. Track officials disqualified Budd, but after reviewing a videotape of the race, determined that no one was at fault.

5. (A) **Judo.** From 1946 to 1972, only one sport for women was added to the Summer Olympics slate: volleyball. Since 1972, several new sports have been added including judo, field hockey, softball, and synchronized swimming.

6. (C) **Olga Korbut.** Korbut, the darling of the 1972 Olympics, also performed the first "Korbut somersault," a backward somersault on the balance beam.

7. (C) **Babe Didrikson.** Didrikson qualified for five different events at the U.S. AAU trials, but Olympic rules limited her participation to only three.

8. (A) **Eleanor Holm.** Holm was a socialite unfamiliar with a stifled social life, and spent much of the nine-day voyage up until the wee hours of the morning. As a consequence, she wound up as a spectator in Berlin. She returned to the U.S. to have a successful career as an actress.

1. What gymnast, who won four medals at the 1984 Olympics, went on to star in the movies "American Anthem" and "American Tiger"?
A. Bart Connor
B. Trent Dimas
C. Kurt Thomas
D. Tim Daggett
E. Mitch Gaylord

2. What gold medal winning heavyweight boxer in the 1968 Olympics starred in his own TV series titled after his first name, the same name he gave to each of his male children?
A. Evander Holyfield
B. Cassius Clay
C. Joe Frazier
D. Ken Norton
E. George Foreman

3. What star athlete burned brightest when he set a world record at the 1976 Olympics while winning the gold in the decathlon before having his star dim a little in such movie fare as "Can't Stop the Music" and "Original Intent"?
A. Daley Thompson
B. Dan O'Brien
C. Bruce Jenner
D. Bill Toomey
E. Rafer Johnson

4. Which of these movie Tarzans did not win a medal in the Olympic Games?
A. Glenn Morris
B. Gordon Scott
C. Herman Brix
D. Johnny Weissmuller
E. Buster Crabbe

5. What swimmer won the gold medal in the 100-meter freestyle at the 1924 Olympics and the 400-meter freestyle in 1924 and 1928, before starring in a series of films as Jungle Jim?
A. Buster Crabbe
B. Red Skelton
C. Johnny Weissmuller
D. Fernando Lamas
E. Duke Kahanamoku

6. Who won the gold medal for the women's all-around in gymnastics in the 1984 Olympics, and then played herself in "Naked Gun 33 1/3: The Final Insult" and "Scrooged"?
A. Mary Lou Retton
B. Shannon Miller
C. Cathy Rigby
D. Olga Korbut
E. Janet Jones

7. What Olympic decathlete starred in his own motion picture biography in 1954?
A. Rafer Johnson
B. Bob Mathias
C. Jim Thorpe
D. Bill Toomey
E. Floyd Simmons

8. The much photographed Donna De Varona won the 1964 Olympic gold medal in the 400-meter individual medley swimming event. Who is her equally beautiful sister?
A. Alley Mills
B. Cybill Shepherd
C. Kim Basinger
D. Elinor Donahue
E. Joanna Kerns

1. **(E) Mitch Gaylord.** "American Anthem" was directed by Albert Magnoli who hoped to make a star of Gaylord as he did with Prince in "Purple Rain." Kurt Thomas also pursued a film career with the 1985 martial-arts movie "Gymkata."

2. **(E) George Foreman.** Foreman went on to win the professional heavyweight championship of the world twice. Warming up his acting muscles in commercials for Meineke mufflers, he landed the starring role in the short-lived sitcom "George."

3. **(C) Bruce Jenner.** A talented self-promoter, Jenner also remained on the front of the Wheaties box for seven straight years.

4. **(B) Gordon Scott.** Crabbe and Weissmuller won gold medals in swimming. Morris was the champion decathlete in the 1936 Olympics. Morris's co-star in "Tarzan's Revenge" was gold medal-winning swimmer Eleanor Holm. Herman Brix pursued a movie career using the name Bruce Bennett after his silver medal in shot put in 1932.

5. **(C) Johnny Weissmuller.** Weissmuller was the first Olympian to swim the 100-meter freestyle in under a minute. He was also the first actor to play Tarzan in a talking picture in "Tarzan the Ape Man" in 1932.

6. **(A) Mary Lou Retton.** Retton has produced a series of videos for children, and was the first woman to appear on the front of the Wheaties box.

7. **(B) Bob Mathias.** Mathias won back-to-back Olympic decathlons in 1948 and 1952. He won the 1952 Olympic decathlon by the largest margin in Olympic history.

8. **(E) Joanna Kerns.** Kerns was a gymnast of national caliber who pursued a career in dancing and acting. She starred as Maggie Seaver on the ABC sitcom "Growing Pains" from 1985-92.

Quiz #48 — **Politics and the Olympics**

1. In 1968, American athletes Tommie Smith and John Carlos were stripped of their medals for appearing at the awards ceremony with a gloved fist salute. In what track and field event did they respectively win the gold and bronze medals?
A. 1500 meters
B. 100-meter hurdles
C. 200-meter dash
D. Javelin
E. Long jump

2. After the 1956 Olympics, 40% of what nation's Olympic team elected to defect rather than return to their home country, recently invaded by the USSR?
A. Czechoslovakia
B. Hungary
C. Yugoslavia
D. Poland
E. Romania

3. The International Olympic Committee took the unusual action of expelling what nation from the Games in 1964 because of political actions within that nation?
A. Egypt
B. Iran
C. South Africa
D. Germany
E. Ireland

4. In 1972, eight Palestinian terrorists invaded the Olympic Village in Munich and killed 11 Israeli athletes and coaches. By what name was this terrorist group known?
A. Black Friday
B. Black September
C. Black Panthers
D. Black Brigade
E. Black Lightning

5. In 1976, African nations withdrew from the Games to protest the participation of what nation that had violated the international ban on competing in South Africa?
A. United States
B. Mexico
C. New Zealand
D. China
E. Norway

6. In 1980, the United States and 34 other nations boycotted the Olympics hosted by the USSR to protest the invasion of what country?
A. Afghanistan
B. Poland
C. Bangladesh
D. Mongolia
E. Turkey

7. How many Olympics were cancelled due to war?
A. 1
B 2
C. 3
D. 4
E. 5

8. In 1936, Jews asked for a boycott of the Berlin Olympics. When the boycott was defeated by a narrow margin, an alternative People's Olympics was scheduled to take place in what country?
A. Spain
B. France
C. Zaire
D. Poland
E. Great Britain

1. (C) **200-meter dash.** Smith and Carlos were both students at San Jose State College in California, and members of the Olympic Project for Human Rights, a group of athletes organized to protest the treatment of blacks in the United States. They appeared on the medal platform with bare feet and a single gloved fist clenched overhead. They later explained that the clenched fists symbolized black strength while the bare feet represented black poverty in the U.S.

2. (B) **Hungary.** The 1956 Games were marked by two boycotts. Holland, Spain, and Switzerland boycotted the Russian invasion of Hungary. Meanwhile, Egypt, Iraq, and Lebanon withdrew to protest the Israeli takeover of the Suez Canal.

3. (C) **South Africa.** South Africa was banned for its segregation policy of apartheid.

4. (B) **Black September.** The terrorists killed two Israelis immediately and held the rest hostage, demanding the release of 200 prisoners from Israeli jails and safe passage out of Germany. At the airport, German sharpshooters opened fire on the terrorists, but in the ensuing battle, all the Israeli hostages were killed. ABC sportscaster Jim McKay was pressed into service by ABC's news division to cover the tragedy. It was his sad duty to inform the world that "they are all gone."

5. (C) **New Zealand.** The boycott, spearheaded by Tanzania, was in protest to New Zealand's rugby team playing in South Africa. The International Olympic Committee claimed it had no authority over rugby teams since rugby was not an official Olympic sport. Iraq and Guyana also joined the African boycott.

6. (A) **Afghanistan.** Unable to come up with any other effective protest, Jimmy Carter banned American athletes from participating in the USSR, threatening to revoke the passport of any athlete who tried. Other nations, like Great Britain and Australia, supported the boycott, but allowed the athletes to decide for themselves.

7. (E) **5.** The 1916 Summer Games, originally awarded to Germany, were cancelled due to World War I. The 1940 and 1944 Summer and Winter Olympics were cancelled during World War II. The 1940 Summer and Winter Olympics were awarded to Japan, but when Japan invaded China, they were taken away.

8. (A) **Spain.** The alternate Olympics was cancelled at the last minute when the Spanish Civil War broke out the day before competition was set to begin.

Quiz #49 — **Olympic Firsts**

1. Who was the first woman diver to win four diving gold medals?
A. Micki King
B. Gao Min
C. Ingrid Kramer
D. Dorothy Poynton
E. Pat McCormick

2. Who was the first female swimmer to win three individual gold medals?
A. Donna De Varona
B. Mary Meagher-Plant
C. Janet Evans
D. Debbie Meyer
E. Kristin Otto

3. Who was the first female American gymnast to win an Olympic gold medal?
A. Cathy Rigby
B. Shannon Miller
C. Julianna McCarthy
D. Mary Lou Retton
E. Kim Zmeskal

4. Who was the first black woman to win an Olympic gold medal?
A. Alice Coachman
B. Ethelda Bleibtrey
C. Dawn Fraser
D. Wyomia Tyus
E. Wilma Rudolph

5. What American athlete was the first to repeat as the gold medalist in the decathlon in the 1948 and 1952 Olympics?
A. Bob Richards
B. Bob Beamon
C. Bob Garrett
D. Bob Seagren
E. Bob Mathias

6. Who was the first athlete to win gold medals in the same event in four consecutive Olympics?
A. Carl Lewis
B. Mark Spitz
C. Matt Biondi
D. Al Oerter
E. Ray Ewry

7. While the U.S. basketball Dream Team has incurred some rancor for the return of several aging pro players over giving an opportunity to younger athletes, it wasn't until the 1952 Olympics that a male athlete played on the U.S. basketball team in consecutive Olympics. Name this former Oklahoma A&M star who won gold medals in 1948 and 1952.
A. Wilt Chamberlain
B. Bob Kurland
C. Clyde Lovellette
D. Alex Groza
E. Bill Russell

8. Who was the first American athlete to win medals in freestyle wrestling in three consecutive Olympic Games?
A. Dan Gable
B. John Davis Jr.
C. Russ Hellickson
D. John Smith
E. Bruce Baumgartner

Answers to Quiz #49 — **Olympic Firsts**

1. **(E) Pat McCormick.** In 1952, McCormick captured both the platform and springboard events, and then repeated both wins in 1956. She was also the first woman to win the prestigious amateur athletics Sullivan Award.

2. **(D) Debbie Meyer.** In Mexico City, at the age of 16, Meyer set Olympic records in the 200-meter, 400-meter, and 800-meter freestyle races. In her career, she set 20 world and 24 American records, at one time holding 5 world records at the same time.

3. **(D) Mary Lou Retton.** Studying under Bela Karolyi, Retton became the first American to take the gold in women's gymnastics all-around competition in 1984.

4. **(A) Alice Coachman.** In 1948, Coachman was the only American woman to win a gold medal in track and field. She qualified for the American team by breaking a 16-year old world record in the high jump at 5'4". She took the gold medal with her first jump of 5' 6.25".

5. **(E) Bob Mathias.** Mathias was also the youngest decathlon winner ever at age 17. He later served in the U.S. Congress for the state of California for four terms.

6. **(D) Al Oerter.** Oerter won gold medals in the discus throw in every Olympics from 1956 through 1968, and set Olympic records in every one. He was the first to throw the discus over 200 feet in Olympic competition in 1964, which he did while suffering from a herniated disk in his back and torn cartilage in his rib cage. Carl Lewis became the second athlete with four consecutive golds in the same event when he won the long jump in Atlanta in 1996.

7. **(B) Bob Kurland.** Kurland, even before George Mikan, was considered the prototype of the seven foot player. He led Oklahoma A&M (which became Oklahoma State) to the NCAA Division I championship in 1945 and 1946, and was elected Outstanding Player in the tournament both years.

8. **(E) Bruce Baumgartner.** Baumgartner, a heavyweight, was also awarded the AAU's Sullivan Award in 1995 as the country's best amateur athlete. He followed John Smith as only the second wrestler to earn that honor.

Quiz #50 — The Olympics: Barcelona 1992

1. What British athlete won the 100-meter sprint, making him the oldest man by four years to ever win this event?
A. Linford Christie
B. Carl Lewis
C. Frankie Fredericks
D. Dennis Mitchell
E. Dave Schreiner

2. Who was the only U.S. boxer to win a gold medal in the 1992 Summer Olympics?
A. Kennedy McKinney
B. Pernell Whitaker
C. Oscar de la Hoya
D. Ray Mercer
E. Eric Griffin

3. Romas Ubartas, who won the silver in the discus throw in 1988 for the USSR, won the gold medal in the same event in 1992, earning the first gold ever for what country?
A. Latvia
B. Lithuania
C. Romania
D. Moldavia
E. Belorussia

4. What country, winning four golds and six silvers in women's swimming in 1992, was criticized for refusing to take part in drug testing prior to the Summer Games?
A. Hungary
B. Cuba
C. New Zealand
D. Japan
E. China

5. What gymnast was the most successful athlete at the 1992 Summer Olympics, earning six gold medals in six events?
A. Lu Li
B. Li Jing
C. Shannon Miller
D. Vitaly Scherbo
E. Tatyana Goutsou

6. Who broke the nine-year-old record of Edwin Moses while winning the 400-meter hurdles?
A. Butch Reynolds
B. Andre Phillips
C. Charley Jenkins
D. Roger Kingdom
E. Kevin Young

7. In 1992, Trent Dimas became the first U.S. athlete in 60 years to win a gold medal in what summer Olympic event?
A. Steeplechase
B. Horizontal bar
C. Pommel horse
D. Greco-Roman wrestling
E. 100-meter backstroke

8. What event earned gold medals for twin sisters Karen and Sarah Josephson and silver for twin sisters Penny and Vicky Vilagos?
A. Volleyball
B. Skeet shooting
C. Table tennis doubles
D. Field hockey
E. Synchronized swimming duet

Answers to Quiz #50 — **The Olympics: Barcelona 1992**

1. **(A) Linford Christie.** Christie was 32 years old when he took the gold. He capped that victory with the world championship in the 100-meter sprint the following year.

2. **(C) Oscar de la Hoya.** De la Hoya proved he was no fluke when he captured the super lightweight crown by becoming the first fighter to defeat the legendary Julio Cesar Chavez in June 1996.

3. **(B) Lithuania.** Lithuania had not been represented in the Summer Olympics since 1928.

4. **(E) China.** No Chinese swimmer had ever won gold before 1992. The Chinese women's team, thought to be quite strong in 1996, had few swimmers make it to the finals.

5. **(D) Vitaly Scherbo.** Scherbo was a member of the Unified Team, but Belorussia's flag was raised, and its national anthem played, during his award ceremonies.

6. **(E) Kevin Young.** Young, an American hurdler, ran the world's first sub-47 second 400-meter hurdles.

7. **(B) Horizontal bar.** Dimas was the first "bartender" to grab the gold since the legendary Dallas Bixler in 1932 in Los Angeles. Dimas was the only male U.S. gymnast to earn gold in 1992.

8. **(E) Synchronized swimming duet.** Synchronized swimming was introduced to the Olympics in 1984. The Josephsons represented the U.S.; the Vilagoses were from Canada.

Quiz #51 — **Fort-itude**

1. The U.S. gold depository is located in Fort Knox, Kentucky. In what city is the U.S. silver depository located?
A. Carson City, NV
B. Annapolis, MD
C. Fort Knox, KY
D. West Point, NY
E. Metropolis, IL

2. What comical TV character was always receiving letters from "Richard Feder of Fort Lee, New Jersey"?
A. Roseanne Roseannadanna
B. Rhoda Morganstern
C. Lou Grant
D. Murphy Brown
E. Jerry Seinfeld

3. Fort Wayne, Indiana was granted an International Hockey League (IHL) franchise in 1952, making its team the oldest active franchise in the league. What is the team's nickname?
A. Ice Dogs
B. Knights
C. Blades
D. Wolves
E. Komets

4. Pretibial fever is a mild disease that was first observed among military personnel at what location?
A. Fort Smith, AK
B. Fort Dix, NJ
C. Fort Benning, GA
D. Fort Hood, TX
E. Fort Bragg, NC

5. What country singer's #1 hits include "Am I Blue," "You Look So Good in Love," "Amarillo by Morning," "Famous Last Words of a Fool," and "Does Fort Worth Ever Cross Your Mind?"
A. George Strait
B. Mickey Gilley
C. Porter Wagoner
D. George Jones
E. Alan Jackson

6. What cartoon character was stationed at Fort Frazzle?
A. Klondike Kat
B. Dudley Do-Right
C. Mighty Mouse
D. Kit Coyote
E. Ricochet Rabbit

7. What fort was the home base for Capt. Wilton Parmenter (Ken Berry) and the members of TV's "F Troop"?
A. Fort Necessity
B. Fort Baxter
C. Fort Ticonderoga
D. Fort Courage
E. Fort Sweetness

8. What fort was under attack when lawyer Francis Scott Key was inspired to write the words that would become "The Star-Spangled Banner"?
A. Fort McHenry
B. Fort Dearborn
C. Fort Ticonderoga
D. Fort Apache
E. Fort Sumter

Answers to Quiz #51 — **Fort-itude**

1. **(D) West Point, NY.** The silver depository is located in the same West Point that has been the seat of the U.S. Military Academy since 1802.

2. **(A) Roseanne Roseannadanna.** Roseanne Roseannadanna was a character played by Gilda Radner on "Saturday Night Live." The real Richard Feder was the brother-in-law of "Saturday Night Live" writer Alan Zweibel.

3. **(E) Komets.** It is spelled Komets with a K because the team was named for the original owner's wife, Kathryn.

4. **(E) Fort Bragg, NC.** The disease, aka Fort Bragg fever, causes a rash to appear on the legs. It is caused by "Leptospira interrogans."

5. **(A) George Strait.** Apart from being one of the more popular traditional country vocalists, George Strait made a foray into acting as the star of the 1991 movie "Pure Country."

6. **(A) Klondike Kat.** Klondike Kat is a fumbling Mountie always in pursuit of the French-accented mouse, Savoir Faire. Klondike's catchphrase was "I'm gonna make mincemeat out of that mouse!" although he was always thwarted by the clever Savoir Faire.

7. **(D) Fort Courage.** Members of "F Troop" included Sgt. O'Rourke (Forrest Tucker) and Corp. Agarn (Larry Storch), two scheming hustlers always out to make a buck; Hannibal Dobbs (James Hampton), the worst bugler in the cavalry; and Pvt. "Eagle Eye" Vanderbilt (Joe Brooks), the sentry whose eyesight was so poor he could barely see beyond his nose.

8. **(A) Fort McHenry.** The flag that flew over Fort McHenry in the famous 1814 battle was sewn by Mary Young Pickersgill and her daughter, Caroline. The flag came through the battle with 11 bullet holes in it. Key witnessed the battle aboard the British flagship Tonnant.

Quiz #52 — **In the Pink**

1. What is the name of the lab where cartoon characters "Pinky and The Brain" live?
A. Delco Labs
B. Toon Labs
C. Brain Labs
D. Acme Labs
E. Snowball Labs

2. Who or what was "The Pink Panther" in the original 1964 "Pink Panther" movie?
A. Automobile
B. Notorious prowler
C. Unusual cat
D. Police detective
E. Rare gem

3. What movie starred Cary Grant as a Naval officer in command of a pink submarine?
A. "Operation Petticoat"
B. "White Water, Blue Water"
C. "Father Goose"
D. "The Hunt for Pink October"
E. "Nobody's Perfect"

4. What actress turned author wrote the novels "Surrender the Pink" and "Delusions of Grandma"?
A. Lilli Palmer
B. Debbie Reynolds
C. Vanna White
D. Pia Zadora
E. Carrie Fisher

5. What Disney film features the songs "Look Out for Mr. Stork," "Casey Junior," and "Pink Elephants on Parade"?
A. "Beauty and the Beast"
B. "The Little Mermaid"
C. "Dumbo"
D. "Saludos Amigos"
E. "Sleeping Beauty"

6. Which of the following ingredients is not usually found in a pink lady cocktail?
A. Lemon juice
B. Grenadine
C. Gin
D. Sweet cream
E. Eggwhite

7. Pinklon "Pinky" Thomas won the WBC heavyweight boxing title in 1984 by defeating what man?
A. Greg Page
B. Mike Weaver
C. Mike Jameson
D. Billy Thomas
E. Tim Witherspoon

8. What is the medical term for "pinkeye"?
A. Conjunctivitis
B. Irisitis
C. Corneaitis
D. Wen
E. Sty

Answers to Quiz #52 — **In the Pink**

1. **(D) Acme Labs.** Acme is the company that also supplied the many defective items used by Wile E. Coyote in his pursuit of the Road Runner. "Pinky and the Brain" originally appeared in segments on "Animaniacs."

2. **(E) Rare gem.** It was a priceless diamond owned by Princess Dala. Its single flaw looked like a pink panther.

3. **(A) Operation Petticoat.** The 1959 film co-starred Tony Curtis and Joan O'Brien. A 1977 TV series sequel starred John Astin in the first season, and Robert Hogan in the second, as the sub commander. Tony Curtis's daughter, Jamie Lee Curtis, appeared on the TV series as Lt. Barbara Duran.

4. **(E) Carrie Fisher.** Fisher's first novel was the best-selling "Postcards from the Edge," the story of a drug-ridden actress with an alcoholic singer-mother which Fisher insists was NOT based on her own life. When the book was turned into a movie in 1990, Fisher also wrote the screenplay.

5. **(C) "Dumbo".** "Dumbo" is one of the shortest feature films made by Disney studios, clocking in at 64 minutes. Other songs in the film include "Song of the Roustabouts," "Baby Mine," and "When I See an Elephant Fly."

6. **(A) Lemon juice.** Take one eggwhite, 1 tsp. grenadine, 1 tsp. sweet cream, and 1.5 oz of gin. Shake ingredients well and serve over cracked ice.

7. **(E) Tim Witherspoon.** Thomas successfully defended his title against Mike Weaver one year later, but lost to Trevor Berbick in March 1986.

8. **(A) Conjunctivitis.** Conjunctivitis is a inflammation of the conjunctiva, the transparent membrane covering the eyeball. When it is inflamed, the normally invisible blood vessels become engorged, making the eye appear red.

Quiz #53 — **Still in the Pink**

1. When, after many years, it was decided to produce "Pink Panther" cartoons in which the cartoon cat actually spoke, what actor was tapped to provide his voice?
A. Tony Danza
B. Matt Frewer
C. Robin Williams
D. Justin Henry
E. John Wesley Shipp

2. Almost 60% of what animals living in Yellowstone National Park were killed by a pinkeye epidemic in 1981-82?
A. Elk
B. Timber wolves
C. Bighorn sheep
D. Grizzly bears
E. Bison

3. What is the title of the two-CD set documenting the 1994 tour of the band Pink Floyd?
A. "The Final Cut"
B. "Pulse"
C. "The Dark Side of the Earth"
D. "A Momentary Lapse of Reason"
E. "The Division Bell"

4. In what American city would you find the Pink Palace Museum?
A. Memphis, TN
B. Jacksonville, FL
C. Madison, WI
D. San Bernardino, CA
E. Denver, CO

5. What singer has recorded albums titled "Little Earthquakes," "Under the Pink," and "Boys for Pele"?
A. Melissa Etheridge
B. Amii Stewart
C. Tori Amos
D. Taylor Dayne
E. Chynna Phillips

6. What crimefighting District Attorney had a naive sidekick named Pinky?
A. Mr. Scarlet
B. Mr. Miracle
C. Mr. Muscles
D. Mr. Terrific
E. Mr. America

7. What pop song hit featured a place with "mirrors on the ceiling, pink champagne on ice"?
A. "Hotel California"
B. "Year of the Cat"
C. "Long Tall Glasses"
D. "Owner of a Lonely Heart"
E. "Cats in the Cradle"

8. What Puccini opera features a Naval officer named Lt. Pinkerton?
A. Tosca
B. La Boheme
C. Le Villi
D. Madama Butterfly
E. Manon Lescault

Answers to Quiz #53 — **Still in the Pink**

1. **(B) Matt Frewer.** Frewer is best known for playing "Max Headroom" and starring in the sitcom "Doctor, Doctor."

2. **(C) Bighorn sheep.** More recently, the bighorns are being threatened by mountain goats creeping into Yellowstone from Idaho, intruding on grazing land.

3. **(B) "Pulse".** The spine of the "Pulse" sets has a red blinking light that is supposed to flash nonstop for more than a year.

4. **(A) Memphis, TN.** The museum was the former home of Piggly Wiggly supermarket magnate Clarence Saunders. The sprawling mansion now hosts a natural and cultural history collection.

5. **(C) Tori Amos.** Amos was signed to Atlantic Records in 1987 where she recorded the ill-fated pop-metal album "Y Kant Tori Read." After changing her style to that of a more introspective balladeer, she released the 1991 album "Little Earthquakes" to positive reviews. The 1994 album, "Under the Pink," yielded the hit singles "God" and "Cornflake Girl."

6. **(A) Mr. Scarlet.** Mr. Scarlet, alias attorney Brian Butler who "discards his legal robes at midnight" to take on crime, appeared in all 69 issues of "Wow Comics" in the 1940s.

7. **(A) "Hotel California".** "Hotel California" was a #1 single and a platinum album for the Eagles in 1977. Along with their "Greatest Hits" album, the Eagles was the first band to see two of their albums reach sales of 10 million copies each.

8. **(D) Madama Butterfly.** Pinkerton has arranged to marry the young and pretty Cio-Cio-San, whom he calls Butterfly, and returns to America. Though she does not hear from him for three years, she remains faithful, having borne his child. When Pinkerton finally returns to Nagasaki with an American wife, Butterfly commits hara-kiri.

Quiz #54 — **The Paper Chase**

1. When paper money was first issued in the U.S. in 1862, who was the only president pictured on any denomination?
A. Thomas Jefferson
B. Abraham Lincoln
C. George Washington
D. James Monroe
E. Franklin Pierce

2. Who became the youngest actress to ever win an Oscar with her 1973 Best Supporting Actress win in "Paper Moon"?
A. Jodie Foster
B. Linda Blair
C. Tatum O'Neal
D. Carrie Fisher
E. Dana Hill

3. What company issued the first paper towels in 1907?
A. Kimberly-Clark
B. Waldorf
C. Georgia Pacific
D. Scott
E. Xerox

4. What song was a hit for both Anita Bryant and Marie Osmond?
A. "Paper Roses"
B. "Paper Moon"
C. "Paper Sun"
D. "Paper Doll"
E. "Paperback Writer"

5. What was the name of Fred Flintstone's paper boy?
A. Jack
B. Kevin
C. Arnold
D. David
E. Rock

6. Whose best friend was a boy named Jackie Paper?
A. Curious George
B. Pippi Longstocking
C. Shirley Temple
D. Puff, the Magic Dragon
E. The Flying Nun

7. "Billy, Don't Be a Hero" was a number one hit in Britain for the group Paper Lace. Before they could release it in the United States, another group released a cover version and hit #1. Name this sneaky American group.
A. First Class
B. Reunion
C. The Kasenatz-Katz Singing Orchestra Circus
D. Cross Country
E. Bo Donaldson and the Heywoods

8. Who played writer George Plimpton in the movie version of his football book "Paper Lion"?
A. Alan Alda
B. Hal Holbrook
C. Martin Sheen
D. Harold Gould
E. George Plimpton

Answers to Quiz #54 — The Paper Chase

1. (B) **Abraham Lincoln.** The first bills offered were the $5 (Alexander Hamilton), $10 (Abraham Lincoln), and $20 (Liberty). They were not legal tender when issued on March 10, 1862, but became so by an act of Congress one week later.

2. (C) **Tatum O'Neal.** O'Neal was 10 years old when the role of young con artist Addie Pray copped her the golden statuette. Her co-star in "Paper Moon" was her father, Ryan O'Neal.

3. (D) **Scott.** The Scott brothers' paper company produced high-quality bathroom tissue. When a factory production error delivered paper too thick and wrinkled to be used as toilet paper, someone came up with the idea of marketing the paper in small sheets calling it "paper towels." The first paper towels were called Sani-Towel, later changed to ScotTowels.

4. (A) **"Paper Roses".** The song, written by Janice Torre and Fred Spielman, was a 1960 hit for Anita Bryant and a 1973 hit for Marie Osmond.

5. (C) **Arnold.** Arnold, whose voice was provided by Don Messick, delivered the "Bedrock Bugle."

6. (D) **Puff, the Magic Dragon.** "Puff, the Magic Dragon" was written by Peter Yarrow and Leonard Lipton and originally recorded by Peter, Paul, and Mary. As the lyrics say: "Little Jackie Paper loved that rascal, Puff..."

7. (E) **Bo Donaldson and the Heywoods.** Paper Lace would not be entirely without success in the U.S. Their single "The Night Chicago Died" hit #1 in August 1974.

8. (A) **Alan Alda.** Plimpton wrote a series of articles for "Sports Illustrated" in 1966 based on his firsthand experience in various sports. He pitched in a major league baseball All-Star Game and boxed a few rounds with Sugar Ray Robinson. "Paper Lion" recounts Plimpton's tryout as a quarterback for the Detroit Lions. The movie "Paper Lion" was the film debut for Alan Alda and Alex Karras (who played himself).

Quiz #55 — "A Midsummer Night's Dream"

1. In Shakespeare's "A Midsummer Night's Dream," who was the King of the Fairies?
A. Lysander
B. Theseus
C. Titania
D. Puck
E. Oberon

2. Which of the following was not one of the fairies in Shakespeare's "A Midsummer Night's Dream"?
A. Mica
B. Peaseblossom
C. Moth
D. Cobweb
E. Mustardseed

3. What Academy Award-winning actress made her film debut in the 1935 production of "A Midsummer Night's Dream"?
A. Anita Louise
B. Katharine Hepburn
C. Luise Rainer
D. Olivia de Havilland
E. Claudette Colbert

4. Who directed and starred in the movie "A Midsummer Night's Sex Comedy"?
A. Alan Alda
B. John Huston
C. Woody Allen
D. Jose Ferrer
E. Ruth Gordon

5. What "Star Trek" character keeps a copy of the "Globe Illustrated Shakespeare" in his cabin always open to "A Midsummer Night's Dream"?
A. Jean-Luc Picard
B. Worf
C. Data
D. James Kirk
E. Deanna Troi

6. The phrase "every mother's son" comes from "A Midsummer Night's Dream." What was the sole top 40 song for the quintet that used the name "Every Mother's Son"?
A. "Psychotic Reaction"
B. "Ain't No Stoppin' Us Now"
C. "Do It Again a Little Bit Slower"
D. "Tracy"
E. "Come on Down to My Boat"

7. Whose festival occurs on the midsummer night?
A. St. Francis of Assisi
B. St. John the Baptist
C. St. Christopher
D. St. Bernard
E. St. Gabriel Possenti

8. In Shakespeare's "A Midsummer Night's Dream," who speaks the exit line: "And if we shadows have offended, think but this and all is mended: that you have but slumbered here, while these visions did appear..."?
A. Oberon
B. Bottom
C. Puck
D. Hermia
E. Helena

1. **(E) Oberon.** The play was thought to have been performed for Queen Elizabeth I, and Oberon narrates a piece of poetic homage to the queen.

2. **(A) Mica.** The four fairies are attendants to Titania, Queen of the Fairies.

3. **(D) Olivia de Havilland.** The Warner Brothers film features some inspired casting such as Joe E. Brown as Flute, James Cagney as Bottom, and Mickey Rooney as Puck. Olivia de Havilland played Hermia in Max Reinhardt's Hollywood Bowl production of the play in 1934, and repeated the role when Reinhardt also directed this film version.

4. **(C) Woody Allen.** The 1982 film is about the sexual antics of a group of couples on a country outing circa 1900. This was the first Woody Allen film to employ Mia Farrow.

5. **(A) Jean-Luc Picard.** The book is open to Act 3, Scene 2, in which Oberon gives Puck a love potion to be administered to Titania.

6. **(E) "Come on Down to My Boat".** "Come on Down to My Boat" hit #8 on the pop charts in July 1967. The group's next three singles made the Billboard top 100, each doing progressively worse. By 1969, the band was relegated to doing school dances and subsequently called it quits.

7. **(B) St. John the Baptist.** St. John's Day is on June 24 with celebration of St. John's Eve on the midsummer eve, commemorating the birth of the saint. In England, John the Baptist is considered the patron saint of the common people.

8. **(C) Puck.** Puck is the mischievous spirit whose antics with a love potion causes commotion among lovers in the play. He is also called Robin Goodfellow.

Quiz #56 — **Senators**

1. Who was the first Senator in office to be elected President?
A. William Henry Harrison
B. John Kennedy
C. Harry Truman
D. Benjamin Harrison
E. Warren Harding

2. What was the nickname of Louisiana Senator Huey Long?
A. Blowfish
B. Kingfish
C. Flying Fish
D. Shark
E. Goldfish

3. Sen. Harrison Williams of New Jersey resigned from the Senate after the Senate Ethics Commitee unanimously voted for his expulsion for his involvement in what scandal?
A. Tailhook
B. Goldfine
C. Teapot Dome
D. Abscam
E. Watergate

4. In what city would you have found the NHL team, the Senators, that won the first Stanley Cup in 1927?
A. Washington, D.C.
B. Quebec
C. Cleveland
D. Ottawa
E. Detroit

5. What U.S. Senator founded the "Golden Fleece Award"?
A. Paul Tsongas
B. Paul Simon
C. William Proxmire
D. Daniel Inouye
E. Margaret Chase Smith

6. What U.S. Senator holds the record for scoring the most points in a NCAA Final Four basketball game?
A. Bill Bradley
B. Jerry West
C. John Glenn
D. Elvin Hayes
E. Austin Carr

7. Julie Andrews played the daughter of a U.S. Senator in what Alfred Hitchcock film?
A. "Topaz"
B. "Family Plot"
C. "Marnie"
D. "Torn Curtain"
E. "The Paradine Case"

8. Who was selected the Senate minority leader in 1994?
A. Richard Gephardt
B. Bob Dole
C. Tom Daschle
D. Edward Kennedy
E. Robert C. Byrd

Answers to Quiz #56 — **Senators**

1. (E) Warren Harding. Harding was elected President in November 1920 and resigned from the Senate in January 1921.

2. (B) Kingfish. Long was assassinated in 1935 by Dr. Carl Weiss who had a personal grievance against Long. Long was the inspiration for the character Willie Stark in Robert Penn Warren's Pulitzer-winning novel "All the King's Men."

3. (D) Abscam. In 1979-80, the FBI ran an undercover operation with a fake company called Abdul Enterprises investigating political corruption that resulted in the conviction of several Congressmen.

4. (D) Ottawa. The original Ottawa Senators lasted from 1917-34 in the NHL.

5. (C) William Proxmire. Proxmire issued a monthly "award" mocking the waste of government funds on unusual research projects, such as a study of the sex life of the Japanese quail.

6. (A) Bill Bradley. Bradley scored 58 points for Princeton in a 1965 game against Wichita State.

7. (D) "Torn Curtain". The film also starred Paul Newman as an American nuclear scientist posing as a defector.

8. (C) Tom Daschle. Daschle was elected as a Senator from South Dakota in 1986. He was elected the Senate Democratic Leader in 1994. Only one Senator — Lyndon Johnson — reached the position with fewer years of service in the Senate.

Quiz #57 — **Treasure Islands 2**

1. What island in Michigan forbids the use of automobiles?
A. Mackinac
B. Sault Ste. Marie
C. Beaver
D. Pelee
E. Manitou

2. Who was the founder of Island Records?
A. Frank Sinatra
B. Jimmy Buffett
C. Luther Campbell
D. Neil Bogart
E. Chris Blackwell

3. What island nation's Capitol building is a replica of the U.S. Capitol?
A. Java
B. Iceland
C. Mauritania
D. Pago Pago
E. Cuba

4. What celebrity owns the island of Tetiroa?
A. Bjorn Borg
B. Marlon Brando
C. Elton John
D. George Steinbrenner
E. Bruce Springsteen

5. What was the name of the island on which journalist Ernie Pyle was killed?
A. Ie Shima
B. Oahu
C. Iwo Jima
D. Tirwawa
E. Timoneng

6. What island is surrounded by the Karimata Strait, the Sunda Strait, and the Strait of Malacca?
A. Tasmania
B. Christmas Island
C. Sumatra
D. Panay
E. Prince Edward Island

7. What sport's Hall of Fame was formerly located in Kings Island, Ohio?
A. Figure skating
B. Diving
C. Professional bowling
D. College football
E. Track and field

8. During World War II, what island was known as "the unsinkable aircraft carrier"?
A. Tonga
B. Hilo
C. New Caledonia
D. Malta
E. Nauru

Answers to Quiz #57 — **Treasure Islands 2**

1. **(A) Mackinac.** MI 185 on Mackinac Island is the only state road in Michigan history that has never had a car accident.

2. **(E) Chris Blackwell.** Blackwell, a white Jamaican, was responsible for discovering such musical talent as Bob Marley, U2, and Melissa Etheridge. Island Records, founded in 1962, was sold to PolyGram in 1989. Label artists have included the Spencer Davis Group, Jethro Tull, Cat Stevens, and King Crimson.

3. **(E) Cuba.** Built in Havana in 1929, the Capitolio is a copy of the U.S. Capitol, although built on a smaller scale.

4. **(B) Marlon Brando.** Tetiroa is located in the Society Islands, a part of French Polynesia in the southern Pacific Ocean. Bjorn Borg owns the island of Kattil, off Stockholm.

5. **(A) Ie Shima.** Pyle was hit by a sniper's bullet on April 18, 1945. The WWII journalist's lively reports of battles and the young men waging war were immensely popular, appearing in syndication in 366 daily U.S. newspapers.

6. **(C) Sumatra.** Sumatra is the world's 6th largest island, with an area of 474,000 square kilometers. Sumatra is an Indonesian island located off the Malay Peninsula, and is one of the Greater Sunda Islands.

7. **(D) College football.** The College Football Hall of Fame was established in 1955 by the National Football Foundation. It moved from Kings Island, Ohio to South Bend, Indiana in the spring of 1994.

8. **(D) Malta.** In World War II, Malta was subjected to more than 1200 air raids, making it the most bombed spot. The collective Maltese people were awarded the George Cross for gallantry by King George VI in 1942.

Quiz #58 — **For the Birds**

1. Which of the following films won Oscars for best film, director, screenplay, actor, and actress?
A. "One Flew Over the Cuckoo's Nest"
B. "The Birds"
C. "Three Days of the Condor"
D. "The Sea Hawk"
E. "The Birdman of Alcatraz"

2. The constellation Aquila is in the form of what bird?
A. Swan
B. Eagle
C. Stork
D. Penguin
E. Pelican

3. "For Your Love" and "Heart Full of Soul" were top 10 hits for what British rock band?
A. Flock of Seagulls
B. Wings
C. The Yardbirds
D. The Fabulous Thunderbirds
E. The Blackbyrds

4. Which of the following is not a water bird?
A. Booby
B. Grebe
C. Shrike
D. Gannet
E. Auk

5. "Keep Your Eye on the Sparrow," sung by Sammy Davis Jr., was the opening theme song of what TV series?
A. "Kojak"
B. "Starsky and Hutch"
C. "Cannon"
D. "Baretta"
E. "Ten Speed and Brownshoe"

6. What was the first bird to leave Noah's Ark?
A. Eagle
B. Dove
C. Raven
D. Duck
E. Owl

7. What bird did Benjamin Franklin suggest as the national emblem for the newly formed United States of America?
A. Bald eagle
B. Turkey
C. Buzzard
D. Rhode Island Red chicken
E. Great horned owl

8. Jean Louise Finch is the narrator of what Pulitzer Prize-winning novel?
A. "The Falcon and the Snowman"
B. "Lonesome Dove"
C. "The Nightingale's Lament"
D. "The Wild Geese"
E. "To Kill a Mockingbird"

Answers to Quiz #58 — **For the Birds**

1. (A) **"One Flew Over the Cuckoo's Nest".** The film, director Milos Forman, writers Lawrence Hauben and Bo Goldman, actor Jack Nicholson, and actress Louise Fletcher all won Oscars in 1975. The only other films to have accomplished a similar feat were "It Happened One Night" in 1934 and "Silence of the Lambs" in 1991.

2. (B) **Eagle.** Prominent in the summer sky of the Northern Hemisphere, Aquila contains the bright star Altair.

3. (C) **The Yardbirds.** "For Your Love" reached #6 on the Billboard charts in the spring of 1965 followed by "Heart Full of Soul" at #9 two months later. Over its history, the group included among its members such legends as Jeff Beck, Jimmy Page, and Eric Clapton. The Yardbirds took their name from British slang for hobo or railroad bum.

4. (C) **Shrike.** The shrike is a bird of prey that captures insects in its beak and then impales them on nearby thorns for "storage."

5. (D) **"Baretta".** "Baretta" was actually a replacement series slapped together by the producers of "Toma." "Toma" was based on a real-life Newark police detective and starred Tony Musante. When Musante decided not to return for a second season, Robert Blake was brought in and David Toma changed into Tony Baretta.

6. (C) **Raven.** A raven "went forth to and fro, until the waters were dried up off the earth" (Genesis 8:7). Noah later sent out a dove which returned with an olive leaf informing him that the floodwaters had abated.

7. (B) **Turkey.** Franklin considered the bald eagle to be a "bird of bad moral character, like those among men who live by sharping and robbing, he is generally poor, and often very lousy. The turkey is a much more respectable bird, and withal a true original bird of America."

8. (E) **"To Kill a Mockingbird".** Jean Louise is nicknamed "Scout." Harper Lee's famous novel included much bird imagery, from the Finch family to the mockingbird metaphor.

Quiz #59 — **Try Try Again**

1. Who created the characters Joe the Joker, Apple Annie, and Nicely-Nicely Johnson?
A. Stefan Zweig
B. Bram Stoker
C. Frank Loesser
D. Ring Lardner
E. Damon Runyon

2. What film critic's reviews have been collected in books titled "Going Steady," "5001 Nights at the Movies," and "Kiss Kiss Bang Bang"?
A. James Agee
B. Dennis Cunningham
C. Gene Shalit
D. Pauline Kael
E. Roger Ebert

3. What animal did Lewis Carroll's Mad Hatter insert into the poem "Twinkle Twinkle Little Star"?
A. Bat
B. Fox
C. Snail
D. Toad
E. Cow

4. What was the name of the loved one seen at the train station in the hit song "Green Green Grass of Home"?
A. Mary
B. Julie
C. Sandy
D. Sue
E. Linda

5. Who won Tony Award nominations for playing Anyanka in "Bajour," Velma in "Chicago," and Rose in "Bye Bye Birdie"?
A. Lola Falana
B. Chita Rivera
C. Mary Martin
D. Ann Reinking
E. Anita Morris

6. Who wrote the oft-misquoted lines: "Water water everywhere / nor any drop to drink"?
A. William Butler Yeats
B. Christopher Columbus
C. Heinrich Heine
D. Samuel Taylor Coleridge
E. Sophocles

7. Whose final film role was as a psychotic tormenting Stefanie Powers in "Die! Die! My Darling"?
A. Veronica Lake
B. Joan Crawford
C. Tallulah Bankhead
D. Rosalind Russell
E. Lana Turner

8. What TV turkey featured regulars called The Unknown Comic and Gene-Gene the Dancing Machine?
A. "The $1.98 Beauty Show"
B. "The Gong Show"
C. "Real People"
D. "Animals, Animals, Animals"
E. "That's Incredible!"

*Answers to Quiz #59 — **Try Try Again***

1. **(E) Damon Runyon.** Damon Runyon's "Guys and Dolls," published in 1931, was a collection of stories about colorful characters in a racy section of Broadway. Frank Loesser won a Tony Award in 1951 for his work on the musical version of "Guys and Dolls."

2. **(D) Pauline Kael.** Kael was the regular film critic for "The New Yorker," until her retirement in 1991. Her second book, "Kiss Kiss, Bang Bang," was published in 1968.

3. **(A) Bat.** The poem recited by the Mad Hatter in "Alice's Adventures in Wonderland" was: "Twinkle twinkle little bat / How I wonder where you're at / Up above the world you fly / Like a teatray in the sky."

4. **(A) Mary.** "Green Green Grass of Home" was written by Curly Putnam and originally recorded by country music legend Porter Wagoner. Tom Jones hit the Billboard top 40 with the song in 1967.

5. **(B) Chita Rivera.** Rivera won a Tony Award in 1984 for "The Rink." At the age of 60, Rivera gave a sensational performance as an exotic film legend in the 1985 movie "Kiss of the Spider Woman."

6. **(D) Samuel Taylor Coleridge.** From his "Rime of the Ancient Mariner," the latter half of this Coleridge quote is often seen as the incorrect "and not a drop to drink."

7. **(C) Tallulah Bankhead.** Bankhead returned to acting after a 12-year hiatus to star as a religious fanatic in this 1965 movie. The movie has also appeared under the title "Fanatic."

8. **(B) "The Gong Show".** Chuck Barris hosted "The Gong Show," an amateur hour gone mad on NBC from 1976-78. Three celebrity panelists judged each act with the option to gong any act before it was completed, eliminating them from being scored. Gene-Gene the Dancing Machine was one of the show's stage hands, an overweight man who shuffled his way onto stage at commercial breaks. The Unknown Comic, who wore a white disco suit and a brown paper bag over his head, was revealed to be stand-up comic Murray Langston.

Quiz #60 — **By the Yard**

1. What was the name of the prisoner's football team headed by quarterback Burt Reynolds in the movie "The Longest Yard"?
A. The Prison Brakes
B. The Junkyard Dogs
C. The Mean Machine
D. The Mad Monsters
E. The Graveyard Shift

2. What rock group was originally known as The New Yardbirds?
A. The Beach Boys
B. Rufus
C. Led Zeppelin
D. The Who
E. Electric Light Orchestra

3. Who set an NFL record in 1970 for kicking a 63-yard field goal, the longest field goal in a regular season game?
A. Tom Dempsey
B. George Blanda
C. Al Del Greco
D. Garo Ypremian
E. Dirk Borgognone

4. What Rudyard Kipling character was captured by the Russians during the Crimean War, but found his way back to his post in the Khyber Pass after spending 30 years in Siberia?
A. Gunga Din
B. Lt. Austin Limmason
C. Major General Stanley
D. Captain George Osborne
E. Captain Vere

5. What was the nickname of the fictional gentleman-thief Michael Lanyard?
A. Bulldog Drummond
B. The Pink Panther
C. The Saint
D. The Thinking Machine
E. The Lone Wolf

6. Actor Clarence Gilyard Jr. was a regular performer on all but which of the following TV shows?
A. "What's Happening Now!!"
B. "CHiPs"
C. "Matlock"
D. "Walker, Texas Ranger"
E. "The Duck Factory"

7. What state claims the resort island of Martha's Vineyard?
A. New York
B. New Hampshire
C. Delaware
D. Rhode Island
E. Massachusetts

8. Scotland Yard refers to the Criminal Investigation Department (C.I.D.) of the London metropolitan police force. Originally established in a 12th-century castle, the unit eventually moved to a building in the Victoria area of London, and was renamed New Scotland Yard. In what year did this move take place?
A. 1890
B. 1919
C. 1954
D. 1967
E. 1980

Answers to Quiz #60 — **By the Yard**

1. (C) **The Mean Machine.** Reynolds wore #22, the same number he wore as a college football player. Reynolds was named All-Southern (1953) and First-Team All-State (1954) while playing for Florida State University. He was being scouted by the pro teams when he was in a car accident that shattered his knees as well as his pro football prospects. Appearing in the "The Longest Yard" as players on the prison guard team were ex-NFL players Ray Nitschke, Mike Henry, and Joe Knapp.

2. (C) **Led Zeppelin.** When the original Yardbirds split up in 1968, Jimmy Page and bassist Chris Dreja launched the New Yardbirds with R&B singer Robert Plant and drummer John Bonham. By the end of 1968, the group had renamed itself Led Zeppelin, borrowing the name from a phrase often used by The Who's drummer, Keith Moon, who described bad gigs as "going down like a lead Zeppelin."

3. (A) **Tom Dempsey.** Dempsey kicked a 63-yard field goal for the New Orleans Saints against the Detroit Lions on November 8, 1970. Dempsey was born without a right hand or toes on his right foot. The NFL passed a rule that future kickers would have to use a normal kicking shoe, inspired by criticism that Dempsey had an unfair advantage with his flat-toed surface. That didn't stop Jason Elam of the Denver Broncos from tying the record in 1998.

4. (B) **Lt. Austin Limmason.** Limmason was featured in Kipling's short story, "The Man Who Was," published in "Life's Handicaps." Limmason is reduced to an amnesiac "limp heap of rags" by the Russians, but recognizes his name on the regimental records just days before he dies.

5. (E) **The Lone Wolf.** Lanyard was the creation of American writer Louis J. Vance in numerous novels between 1918 and 1934. On film, The Lone Wolf was played by Melvyn Douglas, Francis Lederer, and Warren William among others.

6. (A) **"What's Happening Now!!".** Gilyard played motorcycle patrolman Off. Webster on "CHiPs" (1982-83), storyboard artist Roland Culp on "The Duck Factory" (1984), Ben Matlock's legman Conrad McMasters on "Matlock" (1989-93), and Texas Ranger Jimmy Trivette on "Walker, Texas Ranger" (1993-).

7. (E) **Massachusetts.** Martha's Vineyard is located off the southwest coast of Cape Cod, and is part of Dukes County, Massachusetts. The chief town on the island is Edgartown.

8. (D) **1967.** The original home of the London police was Whitehall Place. The back of this building opened onto a courtyard which had been the site of a residence owned by the Kings of Scotland. Used and occupied by the Kings when in London, this residence became known as "Scotland." The courtyard was later used by Sir Christopher Wren and was called "Scotland Yard." The back premises of 4 Whitehall Place, which could be entered from this courtyard, were used as a police station, and so the headquarters of the Metropolitan Police became known as Scotland Yard.

Quiz #61 — If the Shoe Fits

1. While Elvis Presley had a monster hit with his cover version of Carl Perkins's "Blue Suede Shoes," what band had a hit with the flip side of Perkins's single, "Honey Don't"?
A. Spandau Ballet
B. The Beach Boys
C. Fleetwood Mac
D. Herman's Hermits
E. The Beatles

2. The popular baseball movie "Field of Dreams" was based on the book "Shoeless Joe" written by what author?
A. Saul Bellow
B. Harry Chapin
C. Michael Hockinson
D. Dale Jellings
E. W.P. Kinsella

3. What is the secret alter ego of cartoon character Shoeshine Boy?
A. Hong Kong Phooey
B. Super President
C. Underdog
D. Frankenstein Jr.
E. Space Ghost

4. What was the name of the college attended by Dexter Riley (Kurt Russell) in the Disney movies "Now You See Him, Now You Don't," "The Strongest Man in the World," and "The Computer Wore Tennis Shoes"?
A. Medfield
B. Rutgers
C. Faber
D. Bueller
E. Tait

5. What TV husband and father worked as a shoe salesman?
A. Archie Bunker
B. Howard Cunningham
C. Al Bundy
D. Herman Munster
E. John Walton

6. Bill Shoemaker won four Kentucky Derbys before retiring in 1990. Which of the following horses was not a champion for him at the Derby?
A. Ferdinand - 1986
B. Lucky Debonair - 1965
C. Candy Spots - 1963
D. Tomy Lee - 1959
E. Swaps - 1955

7. What is the correct distance between stakes in the game of horseshoes?
A. 20 feet
B. 25 feet
C. 30 feet
D. 35 feet
E. 40 feet

8. What kind of bird is the title character in the Jeff MacNelly comic strip "Shoe"?
A. Robin
B. Baltimore oriole
C. Osprey
D. Purple martin
E. Buzzard

Answers to Quiz #61 — **If the Shoe Fits**

1. **(E) The Beatles.** In 1985, George Harrison and Ringo Starr appeared on the Cinemax special "A Rockabilly Session — Carl Perkins and Friends" and performed "Honey Don't" with Perkins and Eric Clapton.

2. **(E) W.P. Kinsella.** W.P. Kinsella was also the author of "The Iowa Baseball Confederacy." In the movie, Kevin Costner played a character named "Ray Kinsella."

3. **(C) Underdog.** "There's no need to fear! Underdog is here!" Shoeshine Boy transformed into Underdog by ducking into the nearest telephone booth and downing an energy pill he kept in his ring. Wally Cox provided the voices of Shoeshine Boy and Underdog.

4. **(A) Medfield.** The antics of Dexter Riley and his friends always brought out the greedy nature of Dean Higgins (Joe Flynn) at Medfield College and Dean Collingswood (Alan Hewitt) at their rival Springfield State University. Disney got a lot of mileage out of Medfield College. Medfield was attended by Merlin Jones (Tommy Kirk) in "The Misadventures of Merlin Jones" and "The Monkey's Uncle," and was the home of Prof. Ned Brainard (Fred MacMurray) in "The Absent-Minded Professor" and "Son of Flubber."

5. **(C) Al Bundy.** Al Bundy worked as a shoe salesman for Garry's Shoes and Accessories for the Beautiful Woman in the New Market Mall. He once appeared in a TV commercial for Zeus Athletic Shoes.

6. **(C) Candy Spots - 1963.** Candy Spots took 3rd place at the Kentucky Derby in 1963, but went on to win the Preakness Stakes. Bill Shoemaker was the first jockey to earn $1 million in purses. In his career he rode 40,350 mounts and brought in 8,833 wins. When he won the Kentucky Derby in 1986, he was the oldest winning jockey ever at the age of 54.

7. **(E) 40 feet.** President George Bush was a big fan of horseshoes and installed the first horseshoe pit at the White House.

8. **(D) Purple martin.** Shoe's full name is P. Martin Shoemaker. He is the editor of the "Treetops Tattler Tribune" newspaper.

Quiz #62 — **Scandalous!**

1. What "Washington Post" writer won a Pulitzer Prize for her tale of "Jimmy," an 8-year-old heroin addict, only to have the prize taken away?
A. Janet Cooke
B. Lee Bey
C. Jane Bryant Quinn
D. Joan D. Vinge
E. Deborah Blum

2. 14-year-old Jimmy Gronen of Boulder, CO, won what race using an illegal electromagnet?
A. Akron Soap Box Derby
B. Iditarod
C. Junior America's Cup
D. Ironman Triathlon
E. Hell of the West

3. Columbia professor Charles Van Doren was the popular champion on what TV quiz show investigated for providing questions and answers to contestants in advance?
A. "Dotto"
B. "Name That Tune"
C. "Twenty-One"
D. "The $64,000 Challenge"
E. "The $64,000 Question"

4. What popular TV host was ordered to divest himself of music publishing stocks after his suspected participation in the 1959 "Payola" scandal?
A. Johnny Carson
B. Milton Berle
C. Red Skelton
D. Arthur Godfrey
E. Dick Clark

5. What WWII general slapped Pvt. C.H. Kuhl, a shell-shocked soldier at a Sicily military hospital, calling him "a coward and a bastard"?
A. George C. Marshall
B. Bernard Montgomery
C. George Patton
D. Dwight Eisenhower
E. Erwin Rommel

6. What automobile suffered unfavorable publicity when it was reported that rear-end collisions with the car caused the gas tank to explode?
A. Chevrolet Nova
B. Chevrolet Corsair
C. Ford Pinto
D. Isuzu Trooper
E. Lincoln Continental

7. Skier Vladimir "Spider" Sabich was shot to death in 1976 by what actress?
A. Heather Menzies
B. Cheryl Crane
C. Virginia Rappe
D. Claudine Longet
E. Thelma Todd

8. Vanessa Williams was forced to relinquish her Miss America crown in 1984 after nude "Penthouse" photographs of her surfaced. What state had she represented in the pageant?
A. Texas
B. New York
C. Illinois
D. Washington
E. Florida

*Answers to Quiz #62 — **Scandalous!**

1. **(A) Janet Cooke.** Two days after she received the Pulitzer Prize on April 13, 1981, the "Post" announced that the article was a fabrication. Cooke was forced to resign. The feature prize was then awarded to Teresa Carpenter, a freelancer with the "Village Voice." Cooke's name has recently resurfaced as Columbia TriStar paid $750,000 for the rights to her life story.

2. **(A) Akron Soap Box Derby.** Gronen's car was x-rayed after he won in 1973, uncovering an electromagnet in the nose of the car. The magnet was attracted to the iron-plated starting gate, causing the car to lurch forward in an unfair advantage. Gronen's uncle, Robert Lange Sr., an engineer, admitted his participation in the construction of the car. Lange's son, Robert Lange Jr., won the race the year before, but when the judges asked to see his winning car, it was mysteriously missing.

3. **(C) "Twenty-One".** After losing to Van Doren, contestant Herbert Stempel publicly declared the game was fixed. A subsequent investigation by the Special Subcommittee on Legislative Oversight of the House of Representatives led to the downfall of Van Doren and "Twenty-One" producers Jack Barry and Dan Enright. The scandal was the subject of the 1994 movie "Quiz Show."

4. **(E) Dick Clark.** After completing the TV quiz show scandal investigation, the House Special Subcommittee on Legislative Oversight began to scrutinize the rock-and-roll radio industry. It soon emerged that it was common for disc jockeys to plug records in return for gifts and money from record manufacturers or distributors, a practice dubbed "Payola." Dick Clark survived the investigation, but Alan Freed, "The Father of Rock and Roll," was indicted on 26 counts of accepting bribes to play records.

5. **(C) George Patton.** Witnesses reported the misbehavior to Gen. Dwight Eisenhower who flew to Sicily to personally investigate. He ordered Patton to publicly apologize to the soldier and the hospital staff. It was later discovered that Patton also slapped a second soldier in a similar incident.

6. **(C) Ford Pinto.** The Pinto's gas tank was situated only seven inches from the rear bumper. Ford recalled 1.5 million Ford Pintos and Mercury Bobcats to make their tanks less likely to leak or rupture. In 1980, the Ford Company stood accused of reckless homicide in the 1978 deaths of three young women in a 1973 Pinto. Ford was acquitted.

7. **(D) Claudine Longet.** Longet, formerly married to singer Andy Williams, had been Sabich's lover for the preceding two years. Longet claimed Sabich was shot in the abdomen while he was showing her how to operate the .22 caliber pistol. On January 14, 1977, Longet was convicted of criminally negligent homicide, a misdemeanor. Her sentence consisted of two years probation, 30 days in jail, and a $25 fine.

8. **(B) New York.** Miss America pageant officials insisted Williams resign due to a clause in the pageant form she signed stating she had "committed no acts of moral turpitude." Suzette Charles, Miss New Jersey, was runner-up and awarded the crown for the remaining time. Williams survived the scandal and has gone onto a successful recording and movie career. She co-starred with Arnold Schwarzenegger in the movie "Eraser," and her 1992 hit song "Save the Best for Last" spent five weeks at #1 on the Billboard pop charts.

Quiz #63 — On the Spot

1. Koplik's spots are typically regarded as an early sign of what disease?
A. Chicken pox
B. Mumps
C. Shingles
D. Measles
E. Mononucleosis

2. What Italian astronomer discovered the Great Red Spot on the surface of Jupiter?
A. Jean Picard
B. Galileo Galilei
C. Giovanni Cassini
D. Giuseppe Campani
E. Eustachio Divini

3. Which of the following is a pudding served to English schoolchildren?
A. Spotted dick
B. Spotted tommy
C. Spotted don
D. Spotted john
E. Spotted jimmy

4. In what U.S. state was the Civil War battle of Spotsylvania fought?
A. Tennessee
B. Alabama
C. Virginia
D. Pennsylvania
E. Texas

5. Who is the author of the best-selling children's book "Where's Spot?"
A. Bill Martin Jr.
B. Eric Hill
C. Martin Handford
D. Justine Korman
E. Eric Carle

6. What cartoon crimefighter is accompanied by a striped cat named Spot?
A. Minute Mouse
B. Underdog
C. Ricochet Rabbit
D. Crusader Rabbit
E. Hong Kong Phooey

7. How many spots were painted on each of the dalmatian puppies in Disney's animated film "101 Dalmatians"?
A. 10
B. 32
C. 54
D. 78
E. 101

8. In the classic tale, "Treasure Island," which pirate had a stroke and died after he received the Black Spot, a pirate's death notice, from Blind Pew?
A. Ben Gunn
B. Captain Flint
C. Long John Silver
D. Israel Hands
E. Billy Bones

Answers to Quiz #63 — **On the Spot**

1. **(D) Measles.** Koplik's spots, also known as Filatov's spots, are small red spots on the skin. In the center of each spot is a minute bluish-white speck.

2. **(C) Giovanni Cassini.** Giovanni Cassini (1625-1712) is best known for his pioneering achievements in observational astronomy. While he originally studied the sun, an improved telescope lens led to his observation of the planets. Along with the Great Red Spot, Cassini also discovered four of the satellites surrounding Saturn, and the dark division between the A and B rings of Saturn which today bears his name as the "Cassini division."

3. **(A) Spotted dick.** According to a recipe in the "Upstairs Downstairs Cookery Book," spotted dick is made with flour, suet, breadcrumbs, sugar, currants, baking powder, and a pinch of salt. These ingredients are wrapped in a floured cloth and boiled. The pudding is served with custard sauce or a sweetened wine sauce.

4. **(C) Virginia.** In the Spotsylvania campaign of May 1864, Gen. Ulysses Grant hoped to move his army southward through Virginia, enveloping Robert E. Lee's flank as the Northern troops advanced toward Richmond. Fourteen thousand men were killed or injured during the three-week campaign.

5. **(B) Eric Hill.** The popular yellow puppy has appeared in many other books by Eric Hill including "Spot Visits His Grandparents," "Spot's First Walk," "Spot's First Easter," "Spot's Magical Christmas," and "Spot Goes to School."

6. **(E) Hong Kong Phooey.** Whenever police janitor Penrod Pooch learns of a crime, he climbs into a filing cabinet and dons an orange robe and black mask to become crimefighter Hong Kong Phooey. Hong Kong claims to be a master of the martial arts, but actually learned his craft by correspondence course. It if weren't for the efforts of Spot, Hong Kong's feline companion, most of the crimes Hong Kong investigates would remain unsolved.

7. **(B) 32.** Pongo, father of the dalmatian pups, had 72 spots. The task of animating 101 spotted puppies was possible with a revolutionary development called Xerography. The Xerox system allowed the Disney animators to copy initial drawings many times over, eliminating the need to draw 101 separate dogs for the mass puppy scenes.

8. **(E) Billy Bones.** The Black Spot was a dark spot written on a piece of paper, created with a page torn from the Bible.

Quiz #64 — Singing "I Love You"

1. Identify the song with these lyrics: "Hold my hand and promise / That you'll always love me too / Make me know you'll love me / The same way I love you, little girl."
- A. "Hang On, Sloopy" by The McCoys
- B. "Hey Little Girl" by Major Lance
- C. "Come Go with Me" by the Del-Vikings
- D. "New York's a Lonely Town" by the Trade Winds
- E. "I Beg of You" by Elvis Presley

2. Identify the song with these lyrics: "Darling there will never be another / 'Cause I love you so / Don't you ever leave me / Say you'll never go."
- A. "Silly Love Songs" by Wings
- B. "Oh! Carol" by Neil Sedaka
- C. "Count Every Star" by Linda Scott
- D. "In the Still of the Nite" by the Five Satins
- E. "Telephone Line" by ELO

3. Identify the song with these lyrics: "I don't know who you're with / I don't even know where you've gone / My only hope is that someday you might hear this song / And you'll know that I wrote it especially for you / And I love you wherever you are."
- A. "Still" by Bill Anderson
- B. "This Used to Be My Playground" by Madonna
- C. "Right Place Wrong Time" by Dr. John
- D. "Are You Lonesome Tonight?" by Elvis Presley
- E. "For You" by Ricky Nelson

4. Identify the song with these lyrics: "Kinda like sugar / Kinda like spices / Kinda like, like what you do / Kinda sounds funny / But love, honey / Honey, I love you."
- A. "Dance, Dance, Dance" by Chic
- B. "Yummy, Yummy, Yummy" by the Ohio Express
- C. "Sugar Sugar" by the Archies
- D. "Bang Bang" by Cher
- E. "More More More" by the Andrea True Connection

5. Identify the song with these lyrics: "You know I love you / Do anything for you / Just don't mistreat me / And I'll be good to you."
- A. "Sleeping Single in a Double Bed" by Barbara Mandrell
- B. "People" by Barbara Streisand
- C. "Hello Stranger" by Barbara Lewis
- D. "I Know (You Don't Love Me No More)" by Barbara George
- E. "You'll Lose a Good Thing" by Barbara Lynn

6. Identify the song with these lyrics: "Come on and take my hand / Come on baby and be my man / 'Cause I love you, 'cause I want you / Can't you see that I'm lonely?"
- A. "Show Me" by Joe Tex
- B. "Groove Me" by King Floyd
- C. "Love Me" by Yvonne Elliman
- D. "Rescue Me" by Fontella Bass
- E. "Not Me" by the Orlons

7. Identify the song with these lyrics: "I need you / I want you near me / I love you / Yes I do and I hope you hear me."
- A. "Where the Boys Are" by Connie Francis
- B. "Where or When" by Dion and the Belmonts
- C. "When" by the Kalin Twins
- D. "Who Am I" by Petula Clark
- E. "Where Are You" by Dinah Washington

8. Identify the song with these lyrics: "Don't be afraid of me, little girl / 'Cause I love you most in the whole wide world / You know I wouldn't harm a pretty beautiful thing."
- A. "Rama Lama Ding Dong" by the Edsels
- B. "My Ding-a-Ling" by Chuck Berry
- C. "Ka-Ding-Dong" by the G-Clefs
- D. "Ding-a-Ling" by Bobby Rydell
- E. "Ding Dong" by the McGuire Sisters

Answers to Quiz #64 — **Singing "I Love You"**

1. **(E) "I Beg of You" by Elvis Presley.** "I Beg of You" made a 12-week visit to the Billboard Top 100 charts in 1958, peaking at #8. It also reached #5 on the country charts and #4 on the R&B charts.

2. **(B) "Oh! Carol" by Neil Sedaka.** When Neil Sedaka was a member of the Tokens, Carole Klein used to hang around as a fan of the group. After Sedaka released "Oh! Carol," the real Carole put out an answer record called "Oh Neil," which was a flop. After changing her name to Carole King, however, she went on to sell millions of records, peaking in 1971 with the best-selling LP "Tapestry."

3. **(A) "Still" by Bill Anderson.** "Whispering" Bill Anderson spent seven weeks at #1 on the country charts with his self-composed 1963 hit "Still." It also crossed over to the pop charts as his only top 40 pop hit, peaking at #8. As his popularity as a recording artist waned, Anderson found work as a TV host, working on the game shows "The Better Sex" and "Fandango."

4. **(B) "Yummy, Yummy, Yummy" by the Ohio Express.** Although credited to the Ohio Express, the song was really produced by a group of session musicians. Bubblegum music pioneers Jerry Kasenatz and Jeff Katz produced the song as a demo for the Ohio Express. When Neil Bogart, the head of Buddah Records, heard the demo, he said "Get it out and put Ohio Express's name on the label because it's great the way it is." The song peaked at #4 in 1968. The Ohio Express followed it up with songs they really recorded themselves: "Down at Lulu's," "Chewy Chewy," "Sweeter Than Sugar," and "Mercy."

5. **(E) "You'll Lose a Good Thing" by Barbara Lynn.** Singer Barbara Lynn, born Barbara Lynn Ozen, was discovered by a blues artist-deejay named Clarence "Bon Ton" Garlow in 1960. The self-penned "You'll Lose a Good Thing" was her only top 40 hit, peaking at #8 in 1962.

6. **(D) "Rescue Me" by Fontella Bass.** Fontella Bass was discovered in 1960 by blues artist Little Milton. In 1964, Milton took Fontella to Checker Records, the label for which he was recording. "Rescue Me" established Fontella as an R&B star, although she became more jazz-oriented over time.

7. **(C) "When" by the Kalin Twins.** The Kalin twins, Herbie and Harold, got their big break when songwriter Clint Ballard Jr. heard a demo record by the duo and took it to Decca Records. They signed a recording contract with the label in 1958. Later that year "When" became their biggest hit. The song was written by Paul Evans who had his own hit record with the ditty "Seven Little Girls Sitting in the Back Seat."

8. **(C) "Ka-Ding-Dong" by the G-Clefs.** The G-Clefs, comprising the Scott brothers from Roxbury, Massachusetts and Ray Gibson, started out as a gospel group. "Ka-Ding-Dong" was their first pop song, peaking at #24 in 1956. It could have done better except that cover versions were released by both the Diamonds and the Hilltoppers. The song featured 15-year-old Freddy Cannon on lead guitar. The group's biggest hit was "I Understand (Just How You Feel)" in 1961, a number sung to the tune of "Auld Lang Syne."

1. The crime solver in a series of mystery novels by Jonathan Kellerman is Alex Delaware. Although only in his 30s, Delaware has already retired from what profession?
A. Folk singer
B. Game show host
C. Disc jockey
D. Child psychologist
E. Pro bowler

2. One of the most popular female detectives of recent vintage is Linda Barnes's Carlotta Carlysle. Since Carlotta can't make ends meet as a detective for hire, she also works as what?
A. Cab driver
B. Stripper
C. Armored car guard
D. Stuntwoman
E. Martial arts instructor

3. What TV detective worked for a high-tech detective agency called Intertech before striking out on his own?
A. Paul Drake
B. Joe Mannix
C. Richard Diamond
D. Frank Cannon
E. Barnaby Jones

4. What famous detective has an adopted ward named Paul Giacomin who is a professional dancer?
A. Hammer
B. Thorn
C. Scudder
D. Spenser
E. Shaft

5. What author has churned out detective novels for 20 years about a detective who has remained Nameless?
A. James Crumley
B. John Lutz
C. Bill Pronzini
D. Jack Early
E. Ken Kuhlken

6. What were the names of Hanna-Barbera's trench-coat-wearing cat and mouse private investigation team who frequently tracked down missing animals?
A. Woofer and Tweeter
B. Ruff and Reddy
C. Sherlock and Hemlock
D. Superkatt and Junior
E. Snooper and Blabber

7. Hieronymus "Harry" Bosch is a Los Angeles police detective who has more in common with Philip Marlowe than the Dutch painter he was named after. Who is the former "L.A. Times" feature writer who has been rising to the top of the book charts since Harry's first appearance in "The Black Echo"?
A. Michael Connelly
B. Charlie Sallis
C. Michael Connors
D. John Straley
E. Michael Collins

8. What was the first name of the title character in Disney's "The Great Mouse Detective"?
A. Arthur
B. Watson
C. Gaston
D. Tobias
E. Basil

Answers to Quiz #65 — Detective Work

1. **(D) Child psychologist.** Dr. Delaware frequently works as a consultant with the local police force. His best friend is a hulking gay detective named Milo Sturgis. Kellerman, a former child psychologist himself, has written ten Alex Delaware mysteries.

2. **(A) Cab driver.** Carlotta fits her close-to-6' frame into her cab whenever the bills need to be paid and, somehow, she ends up getting involved in a case anyway.

3. **(B) Joe Mannix.** Unlike his counterparts at Intertech, Mannix (played by Mike Connors) was a man of action, and worked by his fists and his wits. After the first season of the show, Mannix worked as his own boss out of an office on the first floor of the building where he lived. Mannix survived more brutal beatings, gunshot wounds, and automobile hit-and-runs than any man before or since.

4. **(D) Spenser.** Spenser took over the raising of young Paul when Paul's less-than-responsible parents were fighting over custody in Robert B. Parker's "Early Autumn." Paul has made several appearances in the Spenser series since, including a central one in "Pastime."

5. **(C) Bill Pronzini.** Pronzini has done Robert B. Parker's Spenser and James W. Hall's Thorn one better by managing to artfully avoid giving his central character either a first or last name for more than 15 acclaimed and honored novels, including "Hoodwink" (which won the first Shamus Award for Best Novel) and "Blue Lonesome."

6. **(E) Snooper and Blabber.** The cartoon characters appeared in segments on "The Huckleberry Hound Show." The duo worked out of the Super Snooper Detective Agency. Both characters were voiced by the legendary Daws Butler.

7. **(A) Michael Connelly.** Connelly has also received praise for the non-Bosch thriller "The Poet."

8. **(E) Basil.** This 1986 animated film was based on Eve Titus's 1974 novel "Basil of Baker Street." Basil is the Sherlock Holmes of the mouse world, living in the cellar at 221-B Baker Street. His companion is Dr. David Q. Dawson, and his landlady is Mrs. Judson. Basil's archenemy is a rat named Ratigan (with the perfectly evil voice of Vincent Price).

Quiz #66 — Aviation History

1. Baron Manfred von Richthofen, aka "The Red Baron" was Germany's top-ranked World War I ace with 80 Allied aircraft shot down. How many kills did America's top ace, Eddie Rickenbacker, have to his credit?
A. 26
B. 36
C. 56
D. 76
E. 96

2. The Enola Gay dropped the atom bomb on Hiroshima. What was the name of the plane that dropped the bomb on Nagasaki?
A. Enterprise
B. Bodega Bay
C. Botany Bay
D. Bock's Car
E. Blue Chip

3. Who was the first female pilot to break the sound barrier?
A. Jacqueline Cochran
B. Pancho Barnes
C. Amelia Earhart
D. Christopher Strong
E. Alexis Carrel

4. What was the name of the plane flown around the world by Wiley Post in his historic 1931 flight?
A. Bobbie Sue
B. Loretta Lynn
C. Winnie May
D. Betsy Lou
E. Mary Kate

5. In 1986, Jeana Yeager and Richard Rutan flew what craft on the first nonstop around-the-world flight?
A. Albatross
B. Voyager
C. Cormorant
D. Courage
E. Endeavour

6. The Robert J. Collier Trophy is presented annually by the National Aeronautic Association for "the greatest achievement in aeronautics or astronautics in American aviation." Who won the first two Collier Trophies, awarded in 1911 and 1912 by the Aero Club of America?
A. Donald Douglas
B. Howard Hughes
C. Glenn Curtiss
D. Wright Brothers
E. Elmer Sperry

7. What Wisconsin city hosts the Annual Experimental Aircraft Association International Fly-In Convention and Sport Aviation Exhibition?
A. La Crosse
B. Rhinelander
C. Milwaukee
D. Oshkosh
E. Lake Geneva

8. What European city was served by an airlift beginning on June 26, 1948 that lasted 277,000 flights?
A. Moscow
B. Paris
C. Prague
D. Rome
E. Berlin

Answers to Quiz #66 — **Aviation History**

1. **(A) 26.** Of the 26 kills, 22 were airplanes and 4 were balloons. After the war, Rickenbacker was a race car driver and once owned the Indianapolis Speedway. He also produced an automobile called the Rickenbacker, advertised with the slogan "A Car Worthy of His Name."

2. **(D) Bock's Car.** Bock's Car, a B-29 bomber, was piloted by Maj. Charles Sweeney on the August 9, 1945 bombing mission.

3. **(A) Jacqueline Cochran.** In 1953, Cochran broke the world speed records for both men and women in a Sabre jet flying 652.552 MPH on a 100-kilometer course. The same year, she became the first woman to fly at Mach 1, the speed of sound. In 1961, she became the first woman to hit Mach 2, twice the speed of sound. Her autobiography, "The Stars at Noon," was published in 1954.

4. **(C) Winnie May.** Post flew his Lockheed Vega nonstop from Los Angeles to Chicago in just over 9 hours. In 1931, he flew it around the world in 8 days, 16 hours. Two years later, in the first solo flight around the world, he cut a full day off his time. His flight inspired the Lockheed slogan "It takes a Lockheed to beat a Lockheed."

5. **(B) Voyager.** The flight took 216 hours, traveling at an average speed of 115 MPH from Edwards AFB and back again. The Voyager is now on display at the Smithsonian Institutiton.

6. **(C) Glenn Curtiss.** Curtiss won in 1911 for the hydro-airplane and in 1912 for the flying boat. Like the Wright Brothers, Curtiss was involved with bicycles before taking to the air. As the first builder of seaplanes in the United States, he won the first contract to build Navy planes in 1917. His best-known airplane is the JN-4, better known as the Jenny. The Robert J. Collier Trophy was named after the first person to purchase a Wright airplane for personal use.

7. **(D) Oshkosh.** The event attracted 855,000 visitors in 1998, the 46th year of the Fly-In. During the week of the Fly-In, Oshkosh's Wittman Regional Airport is the busiest airport in the world. Parked at the airport you'll find more airplanes than all of those in Asia and Europe combined.

8. **(E) Berlin.** The massive airlift provided fuel and food to 2 million West Berliners. They were trapped behind a land and water blockade instituted by the Soviet Union who hoped that the United States would be forced to abandon the city. The Soviets lifted the ban in May 1949, but the airlift continued until the following September.

Quiz #67 — The Grim Reaper

1. "Sickness Unto Death" and "Practice in Christianity" were books written under the pseudonym Anti-Climacus by what philosopher?
A. Georg W. F. Hegel
B. Friedrich Schelling
C. Rene Descartes
D. Søren Kierkegaard
E. Hans Martensen

2. In order to escape the clutches of the Grim Reaper, Bill and Ted best him at what game in the 1991 movie "Bill & Ted's Bogus Journey"?
A. Hangman
B. Battleship
C. Go Fish
D. Stratego
E. Mouse Trap

3. What title is shared by a Benjamin Britten composition and a Thomas Mann novella?
A. "Death Be Not Proud"
B. "Kiss of Death"
C. "Death Valley Days"
D. "A Death in the Family"
E. "Death in Venice"

4. What sport was the subject of the Ernest Hemingway book "Death in the Afternoon"?
A. Bullfighting
B. Tennis
C. Boxing
D. Deep sea fishing
E. Duck hunting

5. In Jack London's "The Sea Wolf," Wolf Larsen had a brother named Death. What was the name of the ship commanded by Death Larsen?
A. Full Moon
B. Jolly Roger
C. Copperhead
D. Viking
E. Macedonia

6. The 1947 crime film "Kiss of Death" featured the evil character Tommy Udo who tied a woman into her wheelchair and pushed her down a flight of stairs. Who portrayed this chilling murderer?
A. Richard Widmark
B. Robert Lansing
C. Raf Vallone
D. Robert Mitchum
E. Victor Mature

7. What 19th-century novel is the sad tale of wealthy young George Aurispa and his mistress, Hippolyte?
A. "Death of a Hero"
B. "The Triumph of Death"
C. "Death Comes for the Archbishop"
D. "The Death Ship"
E. "Freedom or Death"

8. What rap artist recorded the 1991 albums "Death Certificate," "Lethal Injection," and "Kill At Will"?
A. Dr. Dre
B. Terminator X
C. Ice Cube
D. LL Cool J
E. Snoop Doggy Dogg

Answers to Quiz #67 — The Grim Reaper

1. (D) Søren Kierkegaard. Kierkegaard considered publishing the 1849 opus, "Sickness Unto Death," under his own name, but he felt that his study of despair espoused Christian ideals he did not live up to.

2. (B) Battleship. In the sequel to "Bill & Ted's Excellent Adventure," the boys are replaced by robotic doubles who throw them off a cliff. When the Grim Reaper (William Sadler) arrives to escort Bill and Ted to their ultimate destination, he offers them a chance to return to the living if they can beat him at chess. Chess not being their game, the boys best him instead at Battleship, Clue, and Twister.

3. (E) "Death in Venice". "Death in Venice," written in 1912, is Thomas Mann's best known work. It is the tale of an artist named Aschenbach who hopes to escape the death and decay of mortality through the permanence of his art. Benjamin Britten began composing at age five. Britten's opera, "Death in Venice," was created in 1973 when he was 60 years old.

4. (A) Bullfighting. Hemingway philosophizes on life and death using the metaphor of bullfighting in Spain. "Death in the Afternoon" was first published in 1932.

5. (E) Macedonia. Death Larsen's ship, the Macedonia, is a sealing steamer. Death is not only Wolf's brother, but also his mortal enemy.

6. (A) Richard Widmark. Widmark earned an Oscar nomination for his film debut as the nightmarish, giggling psychopath Udo.

7. (B) "The Triumph of Death". Like his father before him, George Aurispa takes a mistress. He discovers, to his disgust, that he is following the same path to gross sensuality that he loathed in his father. Distress leads him to consider suicide. He leaps to his death off a rocky cliff, taking Hippolyte to death with him in his embrace. "The Triumph of Death" was written by Gabriele D'Annunzio in 1894.

8. (C) Ice Cube. Ice Cube has topped the R&B, pop, and rap charts with the albums "AmeriKKKa's Most Wanted," "The Predator," and the platinum-selling "Lethal Injection." The former member of N.W.A. has started an acting career, appearing in "Boyz N the Hood" and "CB4," and writing and starring in the 1995 film "Friday."

Quiz #68 — **An Exaltation of Clarks**

1. T-shirt sales plummeted after Clark Gable removed his shirt and revealed he was not wearing an undershirt in what movie?
A. "Cain and Mabel"
B. "The Misfits"
C. "Idiots Delight"
D. "It Happened One Night"
E. "Gone with the Wind"

2. What U.S. President organized the westward expedition of Lewis and Clark?
A. Abraham Lincoln
B. James Madison
C. James Monroe
D. James K. Polk
E. Thomas Jefferson

3. Spelman College, Morehouse College, and Clark College are all located in what American city?
A. Pittsburgh
B. New York City
C. San Diego
D. Atlanta
E. Seattle

4. Actress Susan Clark married what former athlete turned actor after they played husband and wife in the 1975 TV movie "Babe"?
A. Don Meredith
B. Alex Karras
C. Joe Namath
D. Fred Williamson
E. Fred Dryer

5. What big band singer provided the vocals on the 1947 Ray Noble Orchestra hit "Linda," and became a household name with regular appearances on the radio shows "Here's to Romance" and "The Contented Hour"?
A. Terri Clark
B. Bobby Clark
C. Petula Clark
D. Dee Clark
E. Buddy Clark

6. "I'll Be Seeing You," "Moonlight Becomes You," "Silent Night," and "Let Me Be Your Sweetheart" are song titles used as mystery novel titles by what writer?
A. Carol Clark
B. Walter von Tilburg Clark
C. Mary Higgins Clark
D. Larry Clark
E. Joe Clark

7. Pro Football Hall-of-Famer Dutch Clark had his jersey number retired by the Detroit Lions. What number did he wear?
A. 7
B. 22
C. 37
D. 56
E. 88

8. Country music star Roy Clark won back-to-back Country Music Awards in 1975 and 1976 for Instrumental Group or Band of the Year with what musical partner?
A. Buck Owens
B Jerry Reed
C. Buck Trent
D. Chet Atkins
E. Kenny Rogers

Answers to Quiz #68 — **An Exaltation of Clarks**

1. **(D) "It Happened One Night".** Women swooned when Gable showed off his bare chest, setting the trend for men's fashion for decades to come. Of the scene, Gable said: "That's just the way I lived. I hadn't worn an undershirt since I started school."

2. **(E) Thomas Jefferson.** The 1804 expedition, under the command of Capt. Meriwether Lewis and Capt. William Clark, was to explore the newly acquired Louisiana Territory, and then proceed along the Missouri River. Between May 1804 and November 1805, with a five-month delay when they were frozen in Bismarck during the winter, they traveled 4,134 miles and reached the mouth of the Columbia River.

3. **(D) Atlanta.** Spelman College was founded in 1881, Morehouse College in 1867, and Clark College in 1869. Also located in Atlanta and its suburbs are the Georgia Institute of Technology, Emory University, Beulah Heights College, Oglethorpe University, and Georgia State University.

4. **(B) Alex Karras.** In the 1975 biopic "Babe," Clark played female athlete Babe Didrickson and Karras played her wrestler husband George Zaharias. The duo has also appeared together in the movies "Porky's" and "Maid in America."

5. **(E) Buddy Clark.** Clark performed on many big band records and radio shows without credit. He was just becoming a known name in the business when he was killed in a light plane crash in the middle of Los Angeles while returning from a football game.

6. **(C) Mary Higgins Clark.** Mary Higgins Clark's first book was a biographical novel about George Washington titled "Aspire to the Heavens." Her second book, "Where Are the Children?" started her down the suspense genre road, and onto the best-seller lists in 1975. She has had 15 best-sellers in all.

7. **(A) 7.** Earl "Dutch" Clark was the Detroit Lions' first quarterback, from 1934-38. From 1936-38, he was also the coach of the Lions. He left the Lions in 1939 to coach the L.A. Rams. He was elected to the Pro Football Hall of Fame in 1963.

8. **(C) Buck Trent.** Roy Clark also won the Country Music Award's top honor as Entertainer of the Year in 1973. He was the co-host of "Hee Haw" with Buck Owens from 1969 until the 1980s when Clark and Owens made room for various guest hosts. Banjo picker Buck Trent was also a "Hee Haw" regular.

Quiz #69 — **Teen Angels**

1. Teenage Chris resents his stepfather, and tries to prevent him from learning about the German shepherd Chris has found, but the dog is sick and Chris needs somebody's help. This is the plot of what children's book?
A. "Lad, a Dog"
B. "The Glorious Conspiracy"
C. "Ribsy"
D. "Smoke"
E. "The Animal Family"

2. What teenage musical group was founded by Edgardo Diaz and released their first album, "Los Fantasmos," in 1977?
A. Menudo
B. Frankie Lymon and the Teenagers
C. The Jets
D. New Kids on the Block
E. New Edition

3. What was the name of the black cat owned by cartoon character "Sabrina, the Teenage Witch"?
A. Salem
B. Salty
C. Salome
D. Sam
E. Sinbad

4. Keeping with cartoons, what superhero was accompanied by the twin teenagers Jan and Jayce?
A. Space Ghost
B. The Blue Falcon
C. Captain Marvel
D. Captain Caveman
E. Incredible Hulk

5. What tennis player, at the age of 16, was the youngest ever to win the U.S. Open?
A. Boris Becker
B. Jennifer Capriati
C. Tracy Austin
D. Michael Chang
E. Maureen Connelly

6. What singer had a top 10 hit in 1957 with the song "Teen-Age Crush"?
A. Pat Boone
B. Tommy Sands
C. Fabian
D. Frankie Avalon
E. Frank Sinatra

7. In the movie "Teen Wolf," Michael J. Fox discovers that puberty not only turns him into a werewolf, but also improves his skill at what sport?
A. Surfing
B. Soccer
C. Football
D. Wrestling
E. Basketball

8. Long before Archie Andrews, "Harold Teen" was hanging around the malt shop in his comic strip. Harold and his friends spoke in hep slang with asterisked translations provided for the old fogies. What was Harold's favorite expression?
A. "Boy howdy!"
B. "Bow wow wow!"
C. "Hot pups!"
D. "Great hog!"
E. "Jumpin' catfish!"

Answers to Quiz #69 — **Teen Angels**

1. **(D) "Smoke".** The award-winning "Smoke" was written by William Corbin. It was adapted into a TV movie for "The Wonderful World of Disney" in 1970.

2. **(A) Menudo.** Edgardo Diaz requires members of Menudo to be clean-cut, angelic, and young enough to appeal to Menudo's pre-teen audience base. Band members frequently cycle as they are "retired" upon reaching age 16. About 30 boys have been in the group.

3. **(A) Salem.** Sabrina debuted in Archie Comics in 1962. Salem was a regular character in the "Sabrina" comic book from 1971 to 1983, and has appeared on the cartoon shows "The Archie Comedy Hour with Sabrina," "Sabrina, the Teenage Witch," and "Superwitch," as well as the current live-action ABC-TV series.

4. **(A) Space Ghost.** Space Ghost was an interstellar police officer in Hanna-Barbera cartoons of the 1960s. His patrol assistants were Jan and Jayce, and their pet monkey, Blip. Space Ghost has made a "comeback" with his own talk show on the Cartoon Network.

5. **(C) Tracy Austin.** Austin won the U.S. Open in 1979. In 1978, at age 15, she was the youngest player to ever reach the Wimbledon singles finals. In 1980, she and her brother John were the first brother-sister team to win the Wimbledon mixed doubles championship.

6. **(B) Tommy Sands.** Sands introduced the song on the January 30, 1957 TV production of "Kraft Television Theatre" called "The Singing Idol." Sands appeared in several movies, including "Sing, Boy, Sing," "Babes in Toyland," and "The Longest Day." He was married to Nancy Sinatra from 1960-65. "Teen-Age Crush" was Sands' only top 10 hit.

7. **(E) Basketball.** "Teen Wolf" director Rod Daniel has shown an affinity for canine characters by going on to direct "K-9" and "Beethoven's 2nd."

8. **(C) "Hot pups!".** "Harold Teen" was created by Carl Ed in 1919. In his heyday, "Harold Teen" was also a radio show with Arthur Lake as the title character. By the time Archie Andrews and the Riverdale teens made the scene in the early 1950s, Harold was considered an antique and faded away.

Quiz #70 — **Religious Matters**

1. What religion is practiced by people known as Parsees?
A. Zoroastrianism
B. Shinto
C. Hinduism
D. Baha'i
E. Muslim

2. The New Connexion was a 1797 splinter group from what religious order?
A. Mennonites
B. Baptists
C. Lutherans
D. Catholics
E. Methodists

3. What Baptist preacher spent 12 years in prison for refusing to cease public preaching, and while there wrote the allegorical "Pilgrim's Progress"?
A. John Wesley
B. Walter Rauschenbach
C. Titus Oates
D. Joseph Proud
E. John Bunyan

4. "The Wicked Bible" was printed in London in 1632 by Barker and Lucas. It earned its nickname when the word "not" was left out of which of the Ten Commandments?
A. 3rd
B. 4th
C. 5th
D. 6th
E. 7th

5. What saint, born in Stridon, Dalmatia, wrote many Biblical commentaries and dialogues against Pelagianism, but is better known for the book "On Illustrious Men" and the Latin translation of the Bible?
A. Jerome
B. Agobard
C. Patrick
D Valentine
E. Stephen

6. What was the name of the church where Father Chuck O'Malley was stationed to assist the aging Father Fitzgibbon in the movie "Going My Way"?
A. St. Mary's
B. St. Francis's
C. St. Peter's
D. St. Dominic's
E. St. Timothy's

7. What religious leader strolled barefoot into the town of Lichfield crying "Woe unto the bloody city of Lichfield"?
A. R.W. Little
B. George Fox
C. Jacob Amman
D. John The Baptist
E. John Knox

8. At the Passover Seder dinner, a seat is traditionally left empty for what prophet?
A. Ezekiel
B. Gabriel
C. Elijah
D. Isaiah
E. Jeremiah

Answers to Quiz #70 — **Religious Matters**

1. **(A) Zoroastrianism.** The Parsees are descended from Persian Zoroastrians, followers of the 6th century B.C. Iranian prophet Zoroaster. The Parsees migrated to India to avoid religious persecution by the Muslims.

2. **(E) Methodists.** The autocratic attitude of some Methodist ministers alienated many of the more ardent and democratic spirits and led to a series of splinter groups. Following the New Connexion came the Primitive Methodists in 1811, the Bible Christians in 1815, and the United Methodist Free Churches in 1857.

3. **(E) John Bunyan.** "Pilgrim's Progress" was published in 1678. It details, in symbolic form, the story of Bunyan's own conversion to Puritanism. In its time, "Pilgrim's Progress" was popular with all social classes and a copy could be found in almost every English home.

4. **(E) 7th.** It thus read "Thou shalt commit adultery."

5. **(A) Jerome.** Jerome was commissioned in 382 by the Pope Damascus to produce an acceptable Latin version of the Bible. His translation is known as the Vulgate (from the Latin "editio vulgata" or "common version"). Jerome is traditionally regarded as the most learned of the Latin Fathers.

6. **(D) St. Dominic's.** Barry Fitzgerald (who played Father Fitzgibbon) faced an unusual double competition in the Academy Awards for 1944 when he was nominated for both Best Actor and Best Supporting Actor for the same role. He won the supporting category, losing Best Actor to his co-star, Bing Crosby.

7. **(B) George Fox.** Fox was the founder of the Quakers. In his journal, he says that in 1651 the Lord told him to walk a mile outside of Lichfield, remove his shoes and enter the town crying "Woe unto the bloody city of Lichfield."

8. **(C) Elijah.** According to tradition, the Hebrew prophet, Elijah, will arrive as an announced guest to declare the coming of the Messiah. During the Seder dinner, Biblical verses are read while the door is briefly opened to allow Elijah's entrance.

Quiz #71 — The Jeffersons

1. Which U.S. President has the middle name of Jefferson?
A. Ronald Reagan
B. Jimmy Carter
C. Bill Clinton
D. George Bush
E. Harry Truman

2. Noted American stage actor Joseph Jefferson spent the last 40 years of his career playing what fictional character?
A. Mark Twain
B. Poor Richard
C. Tarzan
D. Robin Hood
E. Rip Van Winkle

3. Who was the sculptor of the bronze figure of Thomas Jefferson at the Jefferson Memorial in Washington, D.C.?
A. Alexander Calder
B. Andrea Riccio
C. Emilio Greco
D. Francesco Messina
E. Rudulph Evans

4. On the TV series "The Jeffersons," what kind of business was run by George Jefferson?
A. Dry cleaners
B. Hardware store
C. Sporting goods store
D. Ice cream shop
E. Fast food restaurant

5. What musical group did Grace Slick leave to become the lead singer of Jefferson Airplane?
A. Appoggiatura
B. Grace & Co.
C. Just Friends
D. Home Influence
E. The Great Society

6. What silent film comedian was born Arthur Jefferson?
A. Harold Lloyd
B. Harry Longden
C. Oliver Hardy
D. Stan Laurel
E. Fatty Arbuckle

7. What TV teacher worked for Jefferson High School?
A. Pete Haynes
B. John Novak
C. Gabe Kotter
D. Lucas Tanner
E. Connie Brooks

8. Washington University is located in St. Louis. Thomas Jefferson University is located in Philadelphia. In what city would you find Washington and Jefferson University?
A. Chestertown, MD
B. Lexington, VA
C. Washington, PA
D. Salt Lake City, UT
E. Seattle, WA

Answers to Quiz #71 — **The Jeffersons**

1. **(C) Bill Clinton.** The only other President with a "presidential" middle name was Ronald Wilson Reagan.

2. **(E) Rip Van Winkle.** Jefferson followed in the footsteps of his father and grandfather (both also named Joseph Jefferson) into the acting career. In 1859, Jefferson had a moderate success with a stage adaptation of Washington Irving's "Rip Van Winkle." While in England in 1865, Jefferson had another version of the play written. The new play played for 170 consecutive performances in London before Jefferson returned to the U.S. He created no new roles after 1865 as his public never tired of seeing him as Rip Van Winkle.

3. **(E) Rudulph Evans.** The colonnade structure over Jefferson was designed by John R. Pope, Otto R. Eggers, and Daniel P. Higgins using the Classical architecture style favored by Jefferson. The monument, situated in East Potomac Park, was dedicated on April 13, 1943.

4. **(A) Dry cleaners.** George opened his first dry cleaning business in Queens before "Movin' on Up" to Manhattan. His main competitor was Feldway Cleaners.

5. **(E) The Great Society.** Two of Jefferson Airplane's hit songs — "White Rabbit" and "Somebody to Love" — were songs Slick originally sang with The Great Society. The Great Society recorded two live albums for Columbia, but they were not released until after Slick had found fame with Jefferson Airplane.

6. **(D) Stan Laurel.** Stan Laurel, born Arthur Stanley Jefferson, was the thinner half of the comic duo Laurel and Hardy. Working for Hal Roach, the duo made nearly 90 comedy films from 1927 to 1951. Laurel worked out most of the two men's comic routines.

7. **(B) John Novak.** English teacher John Novak was played by James Franciscus on the 1960s TV series, "Mr. Novak." On the 1950s TV series "Mr. Peepers," Robinson Peepers, played by Wally Cox, taught science at Jefferson Junior High.

8. **(C) Washington, PA.** Washington and Jefferson played in the 1922 Rose Bowl, matching California in a scoreless tie. The university's athletic teams are called the First Ladies.

Quiz #72 — **Luggage Rack**

1. Bilbo Baggins and Frodo Baggins are characters in a series of novels by what author?
A. Kurt Vonnegut Jr.
B. Roger Zelazny
C. J.R.R. Tolkien
D. Orson Scott Card
E. Ray Bradbury

2. For what baseball team did LeRoy "Satchel" Paige become the oldest man ever to pitch in the major leagues?
A. Washington Senators
B. Kansas City Athletics
C. Cleveland Indians
D. Detroit Tigers
E. St. Louis Browns

3. "The Carpetbaggers," a film version of Harold Robbins' novel, featured one of the longest, most intense fist fights in screen history between what two unlikely actors?
A. John Wayne and Nick Adams
B. Paul Newman and Fredric March
C. Steve McQueen and Jack Elam
D. George Peppard and Alan Ladd
E. Lee Marvin and Sal Mineo

4. In the comic strip "Peanuts," one of Snoopy's favorite WWI tunes is the English march "Pack Up Your Troubles in Your Old Kit Bag and Smile, Smile, Smile." Who wrote this 1915 classic?
A. George Asaf and Felix Powell
B. Alfred Bryan and Al Plantadosi
C. Jack Judge and Harry H. Williams
D. Howard Johnson and Harry MacGregor
E. Geoffrey O'Hara and Billy Murray

5. Packy East was the ring name of a Cleveland professional boxer who went on to much more fame as a comedy performer under what name?
A. Richard Pryor
B. Lou Costello
C. Bob Hope
D. Bill Cosby
E. Drew Carey

6. Who starred in the TV adventure series "Man in a Suitcase"?
A. Richard Bradford
B. James Garner
C. James Arness
D. Robert Conrad
E. Robert Vaughn

7. Henry Dorsett Case was the central character in what Nebula, Hugo, and Philip K. Dick Award-winning novel?
A. "Xenocide" by Orson Scott Card
B. "Islands in the Net" by Bruce Sterling
C. "Headcrash" by Bruce Bethke
D. "Neuromancer" by William Gibson
E. "Terminal Experiment" by Robert J. Sawyer

8. "Leader of the Pack" was a number one hit in 1964 for what girl group?
A. The Ronettes
B. The Angels
C. The Chiffons
D. The Cookies
E. The Shangri-Las

Answers to Quiz #72 — **Luggage Rack**

1. **(C) J.R.R. Tolkien.** Bilbo and Frodo were but two of a lengthy list of characters who populated J.R.R. Tolkien's "The Hobbit" and the "Lord of the Rings" trilogy.

2. **(B) Kansas City Athletics.** Due to the lack of any official birth certificate, Paige's age has been given as anywhere from 59 to 62 years old when he took the mound in relief for the Kansas City A's against the Red Sox on September 25, 1965.

3. **(D) George Peppard and Alan Ladd.** The scene had to be shot over several days as Alan Ladd was suffering from a chronic back problem, advancing age, and the effects of prolonged use of pain killers. "The Carpetbaggers" was Alan Ladd's last American film. He made two more movies in Europe before dying at the age of 51.

4. **(A) George Asaf and Felix Powell.** George Asaf was the pen name of Felix Powell's brother, George Henry Powell. Through its British lyrics, the colloquialisms "lucifer" for match and "fag" for cigarette became popular in the U.S. Other popular WWI songs were "Keep the Home Fires Burning," "When the Lusitania Went Down," "Over There," "Mademoiselle from Armentieres, Parlay-Voo," and "K-K-K-Katy."

5. **(C) Bob Hope.** At the age of 10, Hope won a Charlie Chaplin imitation contest. He did not return to comedy until after failing at his boxing career. He learned that several acts were needed to fill out the bill of a Cleveland theater. He acquired a partner named George Byrne, and together they worked out a dance routine, calling themselves "Two Diamonds in the Rough."

6. **(A) Richard Bradford.** Richard Bradford played John McGill, a former American intelligence agent who had been falsely accused of defecting to Russia. McGill worked as a private detective investigating the European underworld, all the while hoping to find the evidence and people that could prove his innocence. "Man in a Suitcase" ran for four months on ABC in 1968.

7. **(D) "Neuromancer" by William Gibson.** Dubbed by many critics as the "father of cyberpunk" science fiction, Gibson sent his cyberspace cowboy, Henry Case, into battle against artificial intelligences in virtual reality before the term became part of the language.

8. **(E) The Shangri-Las.** The Shangri-Las were a four-girl singing group made up of one pair of sisters, Mary and Betty Weiss, and another pair of sisters, Mary Ann and Marge Ganser, who were twins.

Quiz #73 — **Here Comes the Sun**

1. Which French monarch was nicknamed "The Sun King"?
A. Louis I
B. Louis X
C. Louis XIV
D. Louis XVI
E. Louis XVII

2. One of the Seven Wonders of the Ancient World was the Colossus of Rhodes, a mammoth statue of what sun god?
A. Shamash
B. Ptolemy
C. Ra
D. Quetzalcoatl
E. Helios

3. What big band leader appeared in only two movies — "Sun Valley Serenade" and "Orchestra Wives" — before his untimely death?
A. Eddy Duchin
B. Guy Lombardo
C. Russ Columbo
D. Red Nichols
E. Glenn Miller

4. Who won the 1951 Academy Award for Best Director for "A Place in the Sun"?
A. William Wyler
B. Cecil B. DeMille
C. Billy Wilder
D. George Stevens
E. Alan Smithee

5. What was the first song recorded by Elvis Presley for the Nashville-based Sun Records?
A. "Good Rockin' Tonight"
B. "Old Shep"
C. "That's All Right (Mama)"
D. "Mystery Train"
E. "Uncle Pen"

6. Which cartoon superhero relied on the rays of the sun to provide his superpowers?
A. Aquaman
B. Super Chicken
C. Birdman
D. Firestorm
E. Nova

7. The 1987 movie, "Empire of the Sun," was based on an autobiographical novel by what science fiction author?
A. Brian Aldiss
B. J.G. Ballard
C. Piers Anthony
D. Harlan Ellison
E. Michael Moorcock

8. What city is the host of college football's annual Sun Bowl?
A. El Paso, TX
B. Tempe, AZ
C. Tampa, FL
D. San Diego, CA
E. St. Louis, MO

1. **(C) Louis XIV.** Louis XIV succeeded his father to the throne at age four, and had the longest reign in European history — from 1643 to 1715.

2. **(E) Helios.** The Colossus probably stood 120 feet high and was the work of sculptor Chares. Erected in the 200s B.C., the statue stood on a promontory overlooking the harbor of Rhodes. It fell during an earthquake in 224 B.C.

3. **(E) Glenn Miller.** Miller, the director of the U.S. Air Force Band, disappeared during a plane flight on Christmas Eve 1944. Many years later, it was discovered that Miller's plane was accidentally destroyed by a U.S. WWII bomber dropping excess bombs over the sea, striking the unseen Miller plane below.

4. **(D) George Stevens.** Stevens's competition that year was John Huston for "The African Queen," Elia Kazan for "A Streetcar Named Desire," Vincente Minnelli for "An American in Paris," and William Wyler for "Detective Story."

5. **(C) "That's All Right (Mama)".** Sun Records was founded in 1952 by record producer Sam Phillips who wanted to record rhythm and blues artists and hillbilly (country-western) artists. Elvis Presley's first record (labeled Sun 209) was "That's All Right (Mama)"/"Blue Moon of Kentucky" released in July 1954. The record did not chart nationally, but reached #4 in Memphis, selling fewer than 20,000 copies.

6. **(C) Birdman.** Hanna-Barbera created 38 episodes of "Birdman" for Saturday morning TV in the 1960s. Birdman derived his powers from the Egyptian sun god, Ra, and could transform the energy into destructive sunbolts or an invisible force shield. Helpless when cut off from the sun, Birdman then relied on help from his young companion, Birdboy, or his pet eagle, Avenger.

7. **(B) J.G. Ballard.** Ballard, a British writer, was born in Shanghai in 1930. As a boy, he was interned in a Japanese POW camp as related in the movie "Empire of the Sun." (Ballard had a cameo appearance in the film as a Beefeater.) Many of Ballard's science fiction novels deal with the destruction of Earth, such as "The Wind from Nowhere" (1962), "The Drowned World" (1962), "The Burning World" (1964), and "Crystal World" (1966).

8. **(A) El Paso, TX.** In 1989, John Hancock, corporate sponsor of the Sun Bowl, demanded the word "Sun" be dropped from the name of the annual bowl game. When John Hancock ended their sponsorship in 1993, the "Sun Bowl" name was reinstated.

Quiz #74 — **Bull Pen**

1. Whose first top 40 record was the instrumental "The Lonely Bull (El Solo Toro)" in 1962?
A. Les Paul
B. The Neville Brothers
C. The Amboy Dukes
D. Paul Revere and the Raiders
E. Herb Alpert and the Tijuana Brass

2. On the TV sitcom "Night Court," what was the real first name of the towering bailiff, Bull Shannon?
A. Jupiter
B. Memphis
C. Nostradamus
D. Fabio
E. Pierre

3. The comic strip "Bull Tales" was featured on the pages of the Yale "Daily News." When the comic became nationally syndicated, what was its new title?
A. "Pogo"
B. "Peanuts"
C. "Shoe"
D. "Doonesbury"
E. "Marvin"

4. The NBA's Chicago Bulls were formed in 1966. Who was the last of the original Bulls with the team?
A. Bob Love
B. Don Kojis
C. Bob Boozer
D. Guy Rodgers
E. Jerry Sloan

5. In what movie did Robert Duvall play a frustrated military man named Bull Meechum?
A. "Bull Durham"
B. "The Great Santini"
C. "Lonesome Dove"
D. "The Pursuit of D.B. Cooper"
E. "M*A*S*H"

6. What heavyweight boxing contender was nicknamed "The Wild Bull of the Pampas"?
A. Joe Louis
B. Ingemar Johansson
C. Jerry Martin
D. Phil Bloom
E. Luis Firpo

7. The constellation Taurus (The Bull) contains what orange star that is the 13th-brightest star in the heavens and 45 times larger than our sun?
A. Aldebaran
B. Vega
C. Sirius
D. Arcturus
E. Betelgeuse

8. The tomb of Sioux chief Sitting Bull is commemorated in Sitting Bull Park with a marble pedestal and three-ton granite bust in the town of Mobridge. Mobridge is located in what state?
A. South Dakota
B. North Dakota
C. New York
D. California
E. Oklahoma

Answers to Quiz #74 — Bull Pen

1. **(E) Herb Alpert and the Tijuana Brass.** Among Herb Alpert's musical accomplishments are the founding of A&M Records with Jerry Moss, producing the first session for Jan and Dean, and writing the Sam Cooke hit "Wonderful World."

2. **(C) Nostradamus.** In the final episode of "Night Court," Bull (played by 6'8" Richard Moll) departed with midget aliens for the planet Jupiter.

3. **(D) "Doonesbury".** The strip was renamed after "Bull Tales" lead character, Mike Doonesbury. The strip's creator, Garry Trudeau, got the name Doonesbury by combining "doone," Yale slang for a simpleton, with Pillsbury, the last name of his college roommate.

4. **(E) Jerry Sloan.** Guard-forward Jerry Sloan came to the Bulls from Baltimore. He ended his career in the NBA still playing for Chicago in 1976, and served as the Bulls' head coach from 1980-82.

5. **(B) "The Great Santini".** The target of much of Meechum's fury was his son played by Michael O'Keefe. O'Keefe seems to have a knack for playing sports figures. In "The Great Santini" (1980), he was a local basketball star. In "Caddyshack" (1980), he was a caddy hoping to become a professional golfer. In "The Slugger's Wife" (1985), O'Keefe played a baseball star.

6. **(E) Luis Firpo.** In a September 1923 bout with heavyweight champion Jack Dempsey, Firpo knocked the champion through the ropes in the first round. Dempsey recovered and KO'd Firpo in the second round.

7. **(A) Aldebaran.** Taurus also contains two famous star clusters — the Hyades and the Pleiades (Seven Sisters) — and the Crab Nebula.

8. **(A) South Dakota.** Sitting Bull's remains laid neglected in the Post Cemetery of Fort Yates, North Dakota until they were spirited out of the state by some Mobridge residents. To prevent further movement of the chief's bones, his remains were placed in a shiny new casket and encased in concrete.

Quiz #75 — **Villains**

1. Thurl Ravenscroft, who provided the singing voice for "You're a Mean One, Mr. Grinch" in the annual TV Christmas special "How the Grinch Stole Christmas," is also the voice for what TV ad cartoon character?
A. The Trix Rabbit
B. Lucky the Leprechaun
C. Tony the Tiger
D. Toucan Sam
E. Cap'n Crunch

2. What was the home country of international spies Boris Badenov and Natasha Fatale on "Rocky and His Friends"?
A. Penandpencilvania
B. Pennsylvania
C. Pottsylvania
D. Spotsylvania
E. Transylvania

3. On the children's TV series, "H.R. Pufnstuf," the evil Witchiepoo is hoping to possess a magical talking flute named Freddie. What is the name of the young lad who owns Freddie?
A. Mark
B. Billy
C. Butch
D. Jimmy
E. Johnny

4. Whose archenemy is a megalomaniac frog named Baron Silas Greenback?
A. Danger Mouse
B. Beany and Cecil
C. Underdog
D. Klondike Kat
E. Teenage Mutant Ninja Turtles

5. Which of the following was not a villain featured in the "Dick Tracy" comic strip?
A. Putty Puss
B. Plaster of Paris
C. Mrs. Pruneface
D. Flattop
E. Mumbles

6. What spacefaring hero faced off against the likes of Kul of Eos, Dr. Clysmak, Heng Foo Seeng, and Mook the Moon Man?
A. Space Ghost
B. Doc Savage
C. Captain Video
D. Buck Rogers
E. Commando Cody

7. What was the home world of Flash Gordon's mortal enemy, Ming the Merciless?
A. Mongo
B. Mars
C. Gallifrey
D. Triton
E. Tuska

8. Who is accused of the murder of Dr. Robinson until Tom Sawyer, who witnessed the crime, points out Injun Joe in the courtroom as the real villain?
A. Pa Finn
B. Judge Thatcher
C. Joe Harper
D. Huck Finn
E. Muff Potter

Answers to Quiz #75 — **Villains**

1. **(C) Tony the Tiger.** As a cartoon voice, Thurl Ravenscroft has appeared as The Captain in "101 Dalmatians" (1961) and Thing 1 in "Dr. Seuss' The Cat in the Hat" (1971). As a vocalist, he was a member of the Johnny Mann Singers on their TV show "Stand Up and Cheer."

2. **(C) Pottsylvania.** Badenov's superiors were Mr. Big and Fearless Leader. The voice of Boris was provided by Paul Frees; Natasha was voiced by June Foray, who also did Rocky.

3. **(D) Jimmy.** Jimmy was played by Jack Wild, a young talented musical star who scored big as the Artful Dodger in the Oscar-winning film "Oliver!"

4. **(A) Danger Mouse.** The "evil amphibian" Baron bore a strong resemblance in body shape and voice to actor Sydney Greenstreet. The eyepatch-wearing, white-furred, British secret agent, Danger Mouse was frequently dispatched by the Department of Intelligence to thwart the Baron's schemes.

5. **(B) Plaster of Paris.** Dick Tracy started out as a plainclothes police officer pursuing gang bosses à la John Dillinger. When Prohibition ended, Tracy began facing grotesque villains like Flattop, Flyface, and Mrs. Pruneface whose physical appearances matched their twisted rotten souls.

6. **(C) Captain Video.** As his name suggests, Captain Video was TV's first interplanetary hero. Using his scientific genius and a good right cross, and assisted by the Video Rangers, he traveled in his spaceship, the Galaxy, to wage war on evildoers in the 22nd century. Captain Video's most popular adversary was the lumbering Tobor the Robot.

7. **(A) Mongo.** Flash Gordon and his companions, Dale Arden and Dr. Hans Zarkov, encountered Ming when he set the planet Mongo on a collision course with Earth. From 1936-40, three "Flash Gordon" movie serials were filmed with Charles Middleton perfectly cast as Ming.

8. **(E) Muff Potter.** After Injun Joe's dramatic escape from the courthouse, Tom and Huck ran into him again, watching him unearth a chest of money from the floorboards of an abandoned house. Later, Tom and his lady love Becky Thatcher got lost while exploring a cave and discovered that Injun Joe was in the cave with them. After Tom discovered a distant way out, the cave was sealed and the trapped Injun Joe perished within. Tom and Huck returned to the cave and became wealthy young men when they found the chest of money, worth $12,000.

Quiz #76 — Fire Drill

1. At the same time the Chicago Fire was underway in 1871, a large fire, burning acres of forestland, wiped out what Wisconsin community?
A. Ashland
B. Menominee
C. Marquette
D. Pewaukee
E. Peshtigo

2. The Campfire Girls were founded in 1910 by Dr. Luther Gulick to teach girls the wonders of nature. In what year were boys first allowed to join the organization?
A. 1915
B. 1935
C. 1955
D. 1975
E. 1995

3. "Fire on the Mountain" was a 1996 tribute album by reggae artists performing cover versions of songs from what group?
A. The Grateful Dead
B. The Doors
C. The Beatles
D. The Eagles
E. The Carpenters

4. What football legend once said, "If you aren't fired with enthusiasm, you will be fired — with enthusiasm!"?
A. George Halas
B. Knute Rockne
C. Red Grange
D. Al Davis
E. Vince Lombardi

5. Two sports-based movies have won the Best Picture Oscar. One was "Chariots of Fire" in 1981. What was the other?
A. "Phar Lap"
B. "Rocky"
C. "Raging Bull"
D. "The Champ"
E. "Jim Thorpe — All-American"

6. What comedian was the host of Texaco's "The Fire Chief" radio program?
A. Bert Lahr
B. Milton Berle
C. Lionel Barrymore
D. Ed Wynn
E. Jack Gilford

7. Who wrote "The Fire Next Time," a two-part essay examining the experiences of blacks in the U.S.?
A. Margaret Mead
B. Ralph Ellison
C. Alex Haley
D. James Baldwin
E. Malcolm X

8. To designate the suitability of fire extinguishers for particular fires, fires are classified according to the material being burned. What class of fire must be extinguished by an agent that does not conduct electricity?
A. Class A
B. Class B
C. Class C
D. Class D
E. Class E

Answers to Quiz #76 — **Fire Drill**

1. **(E) Peshtigo.** The Chicago Fire is remembered as one of the great catastrophes of the 19th century. Three hundred people were killed, and 17,000 buildings destroyed in the 1871 fire. At the same time, 1500 people died and 1.2 million acres of forest were burned in the Peshtigo Fire in northwestern Wisconsin.

2. **(D) 1975.** While the Boy Scouts emphasizes hiking and camping, the Campfire Girls are more focused on environmental concerns and outdoor survival skills. Today, there are more than 500,000 members of the Campfire Girls organization.

3. **(A) The Grateful Dead.** Songs on the album include "Casey Jones" by Wailing Souls, "Franklin's Tower" by Steel Pulse, "Eyes of the World" by Freddie McGregor, and "Row Jimmy" by Judy Mowatt. The Neville Brothers were nominated for a Grammy Award for their remake of the Dead's "Fire on the Mountain."

4. **(E) Vince Lombardi.** Vince Lombardi was the coach of the Green Bay Packers during their first two Super Bowl victories in 1966 and 1967. The Super Bowl trophy was renamed the Lombardi Trophy in his honor.

5. **(B) "Rocky".** "Rocky" won Best Picture, Best Director, and Best Film Editing Academy Awards in 1976.

6. **(D) Ed Wynn.** Wynn was one of the first radio performers to insist on working in front of a live studio audience, appearing in make-up and costume to create a theatrical atmosphere for his broadcasts. He also played a fire chief in the Disney film, "The Absent-Minded Professor."

7. **(D) James Baldwin.** With this 1963 publication, Baldwin leapt into the forefront of the civil rights movement. His acclaimed study of the Black Muslim movement was viewed as a warning to whites and touched the conscience of many blacks and whites.

8. **(C) Class C.** Class A fires involve ordinary combustibles, like paper and wood. Class B fires cover flammable liquids, like oil and grease. Class C fires involve electrical equipment. Extinguishers for Class C fires are usually dry chemical, carbon dioxide, or halon. Class D fires are limited to combustible metals, like magnesium. There is no Class E fire.

Quiz #77 — Bits and PCs

1. "Star Trek" star William Shatner appeared in TV commercials for what computer company?
A. IBM
B. Commodore
C. Compaq
D. Texas Instruments
E. Apple

2. What former NFL quarterback was the CEO of the software company KnowledgeWare?
A. Roger Staubach
B. Lynn Dickey
C. Johnny Unitas
D. Bart Starr
E. Fran Tarkenton

3. What organization purchased the first Cray-1 supercomputer in 1976?
A. AT&T
B. Los Alamos National Laboratory
C. Industrial Light and Magic
D. General Dynamics
E. NASA

4. What is the name of the world's fastest chess-playing computer?
A. Deep Blue
B. Deep Thought
C. Chess Whiz
D. Chessmaster 2000
E. Fritz

5. What does the acronym SUN stand for in the name of the computer company Sun Microsystems?
A. Stanford University Network
B. Switch Under Noise
C. Structured Universal Network
D. Supercomputer Ultra Natural
E. Smart User Navigator

6. What computer slang term's origin is often attributed to Admiral Grace Hopper?
A. Newbie
B. MUD
C. Surfing
D. Smiley
E. Bug

7. Apart from being the name of a video game company, "Atari" is also a Japanese word meaning what?
A. Attack
B. Ping pong
C. Paddle
D. Warning
E. Sound

8. What movie pitted corporate librarian Katharine Hepburn against a computer called EMERAC?
A. "Pat and Mike"
B. "Guess Who's Coming to Dinner"
C. "Desk Set"
D. "Quality Street"
E. "Holiday"

Answers to Quiz #77 — **Bits and PCs**

1. **(B) Commodore.** Other celebrity computer endorsers have included Alan Alda for IBM, Bill Cosby for Texas Instruments, John Cleese for Compaq, Dick Cavett for Apple, Dom DeLuise for NCR, Isaac Asimov for Radio Shack, and George Plimpton for Intellivision.

2. **(E) Fran Tarkenton.** When KnowledgeWare found a niche developing software for small companies, its stock soared to $40 a share. Tarkenton was worth $40 million on paper. After the technology failed to pan out, Tarkenton was hit with lawsuits by angry shareholders. Forced to bow out, Tarkenton sold the company to Sterling Software for $5 a share.

3. **(B) Los Alamos National Laboratory.** The ability of the five-ton Cray-1 computer to simulate hydrogen bomb explosions helped propel the nuclear test ban treaty.

4. **(A) Deep Blue.** Deep Blue, created by IBM, is capable of examining 200 million chess positions per second. Following 50 years of computer chess research, Deep Blue defeated chess champion Gary Kasparov in a regulation match in 1997.

5. **(A) Stanford University Network.** Sun was formed in 1982 by Stanford University students after IBM turned down their offer to manufacture computer workstations.

6. **(E) Bug.** Admiral Hooper accepted credit for devising the term "bug" after she found a moth in the Mark II computer at the U.S. Naval Surface Warfare Center, taping the dead insect into her 1945 log. However, the definition of "bug" as a machine defect has appeared in the Oxford English Dictionary as early as 1889 and in Webster's New International Dictionary in 1934.

7. **(D) Warning.** In the game of Go, "atari" is a polite warning to an opponent that he is about to be engulfed. The Atari company was founded as an arcade machine manufacturer in 1972 by Nolan Bushnell, the inventor of the early video game "Pong."

8. **(C) "Desk Set".** The 1957 movie "Desk Set" was part of a series of Spencer Tracy-Katharine Hepburn movies. Tracy plays the inventor of a computer called EMERAC, short for Electromagnetic Memory and Research Arithmetical Calculator. When the computer is installed in the reference library at the Federal Broadcasting System, Tracy runs headlong into the head librarian, Hepburn, who fears she and her workers will be replaced by the machine.

Quiz #78 — **Smell of the Lamp**

1. The language of Lampung is spoken by one million inhabitants of what island nation?
A. Iceland
B. Tonga
C. Papua New Guinea
D. Indonesia
E. New Zealand

2. Diogenes of Sinope walked in broad daylight carrying a lighted lamp saying he was looking for an honest man. In what city did he roam?
A. Utica
B. Athens
C. Rome
D. Sparta
E. Tunis

3. What college was the setting for the popular 1978 movie "National Lampoon's Animal House"?
A. Medfield College
B. Colby College
C. Milton College
D. Rock Island College
E. Faber College

4. In the Disney film "Pinocchio," the boy-puppet is persuaded to go to Pleasure Island by a wicked lad named Lampwick. Because of his bad behavior, which included playing pool, smoking, and drinking beer, Lampwick was turned into what kind of animal?
A. Donkey
B. Goldfish
C. Frog
D. Eel
E. Pig

5. The lampadedromy was a race run in ancient Greece. Contestants carried lit torches, and the winner was the first to finish with his torch still lit. The race was run in honor of which Greek god?
A. Prometheus
B. Mars
C. Zeus
D. Apollo
E. Epimetheus

6. Poet Archibald Lampman is best remembered for his poems on nature collected in "Lyrics of Earth," "Among the Millet," and "At the Long Sault and Other New Poems." What was Lampman's native country?
A. Scotland
B. United States
C. Canada
D. China
E. India

7. The CBS religious program "Lamp Unto My Feet" took its title from the line "Thy word is a lamp unto my feet and a light to my path." This quotation appears in which book of the Bible?
A. Proverbs
B. Matthew
C. Acts
D. Revelations
E. Psalms

8. What name is given to the larval stage of the lamprey?
A. Notochord
B. Brachiopod
C. Hagfish
D. Ammocete
E. Tadpole

Answers to Quiz #78 — **Smell of the Lamp**

1. **(D) Indonesia.** Lampung is spoken primarily on the island of Sumatra. More than 100 languages are spoken in Indonesia, although Bahasa Indonesia is the official language and the one most widely spoken.

2. **(B) Athens.** Legend has it that Diogenes once met Alexander the Great. The dictator introduced himself "I am Alexander the Great." The philosopher replied, "I am Diogenes the Cynic." Diogenes and Alexander supposedly died on the same day. Diogenes never found his honest man.

3. **(E) Faber College.** Due to the popularity of "Animal House," all three major TV networks offered fraternity house sitcoms in the 1978-79 season. ABC's "Delta House" was the official spinoff, set again at Faber College, with John Vernon, Stephen Furst, Bruce McGill, and James Widdoes reprising their "Animal House" roles. It lasted only three months, but outlived NBC's "Brothers and Sisters" (two months) and CBS's "Co-Ed Fever" (one episode).

4. **(A) Donkey.** When Jiminy Cricket learns the boys on Pleasure Island turn into donkeys and are shipped overseas, he rushes to warn Pinocchio. Jiminy and Pinocchio escape by jumping from a high cliff into the sea, but not before Pinocchio has gained the ears and tail of a donkey.

5. **(A) Prometheus.** Prometheus was the god who delivered the secret of fire to man. He was punished by Zeus, bound in unbreakable chains to the rock peak of Caucasus where an eagle would feast on his liver only to have it grow back the next day, and the cycle repeat. Eventually the eagle was slain, and Prometheus freed, by Hercules.

6. **(C) Canada.** Lampman was born in Marpeth, Ontario. He was influenced by English poets, especially Keats, and in turn influenced Canadian poet Bliss Carman.

7. **(E) Psalms.** "Lamp Unto My Feet" was one of TV's longest-running network shows, airing on CBS on Sunday mornings from 1948 to 1979.

8. **(D) Ammocete.** When lampreys hatch they are wormlike larvae called ammocetes (from the Greek for "embedded in sand") which burrow in the stream bottom. After several years, and upon reaching 4-8 inches in length, they metamorphose into the adult form. The sea lamprey has invaded the Great Lakes causing damage to the commercial fishing industry there. The animal is now being controlled by the use of poison to kill off the ammocetes.

Quiz #79 — **Stand Up and Cheer**

1. What comedian's stand-up routine included references to his brother Russell, his enemy, Junior Barnes, and a ancient street game called Buck Buck?
A. Bill Cosby
B. Lenny Bruce
C. Richard Pryor
D. George Carlin
E. Woody Allen

2. What stand-up comic's mind was labeled "button down," inspiring the title of his breakthrough album that became the first comedy album to be deemed gold by the Recording Industry Association of America?
A. Jackie Mason
B. Bob Hope
C. Steve Allen
D. Bob Newhart
E. Rodney Dangerfield

3. Maudie Frickert and Elwood P. Suggins were characters in what zany comic's stand-up act, also showing up on his various TV series?
A. Jackie Vernon
B. Steve Allen
C. Johnny Carson
D. Tim Conway
E. Jonathan Winters

4. What comedian was one of the first to release a book based on some of his routines with his best-seller, "Cruel Shoes?"
A. Steve Allen
B. Jack Paar
C. Steve Martin
D. Woody Allen
E. Carl Reiner

5. What comedian began his career relying heavily on a cast of characters including Scott Lame, weatherman Al Sleet, and sportcaster Biff Barf?
A. Lenny Bruce
B. George Carlin
C. Mort Sahl
D. Woody Woodbury
E. Steve Allen

6. What performer made more appearances than any other stand-up comic on the "Ed Sullivan Show"?
A. Jackie Mason
B. Totie Fields
C. Alan King
D. Phyllis Diller
E. Robert Klein

7. What performer's filmed versions of his shows, "Live in Concert," "Here and Now," and "Live on Sunset Strip," can be found on several prominent film critics' all-time top 10 lists?
A. Richard Pryor
B. Redd Foxx
C. Eddie Murphy
D. George Carlin
E. Steve Martin

8. What stand-up comic's autobiography is titled "Leading with My Chin"?
A. Jay Leno
B. Tim Allen
C. Neil Simon
D. Ellen DeGeneres
E. Jerry Lewis

Answers to Quiz #79 — **Stand Up and Cheer**

1. **(A) Bill Cosby.** Cosby's routines led to a cartoon series about his old neighborhood entitled, "Fat Albert and the Cosby Kids". He also revisited his youth in his 1991 book "Childhood."

2. **(D) Bob Newhart.** Newhart was famous for comedy routines featuring one-sided phone conversations, often set in historical time periods before the advent of the telephone. His 1961-62 variety series on NBC won critical acclaim, and Emmy and Peabody Awards, but not much of an audience. Newhart had better luck with the sitcoms "The Bob Newhart Show" which ran six seasons and "Newhart," on for eight seasons.

3. **(E) Jonathan Winters.** Winters' mid-50s TV series was the first regularly scheduled show to use videotape on a weekly basis. The inventive and spontaneous Winters served as a "spiritual father" to fellow funnyman Robin Williams. Ironically, Williams would become the father of Winters as characters Mork and Mearth on the TV series "Mork and Mindy."

4. **(C) Steve Martin.** Humorist Roy Blount Jr., in his review of the 1977 "Cruel Shoes," commented that Martin had done many wonderfully inventive, funny, and entertaining things such as the "King Tut" song, the bunny ears, and his "Saturday Night Live" ad-libs, but this book was not one of them: "Good writing is something that many a book has done without."

5. **(B) George Carlin.** Before he spouted the seven words you can't say on TV, Carlin had an "Ed Sullivan"-type routine where he play-acted mini-dramas populated with a cast of odd characters. Carlin starred in a short-lived eponymous FOX TV series in 1994 in which he played a grumpy cab driver.

6. **(C) Alan King.** King appeared on "The Ed Sullivan Show" 39 times. He claimed that he thought Sullivan was his adopted father because he spent so much time getting advice from Ed. The acts that appeared most often on Sullivan's show were Topo Gigio (50 times), Wayne and Shuster (46), Rickie Layne (40), and Alan King (39).

7. **(A) Richard Pryor.** Pryor's routines are legendary for his creative use — or overuse — of profanity, and for being a seamless meshing of comedy and tragedy as he shared intimate details of his life. His high-intensity routines have also been captured on the comedy albums "That Nigger's Crazy" and "Is It Something I Said?"

8. **(A) Jay Leno.** Leno's best-seller is a collection of anecdotes — the adventures of a young comic who endures working in strip clubs, a run-in with the mob, sleeping in garages, and dealing with wacky parents to fulfill his dream as the host of "The Tonight Show."

Quiz #80 — My Darling Clementine

1. According to the lyrics of the traditional ballad "O, My Darling Clementine," what size shoes did Clementine wear?
A. 5
B. 6
C. 7
D. 8
E. 9

2. What cartoon character often sang an off-key version of "Clementine"?
A. Yogi Bear
B. Huckleberry Hound
C. Quick Draw McGraw
D. Wally Gator
E. Touche Turtle

3. In 1994, the Clementine probe was employed to obtain detailed mapping of what object in space?
A. Moon
B. Ceres
C. Sun
D. Venus
E. Pluto

4. Who played Marshall Wyatt Earp in the 1946 John Ford-directed classic movie western "My Darling Clementine"?
A. Henry Fonda
B. Jimmy Stewart
C. Kirk Douglas
D. Victor Mature
E. Burt Lancaster

5. What TV character's favorite movie was the 1946 John Ford-directed classic movie western "My Darling Clementine"?
A. Frank Cannon
B. Archie Bunker
C. Jim Rockford
D. Col. Sherman Potter
E. Thomas Magnum

6. Whose recorded version of "Clementine" hit the top 40 charts in 1960?
A. Marty Robbins
B. Bobby Darin
C. Sonny James
D. Elvis Presley
E. Brian Hyland

7. What Academy Award-winning actress played the recurring role of the roguish Clementine Hale on the TV series "Alias Smith and Jones"?
A. Sally Field
B. Julie Andrews
C. Jane Fonda
D. Julie Christie
E. Shirley Jones

8. The Clementine Vulgate Bible issued in 1592 became the authoritative biblical text of the Roman Catholic Church. It was issued by which Pope?
A. Clement I
B. Clement V
C. Clement VIII
D. Clement XIV
E. Damascus

1. **(E) 9.** The third verse of "Clementine" goes: "Light she was and like a fairy, / And her shoes were number nine, / Herring boxes without topses / Sandals were for Clementine." The song was a favorite college song during the Reconstruction period.

2. **(B) Huckleberry Hound.** "The Huckleberry Hound Show" was produced by Hanna-Barbera. It became the first animated series to win an Emmy Award in 1960 when it won for Outstanding Program Achievement in the Field of Children's Programming.

3. **(A) Moon.** In the three months it orbited the moon, Clementine radioed back 1.5 million pictures that will take years to analyze. Clementine was responsible for the discovery of ice at the Moon's South Pole. Like the girl in the song, NASA's Clementine was expected to be "lost and gone forever" after this mission. When its propellant ran out, it went into a solar orbit, but will rendezvous again with Earth in 2003.

4. **(A) Henry Fonda.** "My Darling Clementine" was John Ford's first major motion picture after spending WWII in the Field Photographic Branch of the OSS making propaganda documentaries. For his part in the war effort, Ford was awarded the Naval rank of rear admiral.

5. **(D) Col. Sherman Potter.** On the TV series, "M*A*S*H," Col. Potter (Henry Morgan) said "There are three things that make a good movie — horses, cowboys, and horses."

6. **(B) Bobby Darin.** "Clementine" peaked at #21 on the U.S. charts, and at #8 on the U.K. charts.

7. **(A) Sally Field.** The character of Clementine Hale was introduced to the series in October 1971 to provide some continuing female interest.

8. **(C) Clement VIII.** Pope Clement VIII, born Ippolito Aldobrandini, served as Pope from 1592 until his death in 1605. Among his important contributions were implementing the reforms decreed by the Council of Trent, and establishing Henry IV as the legitimate king of France.

Quiz #81 — Consumer Products

1. The Dassler brothers' running shoes gained popularity after Jesse Owens wore them in the 1936 Summer Olympics. In 1948, the Dassler brothers partnership dissolved. Adi Dassler created Adidas. What shoe company was formed by Rudi Dassler?
A. New Balance
B. Tiger
C. Puma
D. Nike
E. Keds

2. Curity, KD's Honeysuckle, Tiny World, and Chux were early brand names of what product?
A. Toothpaste
B. Laundry soap
C. Sanitary napkins
D. Disposable diapers
E. Baby food

3. "Igloo of Tomorrow" at the 1939 World's Fair in New York exhibited the achievements in air conditioning by what company?
A. Trane
B. Gibson
C. Fedders
D. Sub-Zero
E. Carrier

4. What snack food found success after sponsoring "Howdy Doody" with Clarabell the Clown distributing free samples to children in the Peanut Gallery?
A. Life Savers
B. Cracker Jack
C. Snowballs
D. M&Ms
E. Hostess Twinkies

5. Francis Xavier McNamara was in the tarpaulin business in 1950. While entertaining clients at a New York restaurant, he realized he had forgotten his wallet. McNamara went home and dreamed up what credit card?
A. Diners Club
B. Signet Club
C. Discover
D. Visa
E. American Express

6. What was the only American company producing clothes dryers before World War II?
A. Bendix
B. Speed Queen
C. Maytag
D. Hamilton
E. Kenmore

7. How many holes are in a Ritz cracker?
A. 4
B. 7
C. 16
D. 25
E. 100

8. What big band leader invented the blender in the 1930s to liquefy vegetables for a family member who could not eat solid food?
A. Fletcher Henderson
B. Duke Ellington
C. Russ Columbo
D. Glenn Miller
E. Fred Waring

Answers to Quiz #81 — **Consumer Products**

1. **(C) Puma.** The first modern running shoe was the Trackster introduced by New Balance in 1962. The unseamed shoe had a wide front for comfort and a rippled sole for flexibility and traction. It also incorporated a rubber wedge to elevate the heel and absorb shocks.

2. **(D) Disposable diapers.** In 1961, Procter & Gamble introduced Pampers in Peoria, IL. At 10 cents per diaper, though, they were not economically feasible for many families. Pampers reappeared in 1966 at 6 cents each, and sales took off. In 1961, Chux diapers were suggested by Consumers Union as the "Best Buy Christmas Gift" for the baby who has everything.

3. **(E) Carrier.** In 1922, Carrier introduced the centrifugal refrigeration machine. It provided air conditioning that released cool air from overhead instead of from the floor. The company soon provided total air conditioning at Grauman's Metropolitan Theatre in Los Angeles and J.L. Hudson's department store in Detroit.

4. **(E) Hostess Twinkies.** The Twinkie was invented in 1931 by Jimmy Dewar in an effort to get more use out of the shortcake pans in his bakery. While on a business trip to St. Louis, he saw a billboard advertising Twinkle Toe Shoes from which evolved the Twinkie name.

5. **(A) Diners Club.** The Diners Club card was the first credit card available for multipurpose use — travel and entertainment.

6. **(D) Hamilton.** J. Ross Moore designed the clothes dryer for his mother in North Dakota who was unable to air clothes outside in frigid winter weather. Moore sold his design to the Hamilton Manufacturing Company. Between 1937 and 1941, Hamilton sold 6,000 units.

7. **(B) 7.** The Ritz cracker was introduced in 1934 by the National Biscuit Company. It differed from the traditional soda cracker in that it had more shortening and no yeast, resulting in a crisper, less fluffy cracker. Within three years, Ritz became the top-selling cracker in the world with more than 40 million sold each day.

8. **(E) Fred Waring.** The Waring blender was considered an extravagance at first, but sold well to those interested in liquefied food for health reasons and to bartenders making mixed drinks. To promote more sales, Waring hired a professional to develop blender recipes like hollandaise and mayonnaise, making the blender useful to gourmet cooks.

Quiz #82 — **Bridging the Gap**

1. Who claimed to have leapt from the Brooklyn Bridge in 1886 and survived to tell about it?
A. George Burns
B. Dean Hillestad
C. Larry Weaver
D. Steve Brodie
E. William Doyle

2. What was the title of Alicia Bridges's sole top 10 hit, a disco number from 1978?
A. "You Don't Have to Be a Star"
B. "Disco Inferno"
C. "Emotion"
D. "Best of My Love"
E. "I Love the Night Life"

3. In Norse mythology, what was the name of the rainbow bridge that connected Midgard (Earth) to Asgard?
A. Hela
B. Yggdrasil
C. Bifrost
D. Muspelheim
E. Westby

4. The Howrah Bridge spanning the Hooghly River is considered the world's busiest bridge. It is located in what city?
A. Peking
B. Hanoi
C. Buenos Aires
D. Calcutta
E. Laredo, Texas

5. What was the name of the main character played by Lloyd Bridges on the TV series "Sea Hunt"?
A. Mike Nelson
B. Joe Forrester
C. Rex Kramer
D. Jonathan Turner
E. Max Sutter

6. What city was the setting of the 1837 Supreme Court case involving competition between the Charles River Bridge and Warren Bridge?
A. Seattle
B. Memphis
C Tallahassee
D. Chicago
E. Boston

7. One year after Simon and Garfunkel hit #1 with their version of "Bridge Over Troubled Water" in 1970, what artist's cover version returned the song to the top 10?
A. Glen Campbell
B. Aretha Franklin
C. David Cassidy
D. Dionne Warwick
E. Petula Clark

8. What real life husband and wife team played a well-to-do couple in the movie "Mr. and Mrs. Bridge"?
A. Tom Cruise and Nicole Kidman
B. Bruce Willis and Demi Moore
C. Paul Newman and Joanne Woodward
D. Robert Wagner and Natalie Wood
E. Ronald and Nancy Reagan

Answers to Quiz #82 — **Bridging the Gap**

1. **(D) Steve Brodie.** For a $200 bet, Brodie supposedly jumped off the Brooklyn Bridge on July 23, 1886, although this was never confirmed. He was asked to do it again before witnesses and replied "I done it oncet." Brodie's name made itself into the English language. To "do a Brodie" was to take a leap into the water. Brodie made a short foray into show business. In a New York stage production called "On the Bowery," Brodie thrilled audiences with a reenactment of his famed leap.

2. **(E) "I Love the Night Life".** "I Love the Night Life" found new life in Australia and New Zealand, returning to the music charts in those countries after the song was featured in three different versions on the soundtrack for the movie "The Adventures of Priscilla, Queen of the Desert."

3. **(C) Bifrost.** Bifrost was guarded by Heimdahl, the god of light.

4. **(D) Calcutta.** An estimated 57,000 vehicles and one million pedestrians cross the Howrah Bridge daily. The bridge's official name is Rabindra Setu, in honor of the poet Rabindranath Tagore.

5. **(A) Mike Nelson.** "Sea Hunt" was turned down by all three major TV networks of the time. It became one of the mostly widely syndicated shows of its time, airing from 1957 to 1961. A short-lived update of the series starring Ron Ely (TV's "Tarzan") ran in 1987.

6. **(E) Boston.** State governments promoted development by issuing charters granting corporations the right to exact tolls for the use of bridges or roads they built and maintained. In Charles River Bridge v. Warren Bridge, the U.S. Supreme Court rejected the claim of one such company that its charter granted it a monopoly to run a toll bridge.

7. **(B) Aretha Franklin.** Art Garfunkel returned to "bridge" music when he performed the theme song for the TV series "Brooklyn Bridge" in 1991.

8. **(C) Paul Newman and Joanne Woodward.** Paul Newman and Joanne Woodward appeared together in many movies including "The Long Hot Summer" (1958), "Rally 'Round the Flag Boys!" (1958), "From the Terrace" (1960), "Paris Blues" (1961), "A New Kind of Love" (1963), "Winning" (1969), "WUSA" (1970), "The Drowning Pool" (1975), and "Harry and Son" (1984). Newman directed his wife in the 1972 film version of "The Effect of Gamma Rays on Man-in-the-Moon Marigolds."

Quiz #83 — **Touched by an Angel**

1. What veteran TV actor provided the voice for the unseen Charles Townsend, the boss of "Charlie's Angels"?
A. George Peppard
B. John Forsythe
C. George Hamilton
D. Charles Durning
E. Peter Graves

2. What California Angel pitcher threw two no-hitters during the 1973 season?
A. Jim Bunning
B. Phil Niekro
C. Ferguson Jenkins
D. Nolan Ryan
E. Sparky Lyle

3. One of the first mutant superhero groups created by Marvel Comics was the X-Men. The original members of the X-Men included Angel plus four others. Which of the following was not a charter member of the X-Men?
A. Marvel Girl
B. Cyclops
C. Beast
D. Iceman
E. Magneto

4. Who was nicknamed the "Angel of the Battlefield"?
A. Molly Pitcher
B. Scarlett O'Hara
C. Martha Washington
D. Clara Barton
E. Florence Nightingale

5. The characters of which TV series hung out at the Angel Grove Youth Center?
A. "What's Happening!!"
B. "California Dreams"
C. "Mighty Morphin Power Rangers"
D. "The Donna Reed Show"
E. "Fudge"

6. "Kiss an Angel Good Mornin' " entered the Billboard country music charts 13 days after its singer won the 1971 Country Music Association's Entertainer of the Year award. Who is this country music legend with 28 #1 songs to his credit?
A. Charlie Pride
B. Sonny James
C. Porter Wagoner
D. Ronnie Milsap
E. Conway Twitty

7. In the Bible, Jacob wrestled with an angel. The two were evenly matched, and Jacob refused to let the angel go until the angel blessed him with what new name?
A. Malachi
B. Laban
C. Israel
D. Solomon
E. Joseph

8. "Look Homeward, Angel" was the autobiographical debut novel of what American writer?
A. Ernest Hemingway
B. Kurt Vonnegut Jr.
C. John Galt
D. Jack London
E. Thomas Wolfe

Answers to Quiz #83 — **Touched by an Angel**

1. **(B) John Forsythe.** Following "Charlie's Angels," John Forsythe returned to acting in body and voice as the patriarchical Blake Carrington on the TV nighttime soap "Dynasty."

2. **(D) Nolan Ryan.** Nolan Ryan threw a Major League Baseball record seventh no-hitter in May 1991 at the age of 44. He was the first major league pitcher to sign a million dollar per year contract.

3. **(E) Magneto.** Magneto was the first villain faced by the X-Men. Magneto was also the father of mutant superheroes Scarlet Witch and Quicksilver.

4. **(D) Clara Barton.** At the outbreak of the U.S. Civil War, Clara Barton organized an agency to supply relief to wounded soldiers. Later in Europe to distribute relief supplies during the Franco-German War, she became associated with the International Red Cross. In 1881, Barton established the American National Red Cross. In 1882, she succeeded in having the United States sign the Geneva Agreement on the treatment of the sick, wounded, and dead in battle, and the handling of prisoners of war.

5. **(C) "Mighty Morphin Power Rangers".** Fox's daily "Power Rangers" was derived from a Japanese TV series called "Zyu Rangers." American producer Haim Saban hired American actors to play the teens, splicing in action scenes from the Japanese show. Since all the Power Rangers faces are unseen behind masks and helmets, their voices could be overdubbed in English. The series was an immediate hit with youngsters and has generated millions of dollars in the sale of merchandise. In 1995, the series spawned a major motion picture.

6. **(A) Charlie Pride.** Charlie Pride is one of few black country music superstars. Before hitting his stride as a country singer, Pride pursued a career in baseball. He played for the Memphis Red Sox as a pitcher and outfielder in 1954. While playing semi-pro ball, he was turned down by the California Angels in 1961 and the New York Mets in 1962.

7. **(C) Israel.** While in Bethel, fleeing from his brother, Esau, Jacob dreamed of angels ascending and descending from a ladder to heaven, giving rise to the expression "Jacob's Ladder." Jacob's 12 sons were the ancestors of the 12 tribes of Israel. Israel translates as "he strives with God."

8. **(E) Thomas Wolfe.** While attending Harvard University, Thomas Wolfe was primarily interested in becoming a playwright. Several of his plays were produced there, including "Welcome to Our City" (1923), which introduced the fictional town of Altamont. When "Look Homeward, Angel" was published in 1929, it too was set in Altamont. The citizens of Wolfe's hometown — Asheville, North Carolina — saw through the thin disguise and were angry with Wolfe's characterization of Southern life and society. "Look Homeward, Angel" was adapted into a three-act play by Ketti Frings, winning a 1958 Pulitzer Prize in Drama.

Quiz #84 — **World Novels**

1. In Bram Stoker's 1897 vampire novel, "Dracula," who was Dracula's first victim?
A. Renfield
B. Arthur Holmwood
C. Jonathan Harker
D. Mina Murray
E. Lucy Westenra

2. What novel involved the murders of pawnbroker Alyona Ivanovna and her sister, Lizayeta?
A. "Deadeye Dick"
B. "The Brothers Karamazov"
C. "The Young Guard"
D. "Gorky Park"
E. "Crime and Punishment"

3. What Herman Melville novel was subtitled "The Ambiguities"?
A. "Pierre"
B. "The Confidence-Man"
C. "White-Jacket"
D. "Omoo"
E. "Typee"

4. Frank Churchill, Jane Fairfax and George Knightly are three characters in which Jane Austen novel?
A. "Sense and Sensibility"
B. "Emma"
C. "Northanger Abbey"
D. "Pride and Prejudice"
E. "Mansfield Park"

5. What was the name of Ayla's son in Jean Auel's novel "Clan of the Cave Bear"?
A. Broud
B. Ogg
C. Alexander
D. Worf
E. Durc

6. In what Arthur Hailey novel would you encounter the characters Keycase Milne, Peter McDermott, Dodo Lash, and Christine Francis?
A. "Airport"
B. "Wheels"
C. "The Moneychangers"
D. "Hotel"
E. "Strong Medicine"

7. What was the name of the pony in John Steinbeck's "The Red Pony"?
A. Tumbleweed
B. Pie
C. Gabilan
D. Kathleen
E. Casey

8. Who was deserted on her wedding night by Angel Clare?
A. Elizabeth Bennet
B. Hester Prynne
C. Tess Durbeyfield
D. Becky Sharp
E. Scarlett O'Hara

Answers to Quiz #84 — World Novels

1. **(C) Jonathan Harker.** Harker was a solicitor visiting the Castle Dracula in Transylvania to transact business with Count Dracula. Harker soon discovered he was a prisoner of the Count, encountering phantom vampire women, giant bats, and a pack of wolves that kept him trapped in the castle.

2. **(E) "Crime and Punishment".** Fyodor Dostoyevsky's first novel was the story of Rodion Raskolnikov, an impoverished St. Petersburg student who dreams of committing the perfect crime. While in the act of murdering the pawnbroker, he is surprised by her demented sister, and is forced to kill her too. Ultimately, the murders destroy Raskolnikov as well.

3. **(A) "Pierre".** Most of Herman Melville's novels dealt with life on the sea or in the Pacific islands. "Pierre," Melville's seventh novel, was Melville's experiment to write about some other subject. The deeply pessimistic novel is probably the least read of any of Melville's works.

4. **(B) "Emma".** Emma Woodhouse, the heiress of Hartfield, amuses herself by meddling in matchmaking. Unfortunately, all of her attempts to move relationships along prove to be unwise.

5. **(E) Durc.** Durc's father is the ruthless Broud, son of the clan's chief. Durc was named by Ayla's protector, the Mog-Ur Creb. "Clan of the Cave Bear" was followed by three sequels in Auel's "Earth Children" series.

6. **(D) "Hotel".** "Hotel" was turned into a 1967 movie starring Rod Taylor, Melvyn Douglas, Karl Malden, and Michael Rennie. It was also the basis of a 1983-88 ABC TV series starring James Brolin, Connie Sellecca, and Anne Baxter.

7. **(C) Gabilan.** Along with his many novels, Steinbeck wrote theatrical productions based on his novels "Of Mice and Men" and "The Moon Is Down." He also worked in Hollywood as a screenwriter for the films "The Forgotten Village," "The Pearl," and "Viva Zapata!"

8. **(C) Tess Durbeyfield.** In Thomas Hardy's "Tess of the D'Urbervilles," Tess and Angel indulged in mutual confessions on their wedding night. Although Angel expected to be forgiven for his sinful past, he could not do the same for Tess, who had a child out of wedlock.

Quiz #85 — **Terra Australis**

1. Rabbits imported into Australia by Europeans bred in a massive population explosion since they have no natural enemies on the continent. Where rabbits are viewed as monsters, a movement is afoot to replace the Easter Bunny in Australia with what native animal?
A. Brush wombat
B. Cane toad
C. Bilby
D. Koala
E. Platypus

2. A new design for the Australian flag was proposed in January 1997. What symbol has been removed from the flag?
A. Kangaroo
B. Emu
C. Southern Cross
D. Union Jack
E. Koala

3. Which Australian state capital is named after a former British Prime Minister?
A. Melbourne
B. Sydney
C. Perth
D. Brisbane
E. Adelaide

4. What architect designed the spectacular Sydney Opera House?
A. Mike Davies
B. I.M. Pei
C. Frank Lloyd Wright
D. Owen Luder
E. Jorn Utzon

5. What is the most populous state of Australia?
A. Victoria
B. New South Wales
C. Queensland
D. South Australia
E. Western Australia

6. What body of water separates New Guinea from the Australia continent?
A. Great Australian Bight
B. Timor Sea
C. Arafura Sea
D. Tasman Sea
E. Moreton Bay

7. Ayers Rock, a massive red-tinted natural landform, and The Olgas, a group of gigantic stone domes, are both part of what Australian national park?
A. Finke George
B. Namburg
C. Grampians
D. Uluru
E. Croajingalong

8. Like the United States Congress, the Australian Parliament is made up of a Senate and House of Representatives. How many members make up the Australian Senate?
A. 12
B. 24
C. 76
D. 100
E. 150

Answers to Quiz #85 — Terra Australis

1. **(C) Bilby.** The bilby is a long-nosed, rabbit-eared member of the bandicoot family. Only 5000 bilbies remain in Australia, compared to over 300 million rabbits that cause millions of dollars of agricultural and environmental damage every year.

2. **(D) Union Jack.** The present Australian flag is red, white, and blue. It has a small British Union Jack, five small stars in the shape of the constellation Southern Cross, and a large star representing Australia.

3. **(A) Melbourne.** William Lamb, the second viscount of Melbourne, was the Prime Minister of England from 1834-1841. Melbourne was Australia's first permanent settlement, established in 1835.

4. **(E) Jorn Utzon.** Utzon's 1957 sketches for the Opera House were derided by many critics who considered the building virtually impossible to realize. With the aid of computers, engineers were able to design a feasible construction. The building was completed in 1973. With its large white roof resembling billowing sails, the Opera House is one of the finest modern structures of the Southern Hemisphere.

5. **(B) New South Wales.** According to the 1991 census, 5.7 million people live in New South Wales, followed by 4.2 million in Victoria. New South Wales's capital city, Sydney, also has the largest city population at 3.5 million.

6. **(C) Arafura Sea.** The Arafura Sea is a shallow sea that contains the most eastern islands of the Malay Archipelago, including New Guinea. Australia administered the island as a United Nations trusteeship after WWII, until the independent nation of Papua New Guinea was formed in 1975.

7. **(D) Uluru.** Uluru National Park, located in "the red center" in central Australia, preserves the culture of the Yankuntjatjara and Pitjantjatjara Aboriginal tribes.

8. **(C) 76.** All citizens of Australia 18 years of age or older must vote or they can be fined.

Quiz #86 — Sign of the Donkey

1. In 1948, Southern Democrats from 13 states broke away from the Democratic Party to form the Dixiecrats. Who was their candidate for President?
A. Harry Truman
B. Carl Curtis
C. Strom Thurmond
D. Franklin Roosevelt
E. Robert Dole

2. Who headed "Democrats for Nixon" in 1972?
A. John Kennedy Jr.
B. John Stennis
C. Les Aspin
D. John Connally
E. Peter Fonda

3. Who nominated Al Smith for President at the 1924 Democratic National Convention, dubbing Smith "The Happy Warrior"?
A. Franklin Roosevelt
B. Wendell Willkie
C. Harry Hopkins
D. Eleanor Roosevelt
E. Joseph Kennedy Sr.

4. Who was elected governor of Illinois in 1948 by the largest plurality in the history of the state?
A. Robert Todd Lincoln
B. Leonard Wood
C. George Ball
D. Richard Oglesby
E. Adlai Stevenson

5. Who did Sam Rayburn succeed as Speaker of the House in 1940?
A. John Nance Garner
B. Claude Wright Jr.
C. Joseph W. Martin Jr.
D. William B. Bankhead
E. James G. Blaine

6. Betty Roberts was elected to replace what U.S. Senator from Oregon who died shortly after winning the state's 1974 Democratic primary and the right to face off against incumbent Bob Packwood?
A. Robert J. Walker
B. Wayne Morse
C. Stephen Douglas
D. George Dallas
E. Chad McQueen

7. What Democrat campaigned for President as an Independent using the slogan "Stand Up for America"?
A. Herbert Hoover
B. George Wallace
C. H. Ross Perot
D. Margaret Chase Smith
E. Robert M. La Follette

8. How many Democrats have served as President of the United States in the 20th century?
A. 3
B. 4
C. 5
D. 6
E. 7

Answers to Quiz #86 — **Sign of the Donkey**

1. **(C) Strom Thurmond.** Thurmond received 38 electoral votes on a platform of racial segregation. The 94-year-old Thurmond was re-elected in 1996 to his eighth term in the U.S. Senate. He will be 100 years old when that term comes to an end.

2. **(D) John Connally.** Nixon handpicked the conservative Democrat to head the organization. Nixon named Connally as his Secretary of Treasury in 1971. Although serving in a Republican Cabinet, Connally didn't officially switch parties from Democrat to Republican until 1973. Connally died in 1993 at the age of 76.

3. **(A) Franklin Roosevelt.** FDR referred to Smith as "the Happy Warrior of the political battlefield," borrowing from the 1807 William Wordsworth poem "Character of the Happy Warrior." Smith was a colorful character usually topped by a brown derby and chomping on a cigar.

4. **(E) Adlai Stevenson.** Stevenson served one term as governor before being named the Democratic Party's unsuccessful presidential candidate in 1952 and 1956. He also served as the U.S. Ambassador to the United Nations from 1961 until his death in 1965.

5. **(D) William B. Bankhead.** A member of an old Alabama family, Bankhead was the father of actress Tallulah Bankhead. Rayburn, a Democrat from Texas, was Speaker of the House from 1940-47, 1949-1953, and 1955-61.

6. **(B) Wayne Morse.** Morse was one of only two U.S. Senators who voted against the 1964 Gulf of Tonkin resolution authorizing U.S. involvement in Vietnam. His convictions cost him his Senate seat, losing to Bob Packwood in 1968. In 1974, Moore won the Democratic primary, but died two months later from kidney failure.

7. **(B) George Wallace.** Alabama governor George Wallace represented the American Independent Party in the 1968 presidential race. He received almost 10 million popular votes, about 13% of the total. With his 46 electoral votes, he was the last third party candidate to collect any electoral votes. In 1972, he ran for President again, under the Democratic banner. He was seriously wounded in an assassination attempt at a Laurel, MD shopping mall on May 15, 1972.

8. **(E) 7.** They are: Woodrow Wilson, Franklin Roosevelt, Harry Truman, John F. Kennedy, Lyndon Johnson, Jimmy Carter, and Bill Clinton.

Quiz #87 — **To the Last**

1. Who was the last ruler of the Holy Roman Empire?
A. Charlemagne
B. Otto von Bismarck
C. Pu-Yi
D. Henry VIII
E. Francis II

2. What was the last black-and-white movie to win a Best Picture Oscar?
A. "The Apartment"
B. "Raging Bull"
C. "The Last Picture Show"
D. "Rocky"
E. "Manhattan"

3. Who finished in last place in the 1861 graduating class at West Point?
A. Edgar Allan Poe
B. Jefferson Davis
C. George Armstrong Custer
D. Nathaniel Hawthorne
E. Herman Melville

4. Who was the last U.S. President who was neither a Democrat nor a Republican?
A. Millard Fillmore
B. Benjamin Harrison
C. Ulysses Grant
D. George Washington
E. Chester A. Arthur

5. Whose 37th and last opera was titled "Deidamia"?
A. Giovanni Battista Bononcini
B. George F. Handel
C. Jean-Philippe Rameau
D. Englebert Humperdinck
E. Jean-Baptiste Lully

6. Who was the last batter to lead the American League in RBIs in consecutive seasons?
A. Mickey Mantle
B. Roger Maris
C. Albert Belle
D. Cecil Fielder
E. Cecil Cooper

7. Who was the last mystery guest on the final show of "What's My Line?" in September 1967?
A. Jimmy Carter
B. Ronald McDonald
C. Elizabeth Taylor
D. John Daly
E. John B. Sebastian

8. What famous literary work ends with the words "Shantih, shantih, shantih"?
A. "Twelfth Night"
B. "Ulysses"
C. "The Iliad"
D. "The Waste Land"
E. "The Sound and the Fury"

Answers to Quiz #87 — **To the Last**

1. **(E) Francis II.** The Holy Roman Empire was the medieval state that controlled most of central Europe and Italy under the rule of German kings from 962 to 1806. After the Treaty of Westphalia in 1648, the Empire was little more than a loose confederation of independent principalities. Napoleon I finally destroyed the empire, compelling some German states to secede from the empire. On March 6, 1806, Francis II, who had previously assumed the title emperor of Austria, abdicated as Holy Roman emperor and declared the empire dissolved.

2. **(A) "The Apartment".** Billy Wilder collected three Oscar statuettes in 1960. He won Best Director, followed by Best Screenplay (with his writing partner I.A.L. Diamond), and finally Best Picture. Accepting the Best Picture award, Wilder said, "It would only be proper to cut it in half and give it to the two most valuable players — Jack Lemmon and Shirley MacLaine."

3. **(C) George Armstrong Custer.** Custer rose through the ranks after proving himself to be a daring cavalry officer during the Civil War. In 1874, the Black Hills, a sacred portion of the Sioux reservation, were rumored to be riddled with gold. When the rumors were confirmed, miners swarmed the area. Unwilling to lease or sell the Hills, the Sioux refused to abandon the area. Custer led troops into the area to force the Sioux to retreat. Custer met his match at the Little Bighorn River in the 1876 battle, and neither he nor any of his 250 soldiers survived.

4. **(A) Millard Fillmore.** Fillmore served one term as U.S. President as a Whig from 1850-53, upon the death of Zachary Taylor. He sought the Presidency again in 1856 as the official candidate of the Whigs and the Know-Nothing Party, but carried only Maryland in the election.

5. **(B) George F. Handel.** "Deidamia" premiered in London in 1740, but was unsuccessful at its debut and has been performed only rarely since. The subject of the opera is Trojan War hero Achilles, who married Deidamia, the daughter of Licomede, King of Scryos.

6. **(C) Albert Belle.** In 1995, Belle became the first major league player to hit 50 home runs and 50 doubles in the same season. Belle tied Mo Vaughn for the most RBIs in 1995 with 126, but Belle belted a whopping 148 RBIs in 1996.

7. **(D) John Daly.** "What's My Line" lasted an astounding 17 years on CBS between 1950 and 1967, with John Daly serving as the show's host for the entire run. The show's first mystery guest was New York Yankees shortstop Phil Rizzuto. "What's My Line" won the Emmy Award for Best Quiz or Audience Participation Show three times in 1952, 1953, and 1958.

8. **(D) "The Waste Land".** According to the author, T.S. Eliot, the word "shantih" is the Sanskrit equivalent of "the peace that passeth all understanding."

Quiz #88 — **The Witching Hour**

1. What rock singer reportedly took his stage name as the reincarnation of a 17th-century witch discovered through a Ouija board?
- A. Ozzy Osbourne
- B. Alice Cooper
- C. Frank Zappa
- D. Mott the Hoople
- E. Iggy Pop

2. What company was founded on the basis of a witch hazel extract used as an all-purpose remedy?
- A. Maybelline
- B. L.L. Bean
- C. Pond's
- D. Avon
- E. Seagrams

3. What was the name of the head witch who commended "The Weird Sisters" in Shakespeare's "Macbeth"?
- A. Circe
- B. Hecate
- C. Medea
- D. Endora
- E. Empusa

4. What U.S. Senator's name was attached to a 1985 measure intended to remove witches from the list of religious organizations eligible for tax-exempt status?
- A. Robert Dole
- B. John Glenn
- C. Ted Kennedy
- D. Jesse Helms
- E. Alan Cranston

5. What Arthur Miller story was set at the 1692 Salem Witch Trials?
- A. "The House of the Seven Gables"
- B. "The Crucible"
- C. "The Hairy Ape"
- D. "Death of a Witch"
- E. "I Married a Witch"

6. What fantasy author was the creator of the popular "Witch World" series?
- A. Piers Anthony
- B. C.S. Lewis
- C. Robert A. Heinlein
- D. Andre Norton
- E. Mercedes Lackey

7. What astrologer and nationally syndicated columnist wrote the books "Diary of a Witch" (1968) and "The Complete Art of Witchcraft" (1971)?
- A. Sybil Leek
- B. Morning Glory Zell
- C. Madalyn Murray O'Hair
- D. Patricia Crowther
- E. Marie Laveau

8. What character was condemned as a witch in Sir Walter Scott's novel "Ivanhoe"?
- A. Guinevere
- B. Roxanne
- C. Rowena
- D. Pamela
- E. Rebecca

1. **(B) Alice Cooper.** Alice Cooper was originally the name of a band led by singer Vincent Furnier. When the band broke up, Furnier began a solo career keeping the Cooper name. Alice Cooper's stage show combined heavy rock 'n' roll with a shocking horror show using props like an electric chair, guillotines, boa constrictors, and lots of fake blood. When asked about the veracity of the Ouija board legend, Cooper laughed and said he thought it was a Scrabble board.

2. **(C) Pond's.** In 1875, Theron T. Pond's company opened a manufacturing plant in Brooklyn expanding the line of products to include Extract Soap and Vanishing Cream. Pond's Cold Cream, introduced in 1907, uses essentially the same formula today, and is one of the company's most popular products.

3. **(B) Hecate.** Hecate evolved from a minor Greek deity into the dread goddess of ghosts and the patron of witches. Hecate possessed infernal power, roaming the earth by night with a pack of hellhounds. She was visible only to dogs. If dogs howled in the night, it meant she was about. The mythical sorceress Circe and the witch Medea are sometimes said to be Hecate's daughters.

4. **(D) Jesse Helms.** North Carolina Senator Jesse Helms introduced the measure into tax-reform legislature in the Senate while Rep. Robert Baker of Pennsylvania did the same in the House. The ACLU fought the bill, calling it "the crudest example of First Amendment infringement," and witches organized a letter-writing campaign. Both measures failed to pass.

5. **(B) "The Crucible".** When the play opened in New York in 1953, audience members were struck by the parallels between the Salem Witch Trials and another witch hunt underway by Senator Joseph McCarthy, probing for Communist conspirators in the United States. "The Crucible" was made into a film starring Winona Ryder.

6. **(D) Andre Norton.** In the 1950s and 1960s, Alice Mary "Andre" Norton was one of the few writers producing good science fiction exclusively for the juvenile market. With the introduction of the first Witch World novel, "Witch World," in 1963, she started the ball rolling on a series that has grown into almost 20 novels and short story collections, developing a wider and more mature readership in the process.

7. **(A) Sybil Leek.** Leek gained considerable fame as an advocate for witchcraft in the United Kingdom and the United States. Her trademarks were a cape, loose gowns, and a large pet bird named Mr. Hotfoot Jackson who was usually perched on her shoulder. Leek published more than 60 books before her death in 1983.

8. **(E) Rebecca.** Rebecca, the daughter of Jewish moneylender, Isaac of York, is condemned as a witch and sentenced to be burned at the stake. In desperation, she demands, as her right, a champion to defend her against the charge. At the champion battle, it appears she will go without a champion until a mysterious knight declares himself her champion. It is the badly wounded Ivanhoe who still manages to defeat the Temple champion, Sir Brian de Bois-Guilbert.

Quiz #89 — **Perchance to Dream**

1. What actor, known for starring in more TV series than any other actor, played reporter Tom Nash on the TV series "American Dreamer"?
A. Robert Conrad
B. Robert Urich
C. Larry Hagman
D. Tony Randall
E. Bill Cosby

2. What philosopher stated "I do not believe that I am now dreaming but I cannot prove I am not"?
A. Ludwig Wittgenstein
B. Frank Ramsey
C. Sigmund Freud
D. Rene Descartes
E. Bertrand Russell

3. What band reached mainstream success after following up their alternative rock albums "Gish" and "Lull" with their first major-label release, "Siamese Dream," in 1993?
A. Soundgarden
B. Stone Temple Pilots
C. Garbage
D. Maids of Gravity
E. Smashing Pumpkins

4. "Dream Master," "Dream Warriors," and "Dream Child" are all sequels to what frightening feature film?
A. "A Nightmare on Elm Street"
B. "Altered States"
C. "Police Academy"
D. "Witchboard"
E. "Friday the 13th"

5. What was the name of the girl group at the heart of the Broadway smash musical "Dreamgirls"?
A. The Heartbeats
B. The Slumbers
C. The Dreamlovers
D. The Dreams
E. The Supremes

6. What science fiction movie was based on Philip K. Dick's novel "Do Androids Dream of Electric Sheep?"
A. "Silent Running"
B. "Soylent Green"
C. "Blade Runner"
D. "Total Recall"
E. "Spaceballs"

7. What composer's works include the song cycle "Fringes of the Fleet," the oratorio "The Dream of Gerontius," and the "Enigma Variations"?
A. Leo Delibes
B. Frederick Delius
C. Claude Debussy
D. Edward Elgar
E. Horatio Parker

8. When "I Dream of Jeannie" was revived for the 1985 TV movie update "I Dream of Jeannie: 15 Years Later," who replaced Larry Hagman in the role of astronaut Anthony Nelson?
A. Wayne Rogers
B. Fred Dryer
C. Butch Patrick
D. Tim Daly
E. Richard Benjamin

Answers to Quiz #89 — **Perchance to Dream**

1. **(B) Robert Urich.** Urich's past credits include being a regular on more than ten series including "Vega$," "Spenser: For Hire," "Soap," and as Bob in the tame TV series version of the film "Bob, Carol, Ted and Alice." He also narrated the National Geographic series, "Explorer," for four years. However, in the 1990s, he launched a run of series, "Gavilan," "It Had to Be You," "Crossroads," "The Lazarus Man," and "Love Boat: The Next Wave." All, like "American Dreamer," lasted less than a year.

2. **(E) Bertrand Russell.** Russell wrote "It is obviously possible that what we call waking life may be only an unusual and persistent nightmare." Russell resolved that he could differentiate wakefulness from sleep because "certain uniformities are observed in waking life, while dreams seem quite erratic." The differences between reality and dreams continue to be a favorite topic of argument among philosophers.

3. **(E) Smashing Pumpkins.** Smashing Pumpkins has its roots unabashedly in '70s progressive rock. Led by guitarist/vocalist/songwriter Billy Corgan, the band won a 1997 Grammy for Best Hard Rock Performance for their song "Bullet with Butterfly Wings."

4. **(A) "A Nightmare on Elm Street".** Talented character actor Robert Englund survived as the murderous Freddy Krueger throughout the "Nightmare" series, and appeared on the "Freddy's Nightmares" TV series.

5. **(D) The Dreams.** Jennifer Holliday was discovered by the producers of "Dreamgirls" as "a raw talent" in "Your Arms Are Too Short to Box with God." She was a huge success and won rave reviews as the tragic member of the Dreams, winning the 1982 Tony Award for Best Actress in a musical, beating out co-star Sheryl Lee Ralph. Her showstopping song from the production, "And I Am Telling You I'm Not Going," was a top 25 pop hit as well as a #1 R&B chart-topper in 1982. It also netted her a 1983 Grammy Award for Best Rhythm & Blues Female Solo Vocal.

6. **(C) "Blade Runner".** Philip Kendred Dick was a versatile and prolific science fiction author of the 1950s and '60s. Among his classic novels are "Time Out of Joint" (1959), "The World Jones Made" (1956), "The Man in the High Castle" (1962) which won a 1963 Hugo Award, and "Galactic Pot-Healer" (1969).

7. **(D) Edward Elgar.** It wasn't until the age of 42, with the first performance of the "Enigma Variations" in 1899, that British composer Sir Edward Elgar finally came to the front rank of composers. His best-known piece is "Pomp and Circumstance," heard at countless graduation ceremonies. He was knighted in 1904.

8. **(A) Wayne Rogers.** Jeannie was also the subject of a 1970s CBS cartoon series called "Jeannie" that featured Julie McWhirter as the voice of the animated genie, and Mark Hamill as the voice of her young master, Corey Anders. "Jeannie" was the top-rated animated series of 1973.

1. What is the smallest living breed of tiger?
A. Bengal
B. Indian
C. Sumatran
D. Javan
E. Siberian

2. What actor won a Best Actor Academy Award for his starring role in the 1973 movie "Save the Tiger"?
A. Christopher Lee
B. Ryan O'Neal
C. Jack Lemmon
D. Jack Nicholson
E. James Garner

3. During World War II, what automobile engineer turned to designing military vehicles, most notably, the Tiger tank?
A. Rolls
B. Mercedes-Benz
C. Saab
D. Porsche
E. Daimler

4. On the Chinese calendar, the year of the Tiger is preceded by which of the following?
A. Year of the Hare
B. Year of the Dragon
C. Year of the Snake
D. Year of the Monkey
E. Year of the Ox

5. The last major league pitcher with 30 wins in a single season was what Detroit Tigers hurler?
A. Roger Clemens
B. Jim Kaat
C. Lefty Grove
D. Denny McLain
E. Mickey Lolich

6. What is the name of Tiger's dog in the Bud Blake comic strip "Tiger"?
A. Punkinhead
B. Stripe
C. Hugo
D. Tiger
E. Winnie

7. What is the real first name of golfing sensation "Tiger" Woods?
A. Eldrick
B. Oscar
C. Tony
D. Elvis
E. Louise

8. The Flying Tigers was a group of U.S. civilian volunteer pilots who fought in the China-Burma-India Theater during World War II. Who designed the insignia used by the Tigers?
A. Omar Bradley
B. Winston Churchill
C. Grand Duke Nicholas of Russia
D. Walt Disney
E. John Wayne

Answers to Quiz #90 — **Tiger in Your Trivia**

1. **(C) Sumatran.** Human overcrowding and habitat destruction threaten the future existence of the Sumatran tiger. Fewer than 500 exist in the wild. The average Sumatran tiger weighs 275 lbs., less than half that of the Siberian or Indian tiger.

2. **(C) Jack Lemmon.** Lemmon's competition was Marlon Brando in "Last Tango in Paris," Jack Nicholson in "The Last Detail," Al Pacino in "Serpico," and Robert Redford in "The Sting." Lemmon joins Jack Nicholson, Robert De Niro, and Gene Hackman as the talented actors who have both Best Actor and Best Supporting Actor Oscars.

3. **(D) Porsche.** Ferdinand Porsche and his son, Ferry, were responsible for the initial design of the Volkswagen in 1934. After World War II, the elder Porsche was imprisoned for a time by the French. The Tiger tank was among the heaviest deployed in the war, armed with an 88-millimeter gun.

4. **(E) Year of the Ox.** The most recent Year of the Tiger in the Chinese calendar was 1998, and the next is 2010.

5. **(D) Denny McLain.** McLain's 30 wins came in 1968. As a result of his pitching prowess, McLain was the first player to win the Cy Young and MVP Awards in the same season. The Tigers went on to win the World Series that year with Tigers pitcher Mickey Lolich named MVP with 3 wins.

6. **(B) Stripe.** The cast of "Tiger" is a group of children led by Tiger and his younger brother, Punkinhead. Their friends include the lunkheaded Hugo and the brainy Julian. The strip debuted in 1965, and won the National Cartoonists Society Best Humor Strip of the Year in 1970 and 1978.

7. **(A) Eldrick.** Tiger Woods was the first male golfer to win three consecutive U.S. Amateur Championships. Woods beat Davis Love III in a playoff for his first PGA tour victory at the Las Vegas Invitational in October 1996. Woods had turned pro five weeks earlier.

8. **(D) Walt Disney.** The Flying Tigers was a small combat unit that fought the Japanese against great odds, but managed to win dogfight after dogfight through the use of precision flying and unorthodox strategies. The flyers, recruited by Col. Claire L. Chennault, were absorbed into the U.S. 10th Air Force in July 1942, under the command of Chennault who was promoted to brigadier general.

Quiz #91 — All in the Family 2

1. The father of UN Secretary General Dag Hammarskjöld was the prime minister of what country during World War I?
A. Sweden
B. Norway
C. Denmark
D. Finland
E. Austria

2. Theater critic Pia Lindstrom is the daughter of what late great actress?
A. Ingrid Bergman
B. Carole Lombard
C. Rita Hayworth
D. Joan Crawford
E. Greta Garbo

3. What was the last name of brothers Gene, Joe, Vic, and Ed who made up a popular 1950s vocal group?
A. DiMaggio
B. Chase
C. James
D. Ames
E. Alberts

4. Baseball players Ken Griffey Sr. and Jr. became the first father and son to play on the same major league baseball team as members of what squad in 1989-90?
A. Kansas City Royals
B. Seattle Mariners
C. Milwaukee Brewers
D. Atlanta Braves
E. New York Yankees

5. What costumed crimefighter was the grand-nephew of the Lone Ranger?
A. Batman
B. The Owl
C. Hawkman
D. The Atom
E. Green Hornet

6. What empress plotted against her brother, Caligula, and married her own uncle, Claudius?
A. Poppaea
B. Octavia
C. Cleopatra
D. Agrippina the Younger
E. Lygia

7. What was the name of Screwtape's nephew, the trainee to whom he is writing instructions in C.S. Lewis's "The Screwtape Letters"?
A. Stickman
B. Wormwood
C. Hope
D. Chernobyl
E. Ardeb

8. What President's daughter inspired the name for the Baby Ruth candy bar?
A. Teddy Roosevelt
B. Grover Cleveland
C. Andrew Jackson
D. William Henry Harrison
E. Martin Van Buren

1. **(A) Sweden.** As Prime Minister of Sweden from 1914 to 1917, Knut Hjalmar Hammarskjöld sought to maintain Sweden's neutrality during World War I. He was elected to the Swedish Parliament in 1923, and served as the chairman of the Nobel Prize foundation from 1929-47.

2. **(A) Ingrid Bergman.** Lindstrom spent 23 years as the theater critic for WNBC-TV in New York City. She has a half-brother and two half-sisters (one is actress Isabella Rossellini) through Ingrid Bergman's marriage to director Roberto Rossellini.

3. **(D) Ames.** As a group, the Ames Brothers had 10 top 40 hits on the Billboard pop charts, including three in the top 10: "The Naughty Lady of Shady Lane" (1954), "Tammy" (1957), and "Melodie D'Amour (Melody of Love)" (1957). Youngest brother Ed was also a successful soloist and played Mingo, the Indian friend of TV's "Daniel Boone."

4. **(B) Seattle Mariners.** On September 15, 1990, the Griffeys hit back-to-back home runs for the Mariners.

5. **(E) Green Hornet.** John Reid, aka the Lone Ranger, was the great-uncle of newspaperman Britt Reid, aka the Green Hornet. Both characters were created for radio by Fran Striker and George W. Trendle.

6. **(D) Agrippina the Younger.** Agrippina may have poisoned her husband after she persuaded him to adopt her son, Nero, as his successor. She hoped to rule Rome through Nero, but her woeful family relationships continued as she was put to death in 59 A.D. by order of her son.

7. **(B) Wormwood.** Screwtape instructed his nephew that the art of winning over a young man's soul is not by luring him into a sudden mortal sin but through the temptations offered during daily life. "The safest road to hell is the gradual one...." In the comic strip "Calvin and Hobbes," cartoonist Bill Watterson named Calvin's teacher Miss Wormwood after the apprentice devil.

8. **(B) Grover Cleveland.** It is a popular misconception that the candy was named after baseball legend Babe Ruth, perpetuated by TV commercials featuring the slugger and candy bar together. Ruth Cleveland had been born in the White House. Although a grown woman when the Baby Ruth bar was first sold in 1920, Americans still remembered her fondly. By 1926, the Curtiss Candy Company was selling 5 million of the log-shaped bars daily.

Quiz #92 — **The Long Arm of the Law**

1. George Harrison lost a legal battle when it was ruled that his 1970 hit song "My Sweet Lord" plagiarized what other hit?
- A. "The Lion Sleeps Tonight"
- B. "Venus in Blue Jeans"
- C. "He's So Fine"
- D. "Knock Three Times"
- E. "Ain't No Mountain High Enough"

2. Kathryn Shannon was determined to turn her husband into a nationally known and wealthy criminal. In spite of his nickname, his only major crime was kidnapping, and he never killed anyone. Who was he?
- A. Roger "The Terrible" Touhy
- B. "Pretty Boy" Floyd
- C. "Machine Gun" Kelly
- D. "Lucky" Luciano
- E. Dale "Da Boss" Jellings

3. In what movie did Gregory Peck play attorney Atticus Finch defending a man accused of rape?
- A. "Twelve Angry Men"
- B. "To Kill a Mockingbird"
- C. "Judd for the Defense"
- D. "Defense for the Prosecution"
- E. "Suspect"

4. What book was Mark David Chapman carrying when he was arrested for the murder of John Lennon?
- A. "Catch-22"
- B. "Who's Afraid of Virginia Woolf"
- C. "Logan's Run"
- D. "Roget's Super Thesaurus"
- E. "The Catcher in the Rye"

5. Who campaigned for the office of U.S. President in 1920 from prison?
- A. Elihu Root
- B. Stephen Duggan
- C. Nicola Sacco
- D. Eugene V. Debs
- E. Booth Tarkington

6. The Missouri Compromise was ruled unconstitutional in 1857 by the U.S. Supreme Court after what slave brought suit against his owner's widow, claiming that when he was brought into Illinois, he was legally free by reason of his residence in free territory?
- A. Bill Doggett
- B. Tom Harvey
- C. Dred Scott
- D. Cotton Mather
- E. Chicken George Moore

7. Who called himself "the law West of the Pecos" and named his town Langtry after the English actress Lillie Langtry?
- A. Bat Masterson
- B. Roy Bean
- C. Wyatt Earp
- D. John Henry
- E. Pat Garrett

8. What Heisman Trophy winner could dodge tacklers on the football field, but failed to elude the Omaha police while driving the getaway car in a service station holdup?
- A. Johnny Rodgers
- B. Ernie Davis
- C. O.J. Simpson
- D. Glenn Davis
- E. Johnny Lujack

1. **(C) "He's So Fine".** Harrison said he was inspired to write "My Sweet Lord" after hearing the Edwin Hawkins Singers' version of "Oh Happy Day." "My Sweet Lord" was the first solo Beatles record to reach #1. The song peaked at the end of 1970, but Harrison's royalties were cut off in 1971 due to the plagiarism lawsuit. Five years later, the suit was finally settled. The judge conceded that while Harrison did not consciously intend to copy "He's So Fine," he was still in violation of the copyright law.

2. **(C) "Machine Gun" Kelly.** George "Machine Gun" Kelly's gang kidnapped oilman Charles Urschel in 1933 and collected $200,000. Kathryn wanted Urschel killed, but Kelly thought the death would be "bad for future business." Urschel proved to have an excellent memory, and though blindfolded throughout the ordeal, provided the FBI with enough clues to locate Kelly's Texas hideout. Kathryn "Kit" Kelly was freed from prison in 1958. Kelly died in Leavenworth Prison in 1954.

3. **(B) "To Kill a Mockingbird".** The 1962 film was warmly received by audiences. The Academy of Motion Pictures Arts and Sciences also favored the film, awarding a Best Actor Oscar to Gregory Peck, and Oscars for Best Adapted Screenplay and Best Art Decoration and Set Decoration.

4. **(E) "The Catcher in the Rye".** A TV movie about John Lennon and Yoko Ono was produced in 1985 with an actor named Mark Lindsay selected to star as Lennon. In one of those bizarre coincidences usually only seen on "The X-Files," Lindsay's real name turned out to be Mark Chapman. Lindsay was subsequently replaced.

5. **(D) Eugene V. Debs.** Debs was in prison facing sedition charges for statements made in a 1918 speech in Canton, Ohio. As the representative of the Socialist Party in 1920, Debs garnered 920,000 votes — almost 4 percent of the total national vote.

6. **(C) Dred Scott.** The case of Dred Scott v. Sandford was only the second instance in which the Supreme Court struck down an act of Congress as unconstitutional. The decision had a tremendous impact on the Abolitionist movement as the Supreme Court ruled that no black was a citizen of the U.S. as defined in the Constitution, and therefore could not sue in the courts.

7. **(B) Roy Bean.** Apocryphal tales of Judge Roy Bean include fining a dead man forty dollars for carrying a concealed weapon. Bean was a saloonkeeper with no legal status but his eccentric administration of justice was tolerated by the Texas Rangers since Bean's law was better than no law at all. Lillie Langtry visited her namesake town 10 months after Bean's death.

8. **(A) Johnny Rodgers.** Rodgers, who has described the holdup as a "college prank," was also once jailed for six months for assaulting a cable TV serviceman who was attempting to disconnect Rodgers's service. Rodgers won the Heisman Trophy in 1972 while playing for the University of Nebraska.

Quiz #93 — **A Tough Nut to Crack**

1. Which of the following is a true nut?
A. Pecan
B. Brazil nut
C. Peanut
D. Hazelnut
E. Walnut

2. What American general, when asked by the Germans to surrender on December 22, 1944, replied with one word: "Nuts!"?
A. George Patton
B. Omar Bradley
C. Curtis Lemay
D. Anthony McAuliffe
E. Daniel Sultan

3. What TV series was set at Walnut Grove in Plum Creek, Minnesota?
A. "Life Goes On"
B. "The Waltons"
C. "The Monkees"
D. "Petticoat Junction"
E. "Little House on the Prairie"

4. On what TV series was the comical Rev. Grady Nutt a fixture?
A. "Amen"
B. "Gimme a Break"
C. "The Beverly Hillbillies"
D. "Chico and the Man"
E. "Hee Haw"

5. What color is the meat of the pistachio nut?
A. Green
B. Pink
C. White
D. Blue
E. Yellow

6. What comedy team made their film debut in the 1930 movie "Soup to Nuts"?
A. Olsen and Johnson
B. The Ritz Brothers
C. The Three Stooges
D. The Marx Brothers
E. Laurel and Hardy

7. What country would you be visiting if you found yourself eating bunya nuts?
A. South Africa
B. Canada
C. Australia
D. Mexico
E. Panama

8. Which cast member of "Gilligan's Island" played Junior on the Saturday morning kid's comedy series "Far Out Space Nuts"?
A. Alan Hale Jr.
B. Bob Denver
C. Russell Johnson
D. Dawn Wells
E. Jim Backus

Answers to Quiz #93 — **A Tough Nut to Crack**

1. **(D) Hazelnut.** A true nut is a fruit that consists of an edible hard seed covered with a dry woody shell. Walnuts and pecans are actually drupes — seeds enclosed in a fleshy covering. The peanut is a legume, more pea than nut. The Brazil nut is a regular fruit seed.

2. **(D) Anthony McAuliffe.** Gen. McAuliffe, in command of the 101st Airborne Division and the Combat Command B 10th Armored Division, found his troops surrounded by the Germans at Bastogne, Belgium during the Battle of the Bulge. Given an offer by Gen. Hendrich von Luttwitz to surrender or be annihilated, McAuliffe called von Luttwitz's bluff with one of the most famous one-word quotes in history.

3. **(E) "Little House on the Prairie".** The Ingalls family moved a lot on the series. Towns they called home included Winoka, Minnesota; Burr Oak, Iowa; and Sleepy Eye, Minnesota. With the Walnut Grove set due for destruction, Michael Landon wrote in the obliteration of the town of Walnut Grove into the 1984 TV movie "Little House: The Last Farewell."

4. **(E) "Hee Haw".** The Rev. Grady Nutt was nicknamed "The Prime Minister of Humor." He appeared 11 times on "The Mike Douglas Show" before becoming a "Hee Haw" regular in 1979. Rev. Nutt was killed in an airplane crash near Vinemont, Alabama in 1982.

5. **(A) Green.** If you've ever eaten pistachio ice cream, there is no mistaking the natural color of the nut. Pistachios are often dyed a bright pink for commercial sale.

6. **(C) The Three Stooges.** At the time, the Stooges' head man was Ted Healy, and he was the main attraction of the movie. The Stooges — Moe, Shemp, and Larry — appeared as supporting players. Their parts were so small they didn't even receive billing in the movie's credits.

7. **(C) Australia.** The sweet pine nuts of the large bunya pine are roasted and eaten by the Aborigines.

8. **(B) Bob Denver.** Denver co-starred with Chuck McCann as two NASA janitors who accidentally launch themselves into space. The live action show relied on slapstick and low-budget space monsters for effect. It lasted only for one season on CBS, 1975-76.

Quiz #94 — **Pepper Game**

1. What is the unit for measuring the heat content of hot peppers?
A. Scoville
B. Rodney
C. Scream
D. BTU
E. Bell

2. What actress played the wingwalking ingenue who plummeted to her death from a WWI biplane in the movie "The Great Waldo Pepper"?
A. Noel Neill
B. Margot Kidder
C. Teri Hatcher
D. Susan Sarandon
E. Lois Nettleton

3. Claude Pepper served as a U.S. Senator from 1936-50 and as a U.S. Representative from 1962 until his death in 1989 representing what state?
A. Alabama
B. Georgia
C. Maryland
D. Florida
E. Massachusetts

4. The title song to what Doris Day film was written by Inez James and Buddy Pepper?
A. "Pillow Talk"
B. "Calamity Jane"
C. "With a Song in My Heart"
D. "On Moonlight Bay"
E. "I'll See You in My Dreams"

5. The Peppermint Trolley Company originally recorded the theme song to what TV series, only to be replaced with a new version of the theme song sung by cast members?
A. "Happy Days"
B. "The Patty Duke Show"
C. "The Brady Bunch"
D. "Lancelot Link, Secret Chimp"
E. "Bonanza"

6. What actor was the original joyous dancing "I'm a pepper" man in TV commercials for the Dr Pepper soft drink?
A. Jason Alexander
B. Lee Majors
C. Barry Newman
D. Peter Lawford
E. David Naughton

7. In what state would you find Pepperdine College?
A. Ohio
B. California
C. Florida
D. New York
E. Oregon

8. Amanda Pepper is the Philadelphia prep school English teacher turned detective in novels by what author?
A. Mary Jackson Braun
B. Clifton James
C. Gillian Roberts
D. Angie Dickinson
E. Lori Russell

Answers to Quiz #94 — **Pepper Game**

1. **(A) Scoville.** The Scoville scale for rating the heat generated by peppers was proposed by American pharmacist Wilbur Scoville in 1912. He derived his measurements using the tongues of various taste testers. Modern Scoville measurement is done through a high-tech assay called high-pressure liquid chromatography. The "red Savana" habanero pepper rates the highest on the Scoville scale at 577,000 Scovilles, 15 times hotter than the jalapeno.

2. **(D) Susan Sarandon.** Robert Redford, as Waldo Pepper, performed some of his own wingwalking stunts 3000 feet above the ground, much to the chagrin of the film's producers. "I felt incredible freedom," he said, "but then I thought — what I am doing here?"

3. **(D) Florida.** Pepper served more than 60 years in public office. He was known as a champion of the elderly and the poor. Detractors called him "Red" Pepper for his liberal views, which included providing financial support to the Soviet Union. His unpopular opinions cost him his Senate seat, losing to George Smathers in 1950. After practicing law for a dozen years, Pepper returned to Congress in 1962 as a U.S. Representative. In May 1989, he received the Medal of Freedom, the nation's highest civilian award, five days before his death.

4. **(A) "Pillow Talk".** Pepper and James also wrote the Les Paul-Mary Ford song "Vaya Con Dios." Pepper's real name was Jack Starkey, but while playing the younger brother of actor Jack Pepper in a Broadway musical revue, he became known as "Little Buddy" Pepper. Pepper was the musical accompanist who helped Judy Garland back to her feet after her spill during the opening number at the London Palladium on April 14, 1951. Pepper died February 7, 1993 at the age of 70.

5. **(C) "The Brady Bunch".** The Peppermint Trolley Company's version of "The Brady Bunch" theme song was used only during the initial 1969-70 season, after which a version featuring the Brady kids was used. The Peppermint Trolley Company also recorded the theme song for "Love, American Style."

6. **(E) David Naughton.** Naughton is probably best remembered as the werewolf in John Landis's 1981 comedy-horror movie "An American Werewolf in London." Naughton also starred in a short-lived TV series called "Makin' It" in 1979.

7. **(B) California.** Pepperdine is located in Malibu, California. The sports teams' nickname is the Waves. Pepperdine volleyball teams have won four NCAA national championships.

8. **(C) Gillian Roberts.** The most recent Amanda Pepper mysteries include "In the Dead of Summer" in 1995 and "The Mummer's Curse" in 1996. Gillian Roberts writes mainstream novels using her real name, Judith Greber. Like her detective, Roberts taught school in Philadelphia before her success as a writer.

Quiz #95 — **Famous Russians**

1. Born a Siberian peasant, who gained influence in the court of Nicholas II as the only man able to treat the hemophilia of the heir to the throne, the Tsarevich Alexis?
A. Rasputin
B. Lenin
C. Joseph Stalin
D. Andrey Platonovich Platonov
E. Anton Chekhov

2. What Russian writer coined the term "nihilism"?
A. Boris Pasternak
B. Ivan Turgenev
C. Aleksandr Solzhenitsyn
D. Fyodor Dostoyevsky
E. Karl Marx

3. What composer is generally acknowledged as the founder of the Russian nationalist school?
A. Tsar Alexander II
B. Nikolay Rimsky-Korsakov
C. Aleksandr Borodin
D. Peter Ilich Tchaikovsky
E. Mikhail Glinka

4. Who was the first Russian author to win the Nobel Prize for Literature?
A. Leo Tolstoy
B. Anton Chekhov
C. Maxim Gorky
D. Ivan Alekseyevich Bunin
E. Aleksandr Solzhenitsyn

5. Who helped develop the first hydrogen bomb in the Soviet Union, but won the Nobel Peace Prize as an advocate for human rights and reform in the USSR?
A. Andrey Sakharov
B. Igor Tamm
C. Aleksey Kosygin
D. Yuri Andropov
E. Mikhail Gorbachev

6. Who was the first Russian-born hockey player named captain of an NHL team?
A. Vladislav Tretiak
B. Viktor Nechaev
C. Johnny Gottselig
D. Alexander Mogilny
E. Bobby Hull

7. Who was the first Russian astronaut launched into space on an American space mission?
A. Alex Ignatiev
B. Vladimir Tirov
C. Valentin Tereshkova
D. Yuri Gagarin
E. Sergei Krikalev

8. The first national film school was the Moscow State Film Institute founded in 1919. What noted Russian film director was the school's first principal?
A. Sergei Eisenstein
B. Vladamir Gardin
C. Alexander Dovzhenko
D. Edouard Tisse
E. Vsevolod Pudovkin

Answers to Quiz #95 — **Famous Russians**

1. **(A) Rasputin.** Rasputin, "the Mad Monk," was assassinated by a group of Russian nobles on December 31, 1916. Rasputin proved difficult to kill. When attempts to poison him inexplicably failed, they shot him and threw his body in the Neva River.

2. **(B) Ivan Turgenev.** In his novel "Fathers and Sons," Turgenev coined the term "nihilism" to describe the philosophy of many young revolutionaries who opposed the tsar's government in the latter 1800s.

3. **(E) Mikhail Glinka.** The opera that first brought international fame to Glinka was "Life for the Tsar" in 1836. The opera was renamed "Ivan Susanin" after the Russian Revolution. Glinka traveled a lot, and his love of exotic places infected his composing which became a model for future Russian composers.

4. **(D) Ivan Alekseyevich Bunin.** Bunin won the Nobel Prize in 1933. He is chiefly known for his prose which was a throwback to classical Russian literary style rather than the modernist style of his contemporaries. Also a poet, Bunin did successful translations of Bryon's "Manfred" and "Cain" into Russian. His translation of Longfellow's "Hiawatha" earned him a Pushkin Prize in 1903 by the Russian Academy.

5. **(A) Andrey Sakharov.** Sakharov's first public protest against Khrushchev came in 1961, when he protested against the plan to test a 100-megaton hydrogen bomb in the atmosphere fearing the fallout would endanger many Russian citizens. For the next 20 years, Sakharov continued to be at odds with the Soviet government. In 1975, he was awarded the Nobel Prize for Peace. But by 1980, he was stripped of all honors and exiled to the closed city of Gorky after he publicly denounced the Soviet invasion of Afghanistan and called for a boycott of the Moscow Olympics. Sakharov was released from exile by Mikhail Gorbachev in 1986. He died in December 1989.

6. **(C) Johnny Gottselig.** Gottselig, born in Odessa, captained the Chicago Blackhawks from 1935-40, and later served as their head coach.

7. **(E) Sergei Krikalev.** Krikalev was the 100th passenger of the space shuttle Discovery. His participation in the 1994 Discovery mission was the first U.S.-Russian cooperative space effort since the 1975 Apollo-Soyuz space docking.

8. **(B) Vladamir Gardin.** Gardin filmed the 1915 version of "War and Peace." During the first year of the school's existence, raw film stock was in such short supply that students shot imaginary films with no film in the camera.

Quiz #96 — **Food at the Movies**

1. What flavor of ice cream did Fozzie Bear order for Kermit the Frog from ice cream vendor Bob Hope in "The Muppet Movie"?
A. Chocolate cricket
B. Dragonfly ripple
C. Tutti-frutti termite
D. Weevil vanilla
E. Grasshopper sundae

2. What actress got mashed in the face with a grapefruit by James Cagney in the 1931 movie "Public Enemy"?
A. Joan Blondell
B. Bette Davis
C. Ann Sheridan
D. Mae Clarke
E. Myrna Loy

3. In the comically-redubbed movie "What's Up, Tiger Lily?," Japanese super agent Phil Moskowitz is tracking down a recipe for what?
A. Bathtub gin
B. Microwave popcorn
C. Frosted flakes
D. Egg salad
E. Stewed prunes

4. In what movie does Paul Newman struggle to devour 50 hard-boiled eggs?
A. "Winning"
B. "WUSA"
C. "Cool Hand Luke"
D. "Hud"
E. "The Hustler"

5. Quaker Oats released the Everlasting Gobstopper, Oompa Loompas, and the Super Skrunch Bar in coordination with what children's film?
A. "Child's Play"
B. "Chitty Chitty Bang Bang"
C. "The Phantom Tollbooth"
D. "The Wizard of Oz"
E. "Willy Wonka and the Chocolate Factory"

6. In "Gone with the Wind," what does Scarlett eat that causes her retch and then declare "as God as is my witness, I'll never be hungry again"?
A. Radish
B. Beef jerky
C. Mushrooms
D. Cranberries
E. Cotton balls

7. In what movie does Jack Lemmon prepare spaghetti by using a tennis racket to drain the pasta?
A. "Some Like It Hot"
B. "Mass Appeal"
C. "The Apartment"
D. "Grumpy Old Men"
E. "The Odd Couple"

8. What movie ends with leading man Clint Eastwood being dispatched by a meal of poisoned mushrooms?
A. "Pale Rider"
B. "High Plains Drifter"
C. "Tightrope"
D. "The Beguiled"
E. "Play Misty for Me"

Answers to Quiz #96 — **Food at the Movies**

1. **(B) Dragonfly ripple.** Many stars made cameo appearances in "The Muppet Movie," including James Coburn as a bar owner, Milton Berle as a used car salesman, Steve Martin as an obnoxious waiter, Dom DeLuise as a Hollywood agent, and Orson Welles as a Hollywood mogul.

2. **(D) Mae Clarke.** The scene was inspired by a report of gangster Hymie Weiss hitting his girlfriend in the face with an omelet. "Public Enemy" put Cagney on the cinematic map as the anti-hero gangster for which he would find himself typecast while at Warner Brothers.

3. **(D) Egg salad.** Take one Japanese spy film, hire Woody Allen to create hysterical new dialogue, rename the Japanese hero "Phil Moskowitz," mix in some music from the Lovin' Spoonful, and you've got the recipe for the hilarious "What's Up, Tiger Lily?"

4. **(C) "Cool Hand Luke".** Prison inmate Newman makes a bet that he can eat 50 eggs in an hour. It takes a little help from George Kennedy to keep stuffing them into the mouth of a prone Newman, but he makes it.

5. **(E) "Willy Wonka and the Chocolate Factory".** The 1971 movie was initially a flop, successful only for the song "The Candy Man" which was a #1 hit for Sammy Davis Jr. But the candy put out by Quaker Oats kept the name "Willy Wonka" out in the public, and subsequent reshowings of the movie on TV gained it a following.

6. **(A) Radish.** Scarlett's retching sounds were dubbed from a performance by Olivia de Havilland after Vivien Leigh didn't sound convincing enough.

7. **(C) "The Apartment".** Jack Lemmon starred as an up-and-coming insurance clerk who allows his immoral and married boss, Fred MacMurray, to use his apartment for a rendezvous with elevator girl Shirley MacLaine. When MacMurray gives MacLaine the brushoff, she tries to commit suicide in Lemmon's apartment. Lemmon returns to his apartment in time to save her, and takes the responsibility of nursing her back to health by playing card games and cooking her spaghetti in his own unique style. Eventually, the two fall in love.

8. **(D) "The Beguiled".** Eastwood played a wounded Union soldier taken in by a southern girls' school during the Civil War. Although the girls originally mean to take good care of him, Eastwood becomes the cause of jealousy and bad feelings among the girls, and he does not hesitate to manipulate their feelings to his own end. His bad faith first causes him to lose a leg, and then his life. This haunting 1971 film was one Eastwood's rare box office failures.

Quiz #97 — **Pages of the Calendar**

1. What film directed by Woody Allen featured Jack Warden, Denholm Elliott, and Elaine Stritch?
A. "September"
B. "April in Paris"
C. "The October Revolution"
D. "The Whales of August"
E. "November Affair"

2. What author created the mystery series characters Solar Pons and Dr. Lyndon Parker?
A. May Sarton
B. June Leighton
C. August Derleth
D. Donald May
E. Fredric March

3. "It Might As Well Rain Until September" was the first top 40 hit for what singer/songwriter who would have far greater success as a songwriter for others and for her albums, one of which remained on the LP charts for over a year?
A. Joni Mitchell
B. Laura Nyro
C. Janis Ian
D. Carole King
E. Nanci Griffith

4. What classic TV series starred Spring Byington, Harry Morgan, Verna Felton, and Francis Rafferty?
A. "December Bride"
B. "Tell Me That You Love Me, Junie Moon"
C. "March Madness"
D. "April Dancer"
E. "First Monday in October"

5. Who won Pulitzer Prizes for the plays "The Piano Lesson" and "Fences"?
A. Fredric March
B. Elaine May
C. Archibald Mayerling
D. Edna Mae Ferber
E. August Wilson

6. What cartoon character had nieces named April, May, and June?
A. Daisy Duck
B. Woody Woodpecker
C. Chilly Willy
D. Andy Panda
E. Minnie Mouse

7. Who was the intended assassination victim in the July Plot?
A. Charlemagne
B. Oliver Cromwell
C. Marc Antony
D. Guy Fawkes
E. Adolf Hitler

8. What country adopted "March On, March On" as its national anthem in 1978?
A. China
B. India
C. Vietnam
D. Pakistan
E. Italy

Answers to Quiz #97 — **Pages of the Calendar**

1. (A) "September". Allen originally completed "September" with a different cast of stars including Charles Durning, Sam Shepard, and Maureen O'Sullivan, but when he ran into problems editing the film, he decided to rewrite and reshoot much of it with a different cast.

2. (C) August Derleth. Derleth's sleuths were basically copies of Sherlock Holmes and Dr. John Watson, right down to Dr. Parker's mustache and Pons' home address of 7B Praed Street. Doyle was not writing new Holmes stories, so Derleth received permission to carry on with his imitations. After Derleth's death, the Solar Pons stories were continued by Basil Copper. Although primarily known for other types of writing, the mystery novels of August Derleth are becoming more popular now than when they were originally published.

3. (D) Carole King. King was a member of the Brill Building team of songwriters in the early sixties with her then-husband, Gerry Goffin. She wrote and produced such hits as "Locomotion" for Little Eva and "Will You Love Me Tomorrow" by the Shirelles, to name but a few. Her solo career soared with the release of the monumentally successful LP, "Tapestry," which featured the #1 hit, "It's Too Late," and several other King standards like "You've Got a Friend" and "I Feel the Earth Move."

4. (A) "December Bride". "December Bride" was so successful that it became one of the first TV shows ever to foster a spinoff. The popular Harry Morgan character, Pete Porter, moved to his own series, "Pete and Gladys," which featured his formerly unseen wife, Gladys, played by Cara Williams.

5. (E) August Wilson. Wilson, one of the American stage's foremost black playwrights, won the Pulitzer for "Fences" in 1987 and for "The Piano Lesson" in 1990. He also received plaudits and other awards for his plays, "Joe Turner's Come and Gone" and "Two Trains Running." "Fences" grossed $11 million during its 526 performances on Broadway, earning more money than any nonmusical play before it.

6. (A) Daisy Duck. Daisy Duck made her debut in the 1937 cartoon "Don Donald." She had the same "quacky" voice as Donald until her sixth cartoon appearance, "Cured Duck," in 1945. She then got a clear feminine voice which better matched her personality. Daisy's nieces were introduced in her comic book series by Gold Key.

7. (E) Adolf Hitler. The assassination plot, also known as the Rastenburg Plot and the Stauffenberg Plot, was an attempt by top officers in Hitler's staff to dispose of the dictator in order to clear the way for favorable peace terms with the Allies. On July 20, 1944, Count von Stauffenberg left a bomb in a briefcase under a table at Hitler's headquarters in Rastenberg. The bomb went off, but because an aide had put the briefcase to the far side of the oak support of the conference table, Hitler was spared the brunt of the blast.

8. (A) China. The new anthem had the same music as the old anthem, "March of the Volunteers." The lyrics of the old anthem had fallen into disfavor during the Cultural Revolution. New lyrics included references to Mao Tse-Tung and the Communist Army.

Quiz #98 — Night of the Comet

1. What writer claimed he came in with Halley's Comet and would go out with Halley's Comet?
A. Mark Twain
B. Stephen Crane
C. James Fennimore Cooper
D. Ernest Hemingway
E. Richard Wright

2. What was the name of the female plumber played by Jane Withers in Comet cleanser TV commercials?
A. Alice
B. Josephine
C. Madge
D. Maria
E. Eloise

3. What female astronomer was awarded a gold medal by the King of Denmark for becoming the first person to discover a comet with the use of a telescope?
A. Margaret Palmer
B. Annie Wright
C. Polly Palomar
D. Frances Schlesinger
E. Maria Mitchell

4. "The Comet Man" was a comic book character created for Marvel Comics by what former child star?
A. Bob Denver
B. Tony Dow
C. Spanky MacFarland
D. Bill Mumy
E. Bobby Diamond

5. When the Women's National Basketball Association (WNBA) debuted on June 21, 1997, the WNBA franchise called the Comets was based in what city?
A. Phoenix
B. Sacramento
C. Salt Lake City
D. Houston
E. New York City

6. "The Comet" was the title of a tabloid newspaper on what comic TV series?
A. "Roseanne"
B. "Seinfeld"
C. "The Practice"
D. "Arsenio"
E. "The Naked Truth"

7. What TV western figure rode an intelligent horse named Comet?
A. Artemus Gordon
B. The Virginian
C. Hopalong Cassidy
D. Brisco County Jr.
E. Wild Bill Hickok

8. Prior to being known as rock 'n' rollers Bill Haley and the Comets, what name did Haley's group go by?
A. The Rockets
B. The Downhomers
C. The Saddlemen
D. The Four Seasons
E. The Baptists

Answers to Quiz #98 — **Night of the Comet**

1. **(A) Mark Twain.** Of Halley's Comet, Mark Twain wrote in 1909: "It is coming again next year, and I expect to go out with it. It will be the greatest disappointment of my life if I don't go out with Halley's Comet. The Almighty has said, no doubt: 'Now here are these two unaccountable freaks; they came in together, they must go out together.'" Twain was born in 1835 under Halley's Comet, and true to his word, died upon its return in 1910.

2. **(B) Josephine.** In the 1930s, Jane Withers was a child star in roles as a mischievous child that served as counterpoint to cutesy Shirley Temple. Withers retired from acting in 1947 to raise a family. With her children grown, she made her fortune playing Josephine in TV commercials for 17 years.

3. **(E) Maria Mitchell.** On Oct 1, 1847, Mitchell discovered Comet 1847 VI. In 1850, she became the first woman elected to the American Academy of Arts and Sciences. The former librarian was named the first professor of astronomy at Vassar College.

4. **(D) Bill Mumy.** Bill Mumy played Will Robinson on "Lost in Space." In 1985, Mumy teamed up with fellow actor Miguel Ferrer to create "The Comet Man." Mumy has also written stories for a "Lost in Space" comic book. Mumy has not strayed far from science-fiction television, appearing as a regular on the TV series "Babylon 5."

5. **(D) Houston.** The seven other original teams in the league were the Los Angeles Sparks, Phoenix Mercury, Sacramento Monarchs, Utah Starzz, Charlotte Sting, Cleveland Rockers, and New York Liberty.

6. **(E) "The Naked Truth".** The outrageous ABC TV series that starred Tea Leoni as a photographer of the rich and notorious for the tabloid jumped to NBC in 1997 in a tamer version, moving Leoni to advice column work with George Wendt added to the show as her new boss.

7. **(D) Brisco County Jr.** Bruce Campbell starred as a Harvard-educated bounty hunter in this lighthearted western series that owed a lot to "The Wild Wild West." The series lasted only one year on FOX, but was rerun on TNT.

8. **(C) The Saddlemen.** Haley formed the Saddlemen in 1949 as a country group that added some rhythm and blues into their mix. In 1953, the Saddlemen changed to the Comets, and their first chart hit, "Crazy, Man, Crazy," hit #15 on the Billboard charts. It was the first rock and roll record ever on the chart. In 1955, Bill Haley and the Comets hit #1 with the rock anthem "Rock Around the Clock."

Quiz #99 — To the Last 2

1. Who hit the last home run at Ebbets Field prior to its demolition on February 23, 1960?
A. Roger Maris
B. Willie Mays
C. Duke Snider
D. Mickey Mantle
E. Jackie Robinson

2. What war's last day was May 31, 1902, ending with the Treaty of Vereeniging?
A. Hundred Years War
B. Punic War
C. Boxer Rebellion
D. Boer War
E. Sino-Japanese War

3. What was the last event held at the original Madison Square Garden?
A. Billy Graham revival meeting
B. Premiere of "The Misfits"
C. Mahalia Jackson concert
D. Muhammad Ali fight
E. Westminster Dog Show

4. Its first advertisements read, "Good looking, big and racy. Note the graceful and harmonious lines. Observe the sweep of the fenders and frame." The last one was made in 1957. Name this former luxury automobile.
A. Packard
B. Studebaker
C. Pierce-Arrow
D. Buick
E. Hudson

5. The last wild specimen of what bird was shot down on March 24, 1900 in Ohio?
A. Passenger pigeon
B. Dodo
C. Solitaire
D. Harpy eagle
E. Dusky sparrow

6. What was the last #1 record on the Billboard pop charts for the King of Rock 'n' Roll, Elvis Presley?
A. "Suspicious Minds"
B. "In the Ghetto"
C. "Promised Land"
D. "Don't Cry, Daddy"
E. "My Way"

7. What philosopher's last words were "It is enough"?
A. Immanuel Kant
B. Georg Wilhelm Hegel
C. Lao-Tse
D. Pierre Gassendi
E. Auguste Comte

8. What is the last letter of the Hawaiian alphabet?
A. U
B. W
C. X
D. Y
E. Z

Answers to Quiz #99 — To the Last 2

1. **(C) Duke Snider.** Snider hit a home run off of Phillies pitcher Robin Roberts on September 24, 1957. Two days later, the Brooklyn Dodgers played their final home game at Ebbets, beating the Pirates 2-0. Team owner Walter O'Malley moved the Dodgers to Los Angeles. Ebbets Field was torn down to make way for an apartment building.

2. **(D) Boer War.** The Boer War was a conflict between Dutch farmers who resided on the tip of South Africa and an influx of British settlers who discovered gold in the region in 1885. The British won the war largely due to their overwhelming number of forces.

3. **(E) Westminster Dog Show.** In 1959, businessman Irving Felt bought a majority of the Garden stock and announced he was creating a new facility. The original Garden was a big building, 200 feet wide and 375 feet long, and was most successful as a sports venue, especially for boxing matches. The last event was held on February 13, 1968.

4. **(E) Hudson.** The Hudson models were large showy cars. The Hudson "Super Six" model was a favorite of Prohibition-era gangsters because of its speed. In the 1950s, Americans began to turn away from large cars, and by 1957, the once-glorious Hudson was no more. American Motors president George Romney pointed out that a reduction of just 12 inches in 10,000 cars represented the elimination of two miles of bumper-to-bumper traffic.

5. **(A) Passenger pigeon.** As agriculture spread across the Midwest, the passenger pigeon became regarded as a nuisance. A single large flock could blot out the sun or strip a cornfield in hours. So with poison, with nets, and with guns, man exterminated them. The final living passenger pigeon, a female named Martha, died at the Cincinnati Zoo in 1914. She is preserved at the Smithsonian.

6. **(A) "Suspicious Minds".** Elvis had 17 #1 hits starting with "Heartbreak Hotel" in 1956, and ending with "Suspicious Minds" in 1969. In between, he sat at the top of the charts a total of 79 weeks, more than any other artist.

7. **(A) Immanuel Kant.** Kant was the author of "Critique of Pure Reason." His theory was that the mind was organized through experience, and not a blank slate simply accumulating data. He also attempted to put man and God on a level playing field describing morality in a scientific and ethical, rather than religious, context.

8. **(B) W.** The Hawaiian alphabet has only 12 letters: A E H I K L M N O P U W. Every Hawaiian word and syllable ends with a vowel. Two consonants never occur together without a vowel between them.

Quiz #100 — **Turn of the Century**

1. What literary children's character lived in the Hundred Acre Wood?
A. Winnie-the-Pooh
B. Curious George
C. Madeline
D. Little Red Riding Hood
E. Pippi Longstocking

2. What juvenile singing star played the female title character in the 1937 movie "100 Men and a Girl"?
A. Shirley Temple
B. Deanna Durbin
C. Jane Withers
D. Googie Withers
E. Judy Garland

3. Argus, a creature of Greek mythology with 100 eyes, some of which were always awake, was turned into what bird?
A. Swan
B. Owl
C. Peacock
D. Hummingbird
E. Raven

4. The Hundred Years' War was waged between what two nations?
A. Germany and France
B. Germany and Russia
C. Russia and China
D. England and France
E. England and the United States

5. Whose face appears on the $100 U.S. Savings Bond?
A. Abraham Lincoln
B. Thomas Jefferson
C. Benjamin Franklin
D. Salmon P. Chase
E. Andrew Jackson

6. Bach's "Jesu, Joy of Man's Desiring" was recorded as a 1972 hit pop instrumental called "Joy" by what studio band?
A. Apollo 100
B. Mercury 100
C. Zeus 100
D. Saturn 100
E. Pluto 100

7. As of the end of the 1998 season, what NFL running back had rushed for the most 100-yard games in his career?
A. James Brown
B. Walter Payton
C. O.J. Simpson
D. Barry Sanders
E. Franco Harris

8. What Academy Award-winning movie was advertised as "100% All Talking! 100% All Singing! 100% All Dancing!"?
A. "The Jazz Singer"
B. "An American in Paris"
C. "Singin' in the Rain"
D. "Gold Diggers of 1938"
E. "Broadway Melody"

Answers to Quiz #100 — **Turn of the Century**

1. **(A) Winnie-the-Pooh.** Winnie-the-Pooh originated in two children's books written by A.A. Milne in the late 1920s about his son, Christopher Robin. Younger generations are more familiar with the Disney version of Pooh which appeared in several short films, and a Saturday morning cartoon series. Those interested in purchasing Pooh merchandise will find items that bear the original illustrations by artist E.H. Shepard competing with the Disneyized items.

2. **(B) Deanna Durbin.** The 100 men in the title were not the U.S. Senate, but members of an orchestra led by Leopold Stokowski. The film score earned an Academy Award for Charles Previn. Deanna Durbin's popularity in this and other films meant big money for the impoverished Universal Studios.

3. **(C) Peacock.** Argus was charged by Hera to watch over Io, who was in the form of a cow. When Argus was slain by Hermes, Hera turned Argus into a peacock, placing his eyes in the bird's magnificent tail.

4. **(D) England and France.** The Hundred Years' War was a series of battles between 1337 and 1453 in which English kings attempted to wrest territory from France. In the end, England succeeded only in gaining Calais, and that was returned a century later.

5. **(B) Thomas Jefferson.** Ben Franklin appears on the $100 bill. Andrew Jackson appears on the $100 U.S. Treasury Bond.

6. **(A) Apollo 100.** The song peaked at #6 in January 1972, and was the only hit for the group. The follow-up "Mendelssohn's 4th (2nd Movement)" only reached #94.

7. **(B) Walter Payton.** Payton recorded 77 games in which he had 100 or more yards rushing, including a record-setting 275-yard game. All of these performances and many more contributed to Payton's career NFL record of 16,726 yards rushing.

8. **(E) "Broadway Melody".** "Broadway Melody" won the Best Picture Oscar for MGM in 1928-29. The movie was filled with songs that would become musical standards including "You Were Meant for Me" and the title song. The musical was also innovative for its time because it actually had a plot.

1. What Bob Hope film was a remake of the Damon Runyon classic story, "Little Miss Marker"?
A. "The Lemon Drop Kid"
B. "Candy Pants"
C. "The Princess and the Pirate"
D. "Sweet Talker"
E. "Bon Bon Voyage"

2. What NFL Hall of Fame running back had the nickname "Sweetness"?
A. Karl Sweetan
B. Walter Payton
C. Milt Plum
D. Larry Csonka
E. Jim Kiick

3. Who played ranch foreman Candy Canaday on the TV series "Bonanza" for seven of the series' 20 years?
A. Mitch Vogel
B. Tim Matheson
C. Ken Curtis
D. David Canary
E. Larkin Malloy

4. "The Chocolate War" is a classic, often banned, young adult novel written by what author?
A. Paul Zindel
B. Judy Blume
C. Robert Lipsyte
D. Elizabeth Patterson
E. Robert Cormier

5. Name the singer/songwriter son of a famous novelist whose critically acclaimed first albums were entitled "(Too Long in the) Wasteland" and "Candyland."
A. Jakob Dylan
B. Karl Vonnegut
C. J.B. Doctorow
D. James McMurtry
E. Tommy Lee King

6. Who played curvaceous girl singer Sugar Kane in the 1959 Billy Wilder film "Some Like It Hot"?
A. Jack Lemmon
B. Jayne Mansfield
C. Marilyn Monroe
D. Betty Grable
E. Tony Curtis

7. Known as the Jackie Robinson of basketball, who was the first black player signed by the NBA?
A. Mel "Sugar" Sanders
B. Nat "Sweetwater" Clifton
C. Willie "Sweet William" O'Ree
D. Taft "Taffee" Turner
E. Chuck "Candy" Martin

8. What musical group hit the top 10 on the Billboard pop charts with its first seven singles, starting with "Lost in Love" and "All Out of Love" in 1980, and ending with "Sweet Dreams" and "Even the Nights are Better" in 1982?
A. Air Supply
B. Eurthymics
C. Alabama
D. Aerosmith
E. The J. Geils Band

Answers to Quiz #101 — Sweet Success

1. **(A) "The Lemon Drop Kid".** "The Lemon Drop Kid" introduced the Livingston and Evans Christmas standard, "Silver Bells." The Runyon story was filmed under its original title in 1934 with Adolphe Menjou and Shirley Temple, and again in 1980 with Walter Matthau and Sara Stimson. Hope also starred in "Sorrowful Jones," another film based on the same story.

2. **(B) Walter Payton.** Payton was such a sweet runner that he set the NFL career rushing mark of 16,726 yards. Because of his small stature (5'9", 195 lbs.) and the suspect nature of his competition while playing for tiny Jackson State, Payton was considered something of a risk when drafted by the Chicago Bears.

3. **(D) David Canary.** Canary has achieved even greater success in recent years as an actor, winning an Emmy Award for his portrayal of twins Adam and Stuart Chandler on "All My Children." He also had a regular role on "Another World" and actually began his career as a cast member of the original prime time soap, "Peyton Place."

4. **(E) Robert Cormier.** Cormier's novel was made into a film starring John Glover, Jenny Wright, Adam Baldwin, and Bud Cort and was the directorial debut of actor Keith Gordon. It has also spawned several sequel novels by Cormier, including "Beyond the Chocolate War."

5. **(D) James McMurtry.** "Painting by Numbers," a top 100 hit for McMurtry, got a lot of FM air play from the "Wasteland" release. McMurtry's father, Larry, remains a bit more famous for his "Lonesome Dove" novels and "The Last Picture Show."

6. **(C) Marilyn Monroe.** Considered by many to be her quintessential role, Monroe played "jello on springs" driving Lemmon and Curtis to distraction while they had to remain in drag and feign disinterest.

7. **(B) Nat "Sweetwater" Clifton.** Although Chuck Cooper of the Boston Celtics was the first black player to be drafted by an NBA team, the New York Knicks signed "Sweetwater" Clifton away from the Harlem Globetrotters to steal the Celts' thunder when they opened the season a day earlier than Boston. Thus, Clifton became the first black NBA player. The Knicks' move turned out to be more than a publicity ploy as "Sweetwater" went on to outscore Cooper 5,444 to 2,725 over careers of similar length.

8. **(A) Air Supply.** In 1981, Air Supply also hit the top 10 with "Every Woman in the World," "The One That You Love" (their only #1 song), and "Here I Am." They returned to the top 10 in 1983 for the final time with "Making Love out of Nothing at All."

Quiz #102 — **Glamour Girls**

1. What singer once gave Marilyn Monroe a pet poodle named Mafia?
A. Frank Sinatra
B. Tom Jones
C. Sammy Davis Jr.
D. Dean Martin
E. Fabian

2. Raquel Welch made her first film appearance in a one-line, walk-on performance in what Elvis Presley movie?
A. "Clambake"
B. "Roustabout"
C. "Blue Hawaii"
D. "Kissin' Cousins"
E. "Love Me Tender"

3. What former pin-up was a recurring character in "The Rocketeer" comic books by Dave Stevens?
A. Bettie Page
B. Tempest Storm
C. Virginia Bell
D. Irish McCalla
E. Maria Whittaker

4. What model appeared on the debut cover of John F. Kennedy Jr.'s political magazine, "George"?
A. Elle Macpherson
B. Claudia Schiffer
C. Twiggy
D. Cindy Crawford
E. Anna Nicole Smith

5. What movie actress was discovered at the age of 18 by comedian George Burns?
A. Goldie Hawn
B. Diana Rigg
C. Ann-Margret
D. Demi Moore
E. Elke Sommer

6. In what prison movie did a prisoner ask for, and receive, Rita Hayworth in his prison cell?
A. "Brubaker"
B. "Cool Hand Luke"
C. "White Heat"
D. "Dog Day Afternoon"
E. "The Shawshank Redemption"

7. What Hollywood glamour girl used a bra especially designed for her by Howard Hughes?
A. Ava Gardner
B. Kim Novak
C. Stella Stevens
D. Elizabeth Taylor
E. Jane Russell

8. What Hollywood sex symbol had a 40-18-36 figure and a reported IQ of 160?
A. Tina Louise
B. Mae West
C. Jayne Mansfield
D. Ursula Andress
E. Gina Lollobrigida

Answers to Quiz #102 — **Glamour Girls**

1. (A) **Frank Sinatra.** Ol' Blue Eyes presented Marilyn with the poodle, which she called "Maf," to comfort her after she left her basset hound, Hugo, behind with her ex-husband, Arthur Miller.

2. (B) **"Roustabout".** The plotline of "Roustabout" has Presley as a carnival worker with romantic leanings toward older woman Barbara Stanwyck. Raquel can be seen in the first few minutes of the movie as one of two college girls who drive up to Mother's Tea House with their boyfriends. Her sole line is "Uh, how come they call this place a tea house, dear?"

3. (A) **Bettie Page.** Page, with her black Louise Brooks bangs, and little clothing, posed for cheesecake in dozen's of men's magazines like "Wink," "Eyeful," "Sunbathing," and "Playboy." At the peak of her fame in 1957, she abruptly retired. When "The Rocketeer" was made into a 1991 Disney movie, the character of Bettie was changed to that of a young, wholesome, up-and-coming actress played by Jennifer Connelly.

4. (D) **Cindy Crawford.** Crawford appeared on the 1995 debut issue dressed as George Washington. The next few covers of "George" featured Charles Barkley, Robert De Niro, Howard Stern, and Demi Moore in colonial garb.

5. (C) **Ann-Margret.** Ann-Margret had just left college and was part of a music group called the Subtle Tones. After auditioning for Burns, she and her act were signed as part of his 1960-61 Las Vegas revue act.

6. (E) **"The Shawshank Redemption".** "The Shawshank Redemption" was based on a short story by Stephen King called "Rita Hayworth and the Shawshank Redemption." After seeing the movie "Gilda" in prison, convict Tim Robbins asks go-to man Morgan Freeman to have Rita Hayworth delivered to him. Rita comes to Robbins in the form of a large poster which he hangs on his cell wall.

7. (E) **Jane Russell.** After seeing a picture of Jane Russell, Hughes offered her star billing in the poorly-received western film "The Outlaw." The buxom brunette was fitted in the movie with a special bra designed by Hughes that worked on a series of pulleys. Russell co-starred with fellow sex goddess Marilyn Monroe in the movies "Gentlemen Prefer Blondes" and "Gentlemen Marry Brunettes." Brassieres were good to Russell when later in her career she found a home on TV as the commercial spokeswoman for Playtex, bringing "great news for us full-figure gals."

8. (C) **Jayne Mansfield.** In spite of her high intelligence, Mansfield was typecast as a dizzy blonde. She was willing to joke about her figure, but often went so far as to appear to be mocking herself. She didn't seem to take her career as an actress seriously, so many in Hollywood didn't either. By the end of her career, she was working in nudie films like "Promises! Promises!" and trying out a seamy nightclub act.

Quiz #103 — Cry Wolf

1. Billy DeWolfe provided the voice of the evil magician trying to regain his hat from Frosty the Snowman in the annual CBS Christmas special. What was the magician's name?
A. Winter the Wizard
B. The Burgomaster Meisterburger
C. King Belgarian
D. Dr. Valentine
E. Professor Hinkle

2. Prior to playing "Walker, Texas Ranger" on TV, action star Chuck Norris played a Texas Ranger in what movie?
A. "Lone Wolf McQuade"
B. "Hour of the Wolf"
C. "Never Cry Wolf"
D. "Scream of the Wolf"
E. "The Lone Wolf Keeps a Date"

3. What 1980s rock group had hits with the songs "New Moon on Monday," "The Reflex," and "Hungry Like the Wolf"?
A. Huey Lewis and the News
B. Talking Heads
C. Duran Duran
D. A Flock of Seagulls
E. The Waitresses

4. What actor won a 1996 Grammy Award for Best Spoken Word Album for Children as the narrator of the recording "Prokofiev: Peter and the Wolf"?
A. Morgan Freeman
B. Jack Lemmon
C. Tom Hanks
D. Denzel Washington
E. Patrick Stewart

5. Which of the following writers is considered a leader in the style of writing known as New Journalism?
A. Virginia Woolf
B. Tom Wolfe
C. Wolf Blitzer
D. Peter Wolf
E. Nero Wolfe

6. What element is also known as wolfram?
A. Tungsten
B. Lead
C. Platinum
D. Uranium
E. Neon

7. Who was the police associate of fictional detective Michael Lanyard, better known as The Lone Wolf?
A. Inspector Cardinal
B. Inspector Crow
C. Inspector Chick
D. Inspector Crane
E. Inspector Canary

8. What award-winning author has written about his Vietnam War experiences in "In Pharaoh's Army" and about his childhood in "This Boy's Life"?
A. Geoffrey Wolff
B. Kurt H. Wolff
C. Michael Wolff
D. Robert Jay Wolff
E. Tobias Wolff

Answers to Quiz #103 — Cry Wolf

1. **(E) Professor Hinkle.** Actor Billy DeWolfe, born William Andrew Jones, was noted for his light supporting roles, using his fussy manner, slight lisp and toothy grin for comic effect. His clipped voice was perfect for the cackling Professor Hinkle who was "busy - busy - busy" pursuing Frosty in the 1971 CBS TV special.

2. **(A) "Lone Wolf McQuade".** As the title implies, Norris was more of a one-man army in "Lone Wolf McQuade" than the upbeat team player he portrays on "Walker, Texas Ranger." "Lone Wolf McQuade" marked the transition that turned Norris from a martial-arts star to a mainstream action picture attraction. "Walker, Texas Ranger" debuted in April 1993 and has become an anchor in CBS' Saturday night prime time lineup.

3. **(C) Duran Duran.** Duran Duran, a group of five musicians from Birmingham, England, were named after the villain in the movie "Barbarella." The lead singer was Simon LeBon, but the band contained three lads named Taylor — John, Andy, and Roger — none of whom were related. The band found popularity with its colorful, original videos airing on MTV in the 1980s.

4. **(E) Patrick Stewart.** Patrick Stewart is best recognized in a Starfleet uniform as Capt. Jean-Luc Picard of "Star Trek: The Next Generation." A former member of the Royal Shakespeare Company, Stewart also does a compelling, internationally acclaimed one-man rendition of Charles Dickens's "A Christmas Carol." Stewart has used his magnificent voice as a narrator for "Stargazers" on the Discovery Channel, as an animated character in "The Pagemaker," and in TV commercials for RCA and Porsche.

5. **(B) Tom Wolfe.** New Journalism uses fiction techniques, such as extensive dialogue, detailed descriptions of people and places, and shifting point of view, in nonfiction writing. Tom Wolfe's books carry such colorful titles as "The Kandy-Kolored Tangerine-Flake Streamline Baby," "The Electric Kool-Aid Acid Test," and "Mauve Gloves & Madmen, Clutter & Vine."

6. **(A) Tungsten.** The names tungsten and wolfram have been used interchangeably since the metal was first isolated in 1783. In British and American usage, tungsten is preferred; in Germany and other European nations, wolfram is preferred. On the periodic table, the element usually appears as tungsten, although it has the symbol W. The metal tungsten is used in steels to increase hardness and strength.

7. **(D) Inspector Crane.** The Lone Wolf is a reformed jewel thief who works as a detective among high society. First appearing in print in 1914, the Lone Wolf was played in a series of movies between 1939 and 1943 by Warren William. The Lone Wolf appeared on TV in 1955 played by Louis Hayward.

8. **(E) Tobias Wolff.** Wolff served in the Special Forces in Vietnam in 1964-67. His memoir, "In Pharaoh's Army," is the tale of a young man learning get to by one day at a time, maturing as a person in the middle of a war zone. "In Pharaoh's Army" was nominated for a 1994 National Book Award. Wolff's childhood memoir, "This Boy's Life," was made into a 1993 film starring Robert De Niro, Leonardo DiCaprio, and Ellen Barkin.

Quiz #104 — Check This Out

1. Chinese checkers is played on a board in the shape of a six-pointed star using marbles instead of traditional checkers. Each player begins the game with how many marbles?
A. 10
B. 12
C. 16
D. 24
E. 50

2. What kind of dog was Richard Nixon's beloved Checkers?
A. Welsh Corgi
B. Dalmatian
C. Labrador retriever
D. Basset hound
E. Cocker spaniel

3. What movie took its title from the signature tune of country singer Johnny Paycheck?
A. "Big Trouble in Little China"
B. "Even Cowgirls Get the Blues"
C. "Take This Job and Shove It"
D. "Back to the Future"
E. "Where the Sidewalk Ends"

4. Checkpoint Charlie was a passageway between the free world and the Communist world located in what European city?
A. Hanoi
B. Belgrade
C. Berlin
D. Moscow
E. Stockholm

5. Marla Gibbs starred in the short-lived sitcom, "Checking In," as Florence Johnston, the executive housekeeper at the St. Frederick Hotel. The series was a spinoff of what long-running sitcom on which Gibbs played the outspoken Florence?
A. "Cheers"
B. "Happy Days"
C. "The Jeffersons"
D. "The Mary Tyler Moore Show"
E. "The Andy Griffith Show"

6. According to the lyrics of Chubby Checker's hit "The Twist," which of his relatives really knows how to twist?
A. My Aunt Tish
B. My little sis
C. My favorite niece
D. My brother Mitch
E. My grandmama

7. Cyd Charisse made her dramatic TV debut, and Charles Laughton made his final TV appearance, in episodes of what 1960s detective series that starred Sebastian Cabot as a criminologist?
A. "Check It Out"
B. "Body Check"
C. "Blank Check"
D. "Checkmate"
E. "Cancelled Check"

8. What radio duo made a single foray into film with the weak 1930 comedy "Check and Double Check"?
A. Amos 'n' Andy
B. Stoopnagle and Budd
C. Fibber McGee and Molly
D. Edgar Bergen and Charlie McCarthy
E. Homer and Jethro

Answers to Quiz #104 — **Check This Out**

1. **(A) 10.** Chinese checkers was introduced in the United States in the 1930s. It is based on a checkers-type board game called Halma that was invented around 1880. The objective in both games is to move all your pieces from one side of the board to the other, jumping your own and opponents' pieces to move toward the goal.

2. **(E) Cocker spaniel.** In a 1952 speech on TV, Republican vice-presidential candidate Richard Nixon defended himself against corruption charges of having a secret $18,000 fund. In the speech, he said that he kept only one gift given to him — Checkers the dog who was adored by his children.

3. **(C) "Take This Job and Shove It".** Johnny Paycheck started his music career over 30 years ago as a backup singer for the legendary George Jones. His popularity as a country singer in the 1960s was countered by trouble with drug and alcohol abuse. Paycheck eventually wound up in prison for two years for shooting a man during a barroom brawl. "The Real Mr. Heartache," a collection of Paycheck tunes originally released in the '60s by Little Darlin' Records, has been reissued on CD. Paycheck appeared in the 1981 movie "Take This Job and Shove It" in a bit part as a fry cook.

4. **(C) Berlin.** When the Berlin Wall was erected on June 8, 1961, it blocked off one of the busier German thoroughfares. At this spot, behind guards, barbed wires, and land mines, was a gate through the wall called Checkpoint Charlie. With the destruction of the wall in 1989, Checkpoint Charlie disappeared. Checkpoint Charlie exists now as a thick line of red paint on the ground where it formerly stood.

5. **(C) "The Jeffersons".** "Checking In" lasted less than a month in 1981, while 'The Jeffersons" enjoyed a ten-year run between 1975 and 1985. Right on the tail of "The Jeffersons," Marla Gibbs moved into a starring role on the NBC sitcom "227" for another five years.

6. **(B) My little sis.** Chubby Checker was born Ernest Evans. He owes his professional name to Mrs. Dick Clark. Ernest was an admirer of Fats Domino, and being heavy himself, was nicknamed "Chubby." When Dick Clark's wife, Barbara, watched the teenage Evans performing in the studio, she said, "He looks like a little Fats Domino — like a chubby checker." The name stuck.

7. **(D) "Checkmate".** "Checkmate" co-starred Anthony George and Doug McClure as detectives hired to prevent crimes from happening. Sebastian Cabot found a more sedate role on TV as the portly gentleman's gentleman to Brian Keith, aka "Unca Bill," on "Family Affair."

8. **(A) Amos 'n' Andy.** The radio series featured white men Freeman Gosden and Charles Correll in the roles of stereotypical black characters Amos Jones and Andrew Brown. The title of the 1930 film came from one of the radio show's popular catchphrases. Unlike the 1950s TV series which employed black actors to play Amos 'n' Andy, the 1930 film featured Gosden and Correll performing in blackface.

Quiz #105 — **Flower Power**

1. What flower, which takes its name from the Greek for "gold flower," is a symbol of Japan's Imperial Family?
A. Chrysanthemum
B. Snapdragon
C. Magnolia
D. Begonia
E. Buttercup

2. In the comic strip, "Lil Abner," Abner's mom, Mammy Yokum, shares her first name with what kind of flower?
A. Pansy
B. Poppy
C. Rose
D. Aster
E. Dandelion

3. What flower takes its name from Latin for "little sword"?
A. Godetia
B. Columbine
C. Orchid
D. Filaree
E. Gladiolus

4. What flower was named after a mythological youth who was in love with his own image?
A. Iris
B. Narcissus
C. Celandine
D. Hawthorn
E. Camomile

5. Fictional detective Nero Wolfe has a hobby of growing what kind of flowers?
A. Hibiscus
B. Rose
C. Orchid
D. Daffodil
E. Lily

6. What showy flower, native to Mexico, was named after an 18th-century Swedish botanist?
A. Bougainvillea
B. Joepyeweed
C. Bellflower
D. Dahlia
E. Sunflower

7. What flower, native to Mexico, was named after the American politician and diplomat who brought the flower to the U.S.?
A. Bougainvillea
B. Zinnia
C. Marigold
D. Poinsettia
E. Forsythia

8. Which of the following flowering plants is not poisonous?
A. Poinsettia
B. Hyacinth
C. Lily of the valley
D. Foxglove
E. Star of Bethlehem

Answers to Quiz #105 — Flower Power

1. **(A) Chrysanthemum.** Chrysanthemums have been raised by the Japanese for thousands of years, and the Japanese chrysanthemum is the largest of the mum's varieties. The 16-petal mum is reserved in Japan as the official symbol of the Imperial Family.

2. **(A) Pansy.** Mammy Yokum was named Pansy Hunks until she married Pappy, aka Lucifer Ornamental Yokum.

3. **(E) Gladiolus.** The gladiolus, native to South Africa, has swordlike leaves and funnel-shaped flowers.

4. **(B) Narcissus.** Narcissus scorned the nymph Echo, who, pining over her unrequited love, wasted away to nothing but a voice. When Narcissus was cursed by one of his enemies, "May he who loves not others love himself," the goddess Nemesis caused Narcissus to fall in love with his own image in a pool of water. Narcissus pined away for his own image, staring into the water until he died. The nymphs Narcissus had scorned were kind to Narcissus after his death and sought to give his body a proper burial, but they could not find it. Instead, where he had lain, they found a new blooming flower which they named Narcissus.

5. **(C) Orchid.** Nero Wolfe, created by Rex Stout, owns over 10,000 orchids. The portly Wolfe stands 5'8" tall and weighs almost 300 pounds. He performs his detective work in a most unusual manner. Since he rarely leaves his home, he relies on verbatim reports from his assistant Archie Goodwin.

6. **(D) Dahlia.** The dahlia was named after Anders Dahl, a pupil of Linnaeus. The dahlia is capable of producing a sugar superior to either beet or cane sugar.

7. **(D) Poinsettia.** The flower was named after Joel Roberts Poinsett who later served as Franklin Van Buren's Secretary of War.

8. **(A) Poinsettia.** The poinsettia has had a bum rap since 1919 when an Army officer's two-year-old child died after allegedly eating a poinsettia leaf. Research has proven that the poinsettia is not poisonous, but nearly 66% of those participating in a 1995 Society of American Florists poll stated they still believed the popular Christmas flower was toxic. Eating the hyacinth bulb leads to nausea, vomiting, and diarrhea, and may be fatal. Eating lily of the valley can cause irregular heartbeat and pulse accompanied by upset stomach and mental confusion. Foxglove contains the drug digitalis which can cause dangerously irregular heartbeat and pulse, and may be fatal. Eating the Star of Bethlehem bulb can cause vomiting and nervous excitement.

Quiz #106 — **Alter Egos and Aliases**

1. Who called themselves Carte Blanche and Ann Orson as the writers of the #1 1976 duet "Don't Go Breaking My Heart"?
A. Mike Reno and Ann Wilson
B. Clint Black and Wynonna Judd
C. John Lennon and Yoko Ono
D. Paul and Linda McCartney
E. Elton John and Bernie Taupin

2. Miss White, Miss Black, and Jane were multiple personalities of the title character in what Academy Award-winning movie?
A. "Driving Miss Daisy"
B. "The Three Faces of Eve"
C. "Sybil"
D. "Gilda"
E. "Who's Afraid of Virginia Woolf?"

3. Who posed as a young lawyer named Balthasar in "The Merchant of Venice"?
A. Thalia
B. Juliet
C. Portia
D. Miranda
E. Ariel

4. Jay Garrick, Barry Allen, and Wally West were secret identities of various versions of what costumed comic book crimefighter?
A. The Flash
B. Superman
C. Iron Man
D. Captain America
E. Batman

5. What British novelist wrote magazine serials using the pseudonym "Boz" accompanied by illustrations by an artist who was known as "Phiz"?
A. Lewis Carroll
B. Victor Hugo
C. F. Scott Fitzgerald
D. Charlotte Bronte
E. Charles Dickens

6. What pianist used the pseudonym Walter Busterkeys when he worked in honky tonks?
A. Billy Joel
B. Neil Sedaka
C. Peter Nero
D. Van Cliburn
E. Liberace

7. What was the real name of the woman who became the beloved Dulcinea to a fever-ridden Don Quixote?
A. Eglantine
B. Electra
C. Aldonza
D. Welche
E. Octavia

8. What is the more familiar name of The Earl of Beaconsfield?
A. Parnell
B. Lenin
C. Adolf Hitler
D. Disraeli
E. Mussolini

Answers to Quiz #106 — **Alter Egos and Aliases**

1. **(E) Elton John and Bernie Taupin.** "Don't Go Breaking My Heart" was the first #1 song for Kiki Dee and the sixth for Elton John. It was the first record released on Elton John's Rocket label. Elton John performed the song on "The Muppet Show," trading in Kiki for Miss Piggy. At the end of his 1976 tour, Elton John announced his retirement, which, of course, was not permanent.

2. **(B) "The Three Faces of Eve".** Joanne Woodward won an Oscar for Best Actress playing the three distinct personalities contained in the body of one woman. Eve White was an insecure and emotionally disturbed housewife who transformed into Eve Black, a loose, hedonistic woman. With the help of a psychiatrist (played by Lee J. Cobb), the personalities eventually cancelled each other out to become a well-balanced woman who called herself Jane.

3. **(C) Portia.** Portia wished to aid her friend, Antonio, who is supposed to forfeit a pound of flesh to the merciless usurer, Shylock. Portia called on Bellario, a counsellor in law, who gave her the proper dress and advice on how to proceed as a lawyer. With a letter from Bellario presented to the court, Portia disguised herself as "Balthasar," a young attorney. In court, Portia granted Shylock permission to take his pound of flesh, but added that his bond did not permit him to take any of Antonio's blood, and to spill a drop while taking the flesh would cause Shylock to forfeit his lands and goods to the state of Venice.

4. **(A) The Flash.** The first Flash, Jay Garrick, debuted in 1940. Garrick, a science student, was separating the elements in hard water when he accidentally spilled some vials and was overcome by the fumes. The chemical exposure left him able to move at incredible speeds. Garrick donned a winged metallic helmet reminiscent of the god Mercury. Rather than wear a mask, Garrick was able to blur his face whenever in costume. In the 1960s, the Flash was revived as Barry Allen, a police lab scientist who was splashed with chemicals after lightning struck his lab, turning him into "The Fastest Man Alive." Allen's costume was a full red rubberized body suit. When Allen was killed, his nephew, Wally West, who in a billion-to-one accident was also bathed in chemicals after a lightning strike, took on the mantle. West originally ran side by side with his uncle using the moniker Kid Flash.

5. **(E) Charles Dickens.** While toying with the idea of a career in theater, Charles Dickens began contributing stories and essays to magazines. These writings were collected and reprinted as "Sketches by Boz." Dickens took the pen name from his younger brother's nickname. Shortly after "Sketches" was published in 1836, Dickens was invited to write a comic serial, "The Pickwick Papers." It was a sensational success. "The Pickwick Papers" was originally illustrated by Robert Seymour, but Seymour committed suicide before "Pickwick Papers" appeared in book form. The new illustrator, Hablot Knight Browne, used the pseudonym "Phiz" to harmonize with Dickens's "Boz." Browne went on to provide illustrations for "David Copperfield," "Martin Chuzzlewit," and "Bleak House."

6. **(E) Liberace.** Liberace was born in West Allis, WI, a suburb of Milwaukee. While in his teens, Liberace helped support his family by playing piano in a speakeasy using the alias Walter Busterkeys. Although trained at the Wisconsin College of Music, and performing with the Chicago Symphony at age 14, Liberace was irresistibly drawn to pop music. With his flamboyant appearance, decked out in furs and jewels, his ability to poke fun at himself, and his trademark candelabra, Liberace found popularity with audiences in Las Vegas.

7. **(C) Aldonza.** Miguel Cervantes's "Don Quixote" has been a popular musical subject. The final successful opera for composer Jules Massanet was "Don Quichotte," in 1910, with a libretto by Henri Cain based on Cervantes's "Don Quixote" and Jacques le Lorraine's "Le Chevalier de la Longue Figure." In 1965, Don Quixote made it to Broadway in "Man of La Mancha," starring the incomparable Richard Kiley as the chivalrous knight who introduced the standard "The Impossible Dream."

8. **(D) Disraeli.** Disraeli, a 19th-century British Prime Minister, accepted a peerage in 1876 to become leader of the House of Lords. Disraeli adopted Beaconsfield, a town northwest of London, as his earldom. Beaconsfield was also the home of 18th-century statesman Edmund Burke.

Quiz #107 — Salt Shaker

1. Salt Lake City is the only U.S. state capital with three words in its name. How many U.S. state capitals have two-word names?
A. 6
B. 7
C. 8
D. 9
E. 10

2. What fictional animal, and Disney film star, was created by children's book author Felix Salten?
A. Dumbo
B. Rascal
C. Peter Rabbit
D. Bambi
E. Winnie-the-Pooh

3. The world's highest waterfall is known as Salten Churun Meru in its native country. By what name is it better known to the rest of the world?
A. Horseshoe Falls
B. Angel Falls
C. Niagara Falls
D. Frostbite Falls
E. Raindrop Falls

4. The working title of the Beatles' movie "Help!" shares what name with the second album from the Chicago-based rock group Veruca Salt?
A. "That Boy"
B. "Oh You Kid"
C. "Eight Arms to Hold You"
D. "I Wanna Hold Your Hand"
E. "Give Me a Ring"

5. The worst Indianapolis 500 for recorded fatalities opened with a crash by driver Salt Walther that left Walther badly burned, burned 11 spectators, and wrecked 11 other cars. The same year driver Art Pollard was killed in a crash during practice. During the race, driver Swede Savage crashed, dying later in a hospital. Rushing out to Savage's rescue, one of his crew was hit and killed by a fire truck speeding to the crash. In what year did this disastrous race take place?
A. 1973
B. 1974
C. 1977
D. 1981
E. 1991

6. "A World the Color of Salt" was a highly acclaimed debut novel introducing Smokey Brandon, a forensic pathologist. Name the author who also featured Smokey in the novels "Carcass Trade" and "*".
A. Janet Evanovich
B. Linda Barnes
C. Patricia Cornwell
D. Noreen Ayres
E. Faye Kellerman

7. In what U.S. state would you find the Bonneville Salt Flats?
A. Michigan
B. Washington
C. California
D. Florida
E. Utah

8. Which U.S. President signed the original SALT treaty with the USSR in an effort to curtail the manufacture of nuclear weapons?
A. Richard Nixon
B. Lyndon Johnson
C. John Kennedy
D. Bill Clinton
E. Ronald Reagan

Answers to Quiz #107 — Salt Shaker

1. **(C) 8.** They are Baton Rouge, LA; Carson City, NV; Des Moines, IA; Jefferson City, MO; Little Rock, AK; Oklahoma City, OK; St. Paul, MN; and Santa Fe, NM.

2. **(D) Bambi.** In creating the animated version of "Bambi," Disney made some changes to Salten's story. He dropped the character of Gobo, and added the skunk Flower and the terrifying forest fire scene. Salten wrote a sequel to "Bambi" called "Bambi's Children."

3. **(B) Angel Falls.** Angel Falls is located in the Guiana Highlands of Venezuela. The waterfall drops 3,212 feet and is 500 feet wide at the base. The heavenly name of the falls comes not from its origin being high in the clouds, but from American pilot Jimmy Angel who crash-landed his plane in the jungle discovering the falls.

4. **(C) "Eight Arms to Hold You".** Veruca Salt is noted for having two women on lead vocals and guitar — Nina Gordon and Louise Post. The band's 1994 debut album, "American Thighs," contained fluffy melodies while the new album goes back to heavy metal roots with the aid of Metallica's producer Bob Rock.

5. **(A) 1973.** David "Salt" Walther holds the Indy record for finishing in last place the most times — three — in 1972, 1973 and 1975. Walther later switched to racing hydrofoils.

6. **(D) Noreen Ayres.** Ayres has been praised for the fair, straightforward, and yet entirely feminine portrayal of her main character, who is tough but not in the Chandleresque manner to which many other female detective writers have resorted. Smokey was a former police officer and before that an exotic dancer, the job where she acquired her nickname.

7. **(E) Utah.** The Bonneville Salt Flats in northwestern Utah is the site of the Bonneville Speedway. The impacted ground is extremely level, conducive to speed trials. Several automobile and motorcycle speed and endurance records have been set there.

8. **(A) Richard Nixon.** The Strategic Arms Limitation Talks (SALT) were first suggested by Lyndon B. Johnson in 1967. In 1972, an agreement known as SALT I was signed by Richard Nixon and Leonid Brezhnev. The Salt II negotiations took another seven years to develop the second treaty, signed this time by Jimmy Carter and Brezhnev in 1979. Continuing discussions have been renamed START, for Strategic Arms Reduction Talks.

Quiz #108 — Lunarcy

1. Keith Moon was the legendary free spirit who served as the long-time drummer for what innovative and enduring rock group?
A. The Kinks
B. The Who
C. The Sex Pistols
D. The Rolling Stones
E. The Spencer Davis Group

2. On what TV series would you have found the Blue Moon Detective Agency?
A. "Miami Vice"
B. "Riptide"
C. "The Big Town"
D. "The Detectives"
E. "Moonlighting"

3. What infamous rock and roll iconoclast had children named Moon Unit and Dweezil?
A. Kurt Cobain
B. Tiny Tim
C. Frank Zappa
D. Sigmund Snopek III
E. Alice Cooper

4. What former Athletics pitcher, nicknamed "Blue Moon," was one of the few pitchers sorry to see the institution of the designated hitter rule as he consistently hit over .250 and once hit 5 home runs in a season?
A. Johnny Lee Odom
B. Diego Segui
C. Vida Blue
D. Glenn Abbott
E. Claude Osteen

5. What Hollywood legend played "Moonlight" Graham, the one-game wonder who never realized his dream of batting in a major league game, in the movie "Field of Dreams"?
A. Burt Lancaster
B. Kirk Douglas
C. Wilford Brimley
D. Charlton Heston
E. Don Ameche

6. Writing under one of his given names, William Trogdon was having little success until he broke out with what best-selling travel commentary book, written under the name William Least Heat Moon?
A. "Desert Solitaire"
B. "A Fool's Progress"
C. "Nebraska"
D. "Blue Highways"
E. "Walking the Dead Diamond River"

7. In what movie did Audrey Hepburn sing the Henry Mancini-Johnny Mercer tune "Moon River"?
A. "Breakfast at Tiffany's"
B. "Funny Face"
C. "Lili"
D. "Gigi"
E. "Roman Holiday"

8. What nation's flag features blue, orange, and green horizontal bars superimposed over a crescent moon and an eight-pointed star?
A. Iran
B. Iraq
C. Afghanistan
D. Ukraine
E. Azerbaijan

Answers to Quiz #108 — **Lunarcy**

1. **(B) The Who.** Moon died of a drug overdose in 1978 and was replaced by Kenny Jones. Moon had also begun a fledgling film career and garnered good reviews for his portrayal of "Uncle Ernie" in Ken Russell's cinematic version of the Who's rock opera, "Tommy."

2. **(E) "Moonlighting".** Run by Maddie Hayes (Cybill Shepherd) and her wisecracking employee, David Addison (Bruce Willis), Blue Moon became more an excuse for Maddie and David's romantic love-hate sparring every week than a serious detective outfit. There was much off-screen battling, too, between the show's stars and producer Glenn Gordon Caron, resulting in constant production delays. "Moonlighting" was featured in ABC's Tuesday night line-up from 1985-89.

3. **(C) Frank Zappa.** Once the leader of the legendary Mothers of Invention, Zappa had a solo career marked by disagreements with record companies and a lack of mainstream success. His only top 40 hit was the novelty record "Valley Girl" which featured his daughter, Moon Unit. Both Moon Unit and Dweezil have attempted acting and musical careers. They appeared together in the TV series "Normal Life." Moon was also a regular on the TV series "Fast Times." Dweezil provided the voice of Ajax for the animated series "Duckman."

4. **(A) Johnny Lee Odom.** Odom was overshadowed by stablemates Catfish Hunter, Vida Blue, and Ken Holtzman, but he was instrumental in the A's getting to and winning the World Series in 1972, '73, and '74 as he posted a career record of 2-0 with 0.40 ERA in championship game series, and a 2.08 ERA in World Series play.

5. **(A) Burt Lancaster.** The 1989 film is Lancaster's last theatrical release to date. Lancaster, known for his athletic prowess since his earliest days as a circus acrobat, has also played such sports figures as Jim Thorpe in "Jim Thorpe, All American," boxer Pete Lund in "The Killers," trapeze artist Mike Ribble in "Trapeze," and skydiver Mike Rettig in "The Gypsy Moths."

6. **(D) "Blue Highways".** Least Heat Moon followed this success with another tome about Middle West entitled "PrairyErth."

7. **(A) "Breakfast at Tiffany's".** "Moon River" won the Academy Award for Best Song in 1961. The triumphant Johnny Mercer accepted his Oscar declaring "Martinis for everybody!" The song is often associated with Andy Williams, who sang it at the Oscars show, but it was a top 20 hit for singer Jerry Butler and as an instrumental for Henry Mancini.

8. **(E) Azerbaijan.** Azerbaijan declared independence from the Soviet Union with the collapse of the USSR in 1991.

1. Cilla Black was a popular singer in the U.K. as a member of Brian Epstein's clientele. What was her only top 40 hit in the United States?
A. "Anyone Who Had a Heart"
B. "Only Sixteen"
C. "You're My World"
D. "Gypsies, Tramps and Thieves"
E. "Downtown"

2. Metallis, The Creature King, Zorak, and The Black Widow were members of the rogues' gallery that fought with what cartoon superhero?
A. Hong Kong Phooey
B. Space Ghost
C. Superman
D. Aquaman
E. Atom Ant

3. What was the name of movie cowboy Allan "Rocky" Lane's horse?
A. Black Beauty
B. Black Oak
C. Black Sabbath
D. Blackjack
E. Blackwell

4. Who was the first black pitcher to win a World Series game?
A. Joe Black
B. Ewell Blackwell
C. Jim Blackburn
D. Don Black
E. Lena Blackburne

5. What is the more familiar name of the painting titled "Arrangement in Grey and Black, Number One"?
A. "Mona Lisa"
B. "American Gothic"
C. "Whistler's Mother"
D. "Pop Musik"
E. "The Scream"

6. What was the name of the evil half-brother attempting to usurp the throne of Ruritania in "The Prisoner of Zenda"?
A. The Black Swan
B. Black Michael
C. The Black Rose
D. Blackbeard
E. Black Jack Shellac

7. What band hit the top 40 with remakes of "Crimson and Clover" in 1982 and "Everyday People" in 1983?
A. Joan Jett and the Blackhearts
B. Black Oak Arkansas
C. Black Sabbath
D. The Black Crowes
E. Blackfoot

8. Country singer Clint Black is married to what popular TV actress?
A. Heather Menzies
B. Elizabeth McGovern
C. Demi Moore
D. Faye Dunaway
E. Lisa Hartman

Answers to Quiz #109 — In the Black

1. **(C) "You're My World".** Cilla Black, born Priscilla White in 1943, was signed to a contract with EMI after she was seen by George Martin while he was checking out Gerry and the Pacemakers in Liverpool. Her cover version of the Dionne Warwick hit "Anyone Who Had a Heart" topped the U.K. charts for four weeks in 1964, becoming one of the all-time best-selling singles in the U.K. by a female singer. It failed to make a dent in the Billboard top 40 in the U.S. She had several other top 10 hits in the U.K., including "You've Lost That Lovin' Feeling," "Love's Just a Broken Heart," "Alfie" and "Don't Answer Me." "You're My World," a #1 song in the U.K., was her only American hit, peaking at #26 in 1964.

2. **(B) Space Ghost.** On 1960s TV, Space Ghost was a black-hooded space policeman who patrolled the galaxy with twin teenage wards named Jan and Jace, and their pet monkey, Blip. Space Ghost derived his powers from "power bands" which he wore on his wrists. The bands were capable of producing various rays or force fields. The voice of Space Ghost was provided by former "Laugh-In" regular Gary Owens. More recently, Space Ghost has been the host of a talk show on the Cartoon Network.

3. **(D) Blackjack.** Allan "Rocky" Lane starred in three western serials for Republic Pictures in the 1940s. In 1946, he made the first of seven popular films starring as Red Ryder. In 1947, he began a series of 32 films for Republic that featured Lane with his majestic stallion, Blackjack, and a sidekick named Nugget Clark. The series made Lane a top 10 cowboy star. After his final film appearance, Lane reappeared on TV, in a way. He supplied the voice for TV's talking palomino, Mr. Ed.

4. **(A) Joe Black.** Joe Black won the first game of the 1952 World Series for the Brooklyn Dodgers. The first black player in any World Series game was Jackie Robinson, also for the Brooklyn Dodgers, in 1947. The first black pitcher in a World Series game was Satchel Paige for the Cleveland Indians in 1948.

5. **(C) "Whistler's Mother".** In 1934, the U.S. Postal Service reproduced "Whistler's Mother" on a postage stamp, but added a flowerpot to the left-hand corner of the otherwise empty composition.

6. **(B) Black Michael.** "The Prisoner of Zenda" was written by Anthony Hope in 1894. Black Michael, the illegitimate son of the dying king, makes plans to seize the throne of Ruritania from his weak-willed half-brother, Rudolf. When Rudolf is too drunk to appear for the coronation, he is replaced by a look-alike named Rudolf Rassendyll. Faithful friends hide the real Rudolf while Rassendyll fills in. But soon the real Rudolf is missing — the work of Black Michael, who now plans to do in both Rudolfs.

7. **(A) Joan Jett and the Blackhearts.** "Crimson and Clover" peaked at #7 in 1982, while "Everyday People" crept up to #37 in 1983. The band's biggest hit was the rock anthem "I Love Rock 'n' Roll" which spent seven weeks in the #1 spot in 1982.

8. **(E) Lisa Hartman.** Clint Black and Lisa Hartman Black were married in Houston on October 20, 1991.

Quiz #110 — **The One and Only**

1. Audience members chimed in with announcer George Fenneman when he introduced what quiz show host as "The one! The only!"
A. Groucho Marx
B. Bill Cosby
C. Woody Allen
D. Johnny Carson
E. Ed MacMahon

2. What was the only movie to win the Best Director Oscar while having two directors?
A. "The Alamo"
B. "West Side Story"
C. "An American in Paris"
D. "Jurassic Park"
E. "Blood Simple"

3. Who was the only football player to win the Most Valuable Player Award in the Super Bowl while playing for the losing side?
A. Alan Page
B. Joe Namath
C. Len Dawson
D. Dan Marino
E. Chuck Howley

4. What is the only crime specifically defined in the Constitution of the United States?
A. Murder
B. Adultery
C. Treason
D. Heresy
E. Polygamy

5. Who was the only female athlete allowed to forgo the sex test during the 1976 Summer Olympic Games?
A. Mary Lou Retton
B. Princess Stephanie of Monaco
C. Kristin Otto
D. Steffi Graf
E. Princess Anne of Great Britain

6. Who was the only performer to appear on "American Bandstand" performing live instead of lip-synching?
A. Chubby Checker
B. B.B. King
C. Roy Orbison
D. Johnny Cash
E. Elvis Presley

7. Who is the only person to appear on the cover of "TV Guide" for three consecutive weeks?
A. Lucille Ball
B. Dick Clark
C. Tom Selleck
D. Michael Landon
E. Oprah Winfrey

8. What actress played the only character to be killed in an episode of the campy 1960s TV series "Batman"?
A. Lesley Gore
B. Eva Gabor
C. Anne Baxter
D. Tallulah Bankhead
E. Jill St. John

Answers to Quiz #110 — **The One and Only**

1. **(A) Groucho Marx.** Groucho Marx hosted "You Bet Your Life" from 1950-1961 with sidekick George Fenneman. Ostensibly a quiz show, it was played as much for laughs as Groucho interviewed the contestants prior to the quiz portion of the show. Updated versions of "You Bet Your Life" hosted by Buddy Hackett and Bill Cosby did not fare very well.

2. **(B) "West Side Story".** "West Side Story" was directed by Robert Wise and Jerome Robbins who won dual Best Director Oscars in 1961.

3. **(E) Chuck Howley.** Howley played linebacker for the Dallas Cowboys who lost to the Baltimore Colts in the last seconds of Super Bowl V, 16-13, in 1971. Howley, also the first defensive player to win the MVP Award, picked off two passes.

4. **(C) Treason.** Article III, Section 3 of the U.S. Constitution defines the crime of treason giving the Congress the "Power to declare the Punishment of Treason."

5. **(E) Princess Anne of Great Britain.** Princess Anne participated in the equestrian events. Stella Walsh, who won the women's 100-meter dash in 1932, was later revealed to be male. Dora Ratjen, who finished fourth in the women's high jump in 1936, was barred from competition after it was discovered she was a hermaphrodite, a sexual definition for which athletic competition had not made provisions.

6. **(B) B.B. King.** Lip-synching was a standard practice for convenience sake when "American Bandstand" was a regional show out of Philadelphia, and continued when the show began broadcasting nationally.

7. **(D) Michael Landon.** Memorial issues of "TV Guide" dedicated to Landon on July 13, 1991 and July 20, 1991 were followed by the 2000th issue of the magazine. Among the "TV Guide" covers reproduced on the July 27, 1991 cover was one featuring Michael Landon from "Little House on the Prairie." He had also appeared on the cover just a few weeks earlier on June 8, 1991. Landon also holds the distinction of being the only male actor with three consecutive hit TV series running five seasons or longer each — "Bonanza," "Little House on the Prairie," and "Highway to Heaven."

8. **(E) Jill St. John.** Jill St. John played Molly, an associate of the Riddler, in the show's first dual episodes. While disguised as Robin, she made her way into the Batcave. When her ruse was easily uncovered by Batman, she fell into the Batcave's atomic pile while trying to escape and was vaporized.

Quiz #111 — **Numbers Game**

1. On what track will you find the title train in the song "Chattanooga Choo-Choo"?
A. 8
B. 29
C. 80
D. 94
E. 102

2. How many consecutive strikes are thrown for a perfect 300 game in bowling?
A. 10
B. 11
C. 12
D. 15
E. 20

3. How many #1 songs did Elvis Presley have on the Billboard pop single charts?
A. 10
B. 11
C. 13
D. 18
E. 20

4. How many different colors are found on "premium" squares on a Scrabble board?
A. 4
B. 5
C. 6
D. 10
E. 12

5. How many American battleships were sunk or crippled in the Japanese attack on Pearl Harbor in 1941?
A. 6
B. 7
C. 8
D. 9
E. 10

6. John Tyler had more children than any other U.S. President. How many children did he father?
A. 5
B. 11
C. 12
D. 15
E. 16

7. To block your name and number from appearing on telephones with caller ID in the United States, what four digits should you dial from an Ameritech rotary telephone?
A. 1166
B. 1167
C. 1169
D. 1160
E. 1170

8. If you added up all the numbers appearing in the titles of Academy Award-winning Best Pictures, what would be the total?
A. 1
B. 3
C. 4
D. 12
E. 84

1. **(B) 29.** Written by Mack Gordon and Harry Warren, "Chattanooga Choo-Choo" was a hit song for Glenn Miller & His Orchestra.

2. **(C) 12.** The first gold medal awarded for a perfect game by the American Bowling Congress was to A.C. Jellison in 1909. Pro bowler Bob Learn Jr. has bowled more than 50 perfect games in his career.

3. **(D) 18.** Elvis's first #1 hit was "Heartbreak Hotel" in 1956. His 18th and final #1 single was "Suspicious Minds" in 1969. Only the Beatles have had more #1 singles.

4. **(A) 4.** The colors are pink (double word score), light blue (double letter score), dark blue (triple letter score), and red (triple word score).

5. **(A) 6.** The USS Arizona, USS Utah and USS Oklahoma were sunk. The USS California, USS Nevada, and USS West Virginia were severely damaged.

6. **(D) 15.** Tyler was married twice. He had three boys and five girls with his first wife, and five boys and two girls with his second wife. He fathered the last of his children at age 70.

7. **(B) 1167.** 1160 allows you to block receipt of calls from designated numbers. 1166 is a repeat dial service for reaching numbers with busy signals. 1169 allows automatic callback of the last call received. 1170 cancels call waiting. On push-button phones, "✱" is used in place of the initial "11" digits, e.g., ✱66 is equivalent to 1166.

8. **(E) 84.** The four pertinent titles are: "It Happened One Night" (1934), "Around the World in 80 Days" (1956), "The Godfather, Part II" (1974), and "One Flew Over the Cuckoo's Nest" (1975).

Quiz #112 — Dolled Up

1. When "Hello Dolly" debuted on Broadway in January 1964, who had the lead role in the musical?
A. Rosalind Russell
B. Ethel Merman
C. Barbra Streisand
D. Carol Channing
E. Angela Lansbury

2. In 1977, Xavier Roberts formed a company to create dolls where the employees wore hospital gowns while working since their dolls were "born" instead of manufactured. What did he call these dolls?
A. Zaadi Dolls
B. Boo Babies
C. Beanie Babies
D. Small Fry
E. Cabbage Patch Kids

3. What is the name of the demonic doll featured in the "Child's Play" series of films?
A. Chucky
B. Michael
C. Fats
D. Elvis
E. Myron

4. What lanky actress played a beautiful female robot named Rhoda Miller on the 1960s TV series "My Living Doll"?
A. Juliet Prowse
B. Gwen Verdon
C. Lucille Ball
D. Julie Newmar
E. Geena Davis

5. What is the traditional Japanese puppet theater in which life-size dolls act out a dramatic story accompanied by music from the Japanese samisen?
A. Joruri
B. Mandeville
C. Asahi
D. Bunraku
E. Chikamatsu

6. Four versions of what song hit the pop charts in 1957, with the most successful version reaching #1 as the debut of Buddy Knox and the Rhythm Orchids?
A. "Rag Doll"
B. "Guys and Dolls"
C. "She's a Living Doll"
D. "Don't Call Her Dolly"
E. "Party Doll"

7. What film critic has not reviewed the films of Russ Meyer since he co-authored the screenplay for the 1970 Meyer movie "Beyond the Valley of the Dolls"?
A. Gene Siskel
B. Roger Ebert
C. Gene Shalit
D. Joe Bob Briggs
E. Michael Medved

8. What U.S. President was portrayed by Burgess Meredith in the 1946 movie "Magnificent Doll"?
A. George Washington
B. Abraham Lincoln
C. Ulysses S. Grant
D. John Quincy Adams
E. James Madison

1. **(D) Carol Channing.** Also present in the cast were David Burns, Eileen Brennan, and Charles Nelson Reilly. At the end of its first season, "Hello Dolly" won an astounding 10 Tony Awards, including Best Female Lead in a Musical for Channing. In August 1965, Channing was succeeded in the role by Ginger Rogers. The musical ran for 2,844 performances.

2. **(E) Cabbage Patch Kids.** The dolls were "adopted" by their new owners, complete with proper papers. The names given to the Cabbage Patch Kids came from a 1938 birth register. Coleco Industries, who obtained the rights to make the dolls from Roberts, found themselves the wrathful target of many parents' anger when supply could not keep up with Christmas demand. After the fad ended, Coleco went out of business.

3. **(A) Chucky.** The devil doll is possessed by the spirit of a murderer with the voice of actor Brad Dourif. Chucky has managed to revive for three sequels so far.

4. **(D) Julie Newmar.** Julie Newmar is best remembered as Catwoman on "Batman." Newmar's co-star on "My Living Doll" was Bob Cummings until he quit after 21 episodes and his character was sent packing to Pakistan. The series lasted only one season, 1964-65, on CBS.

5. **(D) Bunraku.** The term bunraku is derived from the name of a 19th-century Japanese puppet troupe organized by puppet master Uemura Bunrakuken. The Bunraku Kyokai performs traditional bunraku in a theater in Osaka.

6. **(E) "Party Doll".** Wingy Manone and Roy Brown charted in the bottom half of Billboard's Hot 100. Steve Lawrence made it up to #5. As the co-writer of "Party Doll," Knox was the first rock artist to write his own #1 song.

7. **(B) Roger Ebert.** The plot of the film centered around an all-girl rock group called the Carrie Nations. The music for the movie was provided by the Strawberry Alarm Clock, who also appeared in the film.

8. **(E) James Madison.** Ginger Rogers played Dolley Madison who, in this film, had an affair with Aaron Burr, played by David Niven.

Quiz #113 — 1967

1. Reese Tatum, a lead player of the Harlem Globetrotters, died in 1967 at the age of 45. What was Tatum's avian nickname?
A. Swan
B. Robin
C. Goose
D. Meadowlark
E. Cardinal

2. What father-daughter duo had a 1967 hit song with "Somethin' Stupid"?
A. Frank and Nancy Sinatra
B. Neil and Dara Sedaka
C. Pat and Debby Boone
D. John and Bonnie Raitt
E. Nat King and Natalie Cole

3. Who scored the first touchdown in Super Bowl history for the Green Bay Packers in 1967?
A. Max McGee
B. Carroll Dale
C. Bart Starr
D. Forrest Gregg
E. Vince Lombardi

4. Norman Mailer won a Pulitzer Prize for what narrative about the 1967 Peace March in Washington, D.C.?
A. "Knife in the Water"
B. "Armies of the Night"
C. "The Executioner's Song"
D. "The Winds of War"
E. "Fire in the Lake"

5. In 1967, the U.S. launched several spacecraft in what series to study the lunar surface?
A. Surveyor
B. Stockholm
C. Ranger
D. Apollo
E. Von Braun

6. What U.S. ship was attacked by Israeli planes and torpedos near the Sinai Peninsula on June 8, 1967?
A. Maine
B. Pueblo
C. America
D. Saratoga
E. Liberty

7. What Cincinnati Reds player won the 1967 All-Star Game for the National League with a 15th-inning home run?
A. Pete Rose
B. Johnny Bench
C. Ron Cey
D. Tony Perez
E. Cesar Cedena

8. What film won the 1967 Best Picture Awards from the New York Film Critics Circle Awards, the Golden Globes, and the Academy Awards?
A. "The Graduate"
B. "In the Heat of the Night"
C. "Paint Your Wagon"
D. "Bonnie and Clyde"
E. "The Hustler"

Answers To Quiz #113 — 1967

1. **(C) Goose.** The Harlem Globetrotters were originally formed as a serious basketball team, winning the World Professional Tournament in 1940 against the Chicago Bruins. It was the signing of "Goose" Tatum as "the clown prince of basketball" and the creative ballhandling of Marques Haynes that started the gradual shift from purely competitive basketball to the novel entertainment spectacle that is Globetrotter basketball. Tatum and Haynes were succeeded by Meadowlark Lemon and Curly Neal.

2. **(A) Frank and Nancy Sinatra.** "Somethin' Stupid" is the only father-daughter single to reach #1 on the Billboard pop charts. Frank and Nancy also had individual singles reach #1 — "Strangers in the Night" for Frank, and "These Boots Are Made for Walkin'" for Nancy. The only other father-daughter team with individual #1 songs is Pat and Debby Boone, with "Moody River" for Pat and "You Light Up My Life" for Debby.

3. **(A) Max McGee.** McGee scored on a 37-yard touchdown pass from Bart Starr to lead the Packers to a 35-10 victory over the Kansas City Chiefs. McGee, who expected to be warming the bench throughout the game, had snuck out of his room after curfew and stayed out the entire night before the game. When Boyd Dowler got hurt, Vince Lombardi surprised the exhausted McGee by putting him into the game. McGee had his finest hour, catching seven passes and scoring two touchdowns.

4. **(B) "Armies of the Night".** The antiwar march held Oct 21-22, 1967, protesting the U.S. involvement in Vietnam, drew more than 50,000 participants, including Mailer. Some marchers were arrested in a clash with police and troops outside the Pentagon. Mailer won a second Pulitzer Prize in 1980 for "The Executioner's Song," his tale of murderer Gary Gilmore.

5. **(A) Surveyor.** Surveyor 3 was launched on April 17. Surveyor 4 was launched on July 4, but lost contact with NASA just before making lunar contact. Surveyor 5 was launched on September 8. Surveyor 6 was launched on November 5. After recording data and taking pictures, Surveyor 6 lifted off the moon's surface and landed a few feet away to photograph its own original landing site. It was the first spacecraft to lift off from the moon.

6. **(E) Liberty.** The USS Liberty, a communications ship, was in international waters at the time of the attack. Thirty-four seamen were killed and 171 were wounded. Israel later apologized for the accidental attack, saying they had mistaken the ship for an Egyptian freighter in the heat of the Six Day War. The apology was accepted, but the reasons for the attack continued to be debated.

7. **(D) Tony Perez.** Perez was named MVP for the 1967 All-Star Game. Perez was also a member of the "Wheeze Kids," the 1983 Philadelphia Phillies that won the National League pennant with Joe Morgan, Pete Rose, and Perez all over the age of 40.

8. **(B) "In the Heat of the Night".** "In the Heat of the Night" also earned a Best Actor Oscar for Rod Steiger, and a Best Screenplay Based on Material from Another Medium for Sterling Silliphant.

Quiz #114 — **The Cat's Meow**

1. Which album by Cat Stevens features a picture of a trash can on the cover?
A. "Mona Bone Jakon"
B. "Tea for the Tillerman"
C. "Three"
D. "Buddha and the Chocolate Box"
E. "Cat Stevens' Greatest Hits"

2. Who starred on TV as the cat burglar "T.H.E. Cat"?
A. Robert Wagner
B. Ralph Taeger
C. Max Von Sydow
D. Lee Van Cleef
E. Robert Loggia

3. Who played the dual roles of Kid Sheleen and Tim Strawn in the comedy-western "Cat Ballou"?
A. Charles Nelson Reilly
B. Clint Eastwood
C. Eli Wallach
D. Elliott Gould
E. Lee Marvin

4. What comic strip cat is owned by the Nutmeg family?
A. Garfield
B. Heathcliff
C. Fritz the Cat
D. Top Cat
E. Felix the Cat

5. What breed of cat was kept as a White House pet by Presidents Rutherford B. Hayes and Jimmy Carter?
A. Siamese
B. Angora
C. Tabby
D. Manx
E. Persian

6. What baseball pitcher, nicknamed "The Cat," won three games in the 1946 World Series for the St. Louis Cardinals?
A. Jim Kaat
B. Harvey Haddix
C. Harry Brecheen
D. Andres Galarraga
E. Christy Mathewson

7. What mystery author wrote "The Cat Who Knew a Cardinal," "The Cat Who Moved a Mountain," "The Cat Who Talked to Ghosts," and "The Cat Who Saw Red"?
A. Ellery Queen
B. Peter Straub
C. Michael Bond
D. Lilian Jackson Braun
E. Leslie Charteris

8. What breed of cat was featured as the first stuffed animal from Ty, the company responsible for the Beanie Babies craze?
A. Blue Point
B. Assamese
C. Himalayan
D. Tabby
E. Manx

Answers to Quiz #114 — The Cat's Meow

1. **(A) "Mona Bone Jakon".** "Mona Bone Jakon" was released in 1970 but was overshadowed by the more successful "Tea for the Tillerman" released in the same year. Peter Gabriel played flute on the album. Stevens became a Muslim in 1979, adopting the name Yusef Islam, and retired from music.

2. **(E) Robert Loggia.** Thomas Hewitt Edward Cat was a former cat burglar who hired himself out as a bodyguard, working out of his friend Pepe's café, Casa del Gato (House of the Cat).

3. **(E) Lee Marvin.** The title character, a prim schoolmarm who becomes a gunfighter, was played by Jane Fonda. When Fonda's father is gunned down by the evil Tim Strawn, she hires Strawn's twin brother, Kid Sheleen, as her champion. Sheleen, however, is so perpetually inebriated he can't hit the broad side of a barn. Lee Marvin won a Best Actor Oscar for his work in "Cat Ballou."

4. **(B) Heathcliff.** George Gately's "Heathcliff" debuted in 1973. Heathcliff's owners include Iggy, Marcy, and Grandpa and Grandma. His nemesis is Spike the bulldog, and his girlfriend is the Persian cat, Sonja.

5. **(A) Siamese.** Hayes is credited with introducing the Siamese cat to the U.S. Amy Carter's Siamese cat was named Misty Malarky Ying Yang. Abraham Lincoln is believed to have owned the first White House cat. Others have included Tom Quartz (Teddy Roosevelt), Tiger (Coolidge), Tom Kitten (Kennedy), and Socks (Clinton).

6. **(C) Harry Brecheen.** Brecheen, a southpaw, used his screwball to shut out the Boston Red Sox in Game 1 of the 1946 World Series, was the winning pitcher in Game 6, and pitched relief to win Game 7. He was the first pitcher in 26 years to win three games in a single Series, and his .083 career Series ERA is still the best in history. Brecheen served as the pitching coach for the Baltimore Orioles for 14 years after retiring from play.

7. **(D) Lilian Jackson Braun.** Braun started the "Cat" mystery series with "The Cat Who Could Read Backwards" in 1966. The books feature amateur sleuth Jim Qwilleran with his psychic Siamese cats, Koko and Yum Yum. After two more books, she abandoned her literary career to continue her work as an editor for the "Detroit Free Press." In 1986, she returned to writing the series with "The Cat Who Saw Red," earning an Edgar Award nomination from the Mystery Writers of America. She has written more than 20 "Cat" novels and stories.

8. **(C) Himalayan.** Ty Warner left the Dakin toy company to sell a line of understuffed floppy cats. The cats eventually evolved into the smaller stuffed critters introduced as Beanie Babies in 1993. The Ty company employs an unusual marketing strategy with minimal advertising, no licensing deals, and no sales through national chain stores. Relying on small specialty shops, Ty sells a variety of animal characters, but no store can purchase more than 36 of each character per month.

Quiz #115 — A Honey of a Quiz

1. What mellow-voiced singer had a monster hit record in 1968 with the ballad "Honey"?
A. Joe Jackson
B. Tom Jones
C. Bobby Goldsboro
D. Glen Campbell
E. Roger Miller

2. Former Led Zeppelin members Robert Plant and Jimmy Page were members of what 1980s supergroup along with Jeff Beck and Nile Rodgers?
A. A Taste of Honey
B. The Honeycombs
C. Honeysuckle Rose
D. The Honeydrippers
E. Honeymoon Suite

3. Harold L. Davis's 1935 novel, "Honey in the Horn," was a realistic tale of frontier life in what U.S. state?
A. Nebraska
B. Arkansas
C. Kansas
D. Idaho
E. Oregon

4. Which U.S. state was the largest producer of honey in 1996?
A. Florida
B. Texas
C. California
D. Minnesota
E. Kansas

5. What was the name of the pet ocelot owned by the beautiful TV detective "Honey West"?
A. Bruce
B. Elvis
C. Clint
D. Morrison
E. Midnight

6. Honey Ryder was the Bond girl in which James Bond movie?
A. "Goldeneye"
B. "Dr. No"
C. "Goldfinger"
D. "Diamonds Are Forever"
E. "You Only Live Twice"

7. Which U.S. President had a presidential yacht called the "Honey Fitz"?
A. Franklin D. Roosevelt
B. Harry Truman
C. John Kennedy
D. George Bush
E. Ronald Reagan

8. "Hee Haw Honeys" was a sitcom spin-off of the syndicated cornball country comedy show "Hee Haw." Which of the following actors was not a cast member on both shows?
A. Misty Rowe
B. Lulu Roman
C. Gailard Sartain
D. Kenny Price
E. Kathie Lee Gifford

Answers to Quiz #115 — **A Honey of a Quiz**

1. **(C) Bobby Goldsboro.** "Honey" spent five weeks at #1 on the Billboard pop charts and three weeks at #1 on the Billboard country singles charts. Although Bobby Goldsboro wrote many of his other hits, "Honey" was a composition from songwriter Bobby Russell. Russell also wrote another #1 song, "The Night the Lights Went Out in Georgia," recorded by his then-wife, Carol Lawrence.

2. **(D) The Honeydrippers.** The Honeydrippers had only one top 10 hit, "Sea of Love," in 1984.

3. **(E) Oregon.** Davis, an Oregon native, won the Pulitzer Prize for fiction and the $7,500 Harper Prize in 1935 for his novel. He is also the author of the frontier novels "Beulah Land" and "Winds of Morning."

4. **(C) California.** In 1996, California produced 27 million pounds of honey vs. 25 million pounds produced in the #2 state, Florida.

5. **(A) Bruce.** Anne Francis starred as the alluring "Honey West," a slinky but deadly detective who often wore black turtlenecks and tooled around town in her sports car. "Honey West," a spin-off of "Burke's Law," aired on ABC in the 1965-66 season.

6. **(B) "Dr. No".** Honey Ryder, played by Ursula Andress, was the original Bond girl in the 1962 Sean Connery movie, "Dr. No." Andress made an unforgettable entrance, emerging from the sea clad in a dazzling white bikini.

7. **(C) John Kennedy.** The "Honey Fitz" was named after John "Honey Fitz" Fitzgerald, John F. Kennedy's grandfather. Fitzgerald was the first Irish-American mayor of Boston.

8. **(E) Kathie Lee Gifford.** Gifford, then billed as Kathie Lee Johnson, played Kathie Honey. Kathie was the daughter of Kenny and Lulu Honey, owners of Honey's Club, where Kathie worked as a waitress. Gifford did not appear on "Hee Haw," but did a stint as the regular vocalist, singing lots of "la la la," on the syndicated TV game show "Name That Tune."

Quiz #116 — **Nicknames**

1. What Oscar-winning actress was nicknamed "The Viennese Teardrop"?
A. Hedy Lamarr
B. Luise Rainer
C. Rita Hayworth
D. Ingrid Bergman
E. Sally Field

2. What star of the silent screen was nicknamed "The Magnificent Wildcat"?
A. Clara Bow
B. Mary Pickford
C. Pola Negri
D. Theda Bara
E. Pearl White

3. What Scottish writer, born in the 18th century, was known as the "Ettrick Shepherd"?
A. James Hogg
B. Robert Burns
C. William Wallace
D. Sir Walter Scott
E. Robert the Bruce

4. What British musical star of stage and screen was nicknamed "The Dancing Divinity"?
A. Julie Andrews
B. Anna Neagle
C. Deanna Durbin
D. Judy Garland
E. Jessie Matthews

5. What nickname was shared by bluesman John Estes, country singer Thomas Paulsley LaBeef, and basketball player Eric Floyd?
A. Happy
B. Grumpy
C. Doc
D. Sleepy
E. Dopey

6. What baseball slugger was nicknamed "The Million Dollar Baby from the 5 & 10 Cent Store"?
A. Carl Yastrzemski
B. Hack Wilson
C. Lou Gehrig
D. Roger Maris
E. Home Run Baker

7. What aircraft was nicknamed "The Lead Sled" and "The Squash Bomber"?
A. Cessna T-37
B. Lockheed U-2
C. Republic F-105
D. Lockheed SR-71
E. Convair TF-102

8. What American city has been nicknamed "The Athens of America" and "The Cradle of Liberty"?
A. Philadelphia
B. Atlanta
C. Washington, D.C.
D. Boston
E. Albany, NY

Answers to Quiz #116 — **Nicknames**

1. **(B) Luise Rainer.** Luise Rainer is the only actress to win back-to-back Academy Awards for Best Actress as Anna Held in "The Great Ziegfeld" (1936) and as O-Lan in "The Good Earth" (1937).

2. **(C) Pola Negri.** Pola Negri was one of the first European stars to hit it big with the American movie-going public. Her German films were a sensation, and American studios clamored to bring her to America. Her American films, however, always seemed to be lacking. As the talkie came in, Hollywood discovered that Negri had a nice singing voice but spoke with a heavy accent. She returned to Germany in the 1930s, as a favorite of Hitler, but returned to America after war broke out, and retired to live in Texas.

3. **(A) James Hogg.** Hogg came by the nickname honestly. He was born in Ettrick, Scotland and inherited the occupation of shepherd from his family. Hogg is remembered for his poetry celebrating the Celtic folklore tradition. Although he had little formal education, Hogg was encouraged to write by his friend Sir Walter Scott. Hogg's greatest work was "The Queen's Wake" published in 1813.

4. **(E) Jessie Matthews.** Jessie Matthews was a popular star of light musicals and musical comedy in Great Britain in the 1930s. Ten of her 17 movies were musicals. She was also known as the voice of Mrs. Dale in the long-running radio show "Mrs. Dale's Diary."

5. **(D) Sleepy.** Sleepy John Estes was a Tennessee-based singer and guitarist well-entrenched in the country blues tradition. Estes got his nickname because of his propensity to take naps. He wrote songs that commented on social conditions, especially those of the 1930s. "Someday, Baby" (also known as "Worried Life Blues"), his most noted release, eventually became one of Estes's trademark numbers and a blues standard. Estes died in 1977. Sleepy La Beef's music is hard to pigeonhole, as he is comfortable with honky-tonk, blues, and rockabilly. With a career extending over the past 40 years, La Beef has become known as a human jukebox with a working knowledge of over 6,000 songs. La Beef's latest album, released in 1996, is "I'll Never Lay My Guitar Down." Eric "Sleepy" Floyd played an NBA record 64 minutes in one game for the Golden State Warriors on February 1, 1987.

6. **(B) Hack Wilson.** Lewis Robert "Hack" Wilson played only 12 seasons (1923-35), but won 4 home run crowns, and led the league twice in RBIs and walks. In 1930, he hit 56 home runs, a National League record that stood until 1998. He hit a total of 244 home runs, and maintained a career batting average of .307.

7. **(C) Republic F-105.** The fighter-bomber was known as the Thunderchief, but also bore the undignified nicknames of "Thud," "Ultra Hog," and "Iron Butterfly". The Thunderchief was the heaviest U.S. single-engine, single-seat fighter ever. The nickname "Squash Bomber" came about because the pilot always had the option to shut down his engine and squash his target. The Thunderchief flew over 100,000 missions in Vietnam.

8. **(D) Boston.** Boston is also nicknamed "Bean Town," "The City of Kind Hearts" (by Helen Keller and her teacher, Anne Sullivan), "The Hub of the Universe," and "The Literary Emporium."

Quiz #117 — Silly Songs

1. "Weird Al" Yankovic has had two parody songs on the Billboard top 40 charts. The most recent was "Smells Like Nirvana" in 1992, a parody of Nirvana's "Smells Like Teen Spirit." What was the other hit for Yankovic?
A. "Another One Rides the Bus"
B. "Eat It"
C. "I Think I'm a Clone Now"
D. "Like a Surgeon"
E. "Fat"

2. What 1966 novelty song by "Napoleon XIV" has the same song on the "B" side of the single but recorded backwards?
A. "Get Down"
B. "I'm in Love with My Little Red Tricycle"
C. "Disco Duck"
D. "They're Coming to Take Me Away, Ha-Ha"
E. "Pac-Man Fever"

3. According to a silly song sung by Shirley Temple in the movie "Curly Top," what did she find "in her soup"?
A. Pickle Relish
B. Animal Crackers
C. Poison Ivy
D. Sweat Socks
E. Alligator Pears

4. What vegetable "That Ate Chicago" commented, "Neat, sweet just like sugar"?
A. Eggplant
B. Kumquat
C. Chicory
D. Rhubarb
E. Carrot

5. According to the Herman Hermits tune, "I'm Henry the VIII, I Am," the girl would marry only men named Henry, and not men with what other names?
A. Joe or Paul
B. Allen or Zacariah
C. Richard or Peter
D. Jimmy or Barry
E. Willy or Sam

6. Homer and Jethro parodied "The Battle of New Orleans" into a song that takes place at a summer camp called "The Battle of" what?
A. Asuza
B. Chickamauga
C. Camp Cherokee
D. Cincinnati
E. Kookamonga

7. "Big Bopper's Wedding" was the flip side of what 1958 hit single that was essentially one long phone call from the singer's girlfriend?
A. "Chantilly Lace"
B. "Last Kiss"
C. "Yummy, Yummy, Yummy"
D. "Billy, Don't Be a Hero"
E. "La Bamba"

8. What song introduced in 1923 by songwriters Frank Silver and Irving Cohn was based on a real-life conversation with a Greek grocer?
A. "Mairzy Doats"
B. "If You Knew Susie"
C. "Yes! We Have No Bananas"
D. "I Wish I Could Shimmy Like My Sister Kate"
E. "Who Threw the Overalls in Mrs. Murphy's Chowder?"

Answers to Quiz #117 — **Silly Songs**

1. (B) **"Eat It"**. Yankovic's musical career began by sending homemade recordings, made in his bathroom on the accordion, to wacky radio personality Dr. Demento. Yankovic's first commercial recording, "My Bologna" on Capitol Records, came about with the help of The Knack, the band whose "My Sharona" was parodied. Yankovic's success has been boosted by Michael Jackson, who allowed Yankovic to record parodies of "Beat It" ("Eat It") and "Bad" ("Fat").

2. (D) **"They're Coming to Take Me Away, Ha-Ha"**. "Napoleon XIV" was, in fact, songwriter Jerry Samuels. "They're Coming to Take Me Away, Ha-Ha" is about a man who goes insane when his beloved dog leaves him. The song was originally released in 1966 and reached #3 on the Billboard charts, but disappeared after only five weeks when radio stations refused to play the song due to its controversial subject matter. The song resurfaced as a single in 1973, reaching #87 on the charts. The song was also recorded later as a disco song by Tiny Tim.

3. (B) **Animal Crackers.** "Animal Crackers in My Soup" was written by Irving Caesar, Ted Koehler, and Ray Henderson. Caesar also wrote Al Jolson's biggest hit, "Swanee," and "Tea for Two" for the musical "No, No Nanette."

4. (A) **Eggplant.** "The Eggplant That Ate Chicago" was a minor hit in 1966 for the band Dr. West's Medicine Show and Junk Band. "Dr. West" had a bigger hit under his real name, Norman Greenbaum, with "Spirit in the Sky" in 1970. Another Dr. Demento favorite in the same vein was "The Cockroach That Ate Cincinnati" by Rose and the Arrangement.

5. (E) **Willy or Sam.** "I'm Henry the VIII, I Am" was written in 1911 and popularized by music hall comedian Harry Champion. The Hermits recorded the song after they discovered Americans liked a sound different from the Beatles, especially the old music hall songs. The Hermits had the music for "Henry" but not the words, which they couldn't fully remember. Hence, lead singer Peter Noone proclaims, "Second verse, same as the first." "Henry" was a #1 song in the U.S. in 1965, but was considered too ethnic for release as a single in Great Britain.

6. (E) **Kookamonga.** The country comedy due of Henry "Homer" Haynes and Kenneth "Jethro" Burns was country's foremost comedy duo from the 1940s until Homer's death in 1971. Jethro went on to work with folk singer Steve Goodman.

7. (A) **"Chantilly Lace"**. Jape "J.P." Richardson was a Texas disc jockey who preferred to be known as "Big Bopper." He wrote the Johnny Preston hit "Running Bear," and hit the top 10 on his own in 1958 with "Chantilly Lace." Richardson would attain rock 'n' roll immortality when he died in the same 1959 plane crash that claimed the lives of Buddy Holly and Ritchie Valens.

8. (C) **"Yes! We Have No Bananas"**. Mirror-image songs enjoyed popularity in 1923, with such titles as "I Won't Say I Will, But I Won't Say I Won't," "Mamma Loves Papa — Papa Loves Mamma," and "I Cried for You, Now It's Your Turn to Cry Over Me."

Quiz #118 — **The Wizard of Oz**

1. Gene Hackman and Al Pacino starred together in what 1973 film?
A. "Scarecrow"
B. "The Wind and the Lion"
C. "Tin Men"
D. "Ozzie and Phil"
E. "Dr. Syn, Alias the Scarecrow"

2. The International Film Company was a cover business for a covert government spy agency in what TV series?
A. "Kansas City Confidential"
B. "Hart to Hart"
C. "The Wizard"
D. "Pinky and the Brain"
E. "Scarecrow and Mrs. King"

3. Legendary shortstop Ozzie Smith, nicknamed "The Wizard of Oz," replaced what equally legendary sportscaster as the host of the popular syndicated series, "This Week in Baseball"?
A. Vin Scully
B. Marv Albert
C. Mel Allen
D. Bob Costas
E. Curt Gowdy

4. "Which Way You Goin' Billy" was a #2 hit in 1970 for what group?
A. Toto
B. Kansas
C. The Poppy Family
D. Royal Lionsmen
E. The Lollipop Guild

5. Which franchise in the Canadian Football League is nicknamed the Lions?
A. Calgary
B. Winnipeg
C. Saskatchewan
D. Memphis
E. British Columbia

6. Immortal jazz pianist Willie Smith went by what nickname?
A. The Scarecrow
B. The Lion
C. The Wiz
D. The Tornado
E. Woody

7. Don DeFore, Lyle Talbot, Mary Jane Croft, Frank Cady, and June Blair were all regulars at one time or another on what TV series?
A. "The Wizard"
B. "Hart to Hart"
C. "Wizard of Odds"
D. "The Adventures of Ozzie and Harriet"
E. "Oswald the Rabbit"

8. What British invasion band beat the Beatles to #1 with a hit song entitled "Telstar"?
A. Toto
B. The Scarecrows
C. Tin-Tin
D. White Lion
E. The Tornadoes

1. **(A) "Scarecrow".** "Scarecrow," a film about two hapless drifters trying to make good as partners, is the only film thus far to feature a pairing of veteran actors Hackman and Pacino. Both won Oscars in 1992 — Pacino for Best Actor in "Scent of a Woman" and Hackman for Best Supporting Actor in "Unforgiven." Hackman had previously won Best Actor as Popeye Doyle in "The French Connection."

2. **(E) "Scarecrow and Mrs. King".** Scarecrow was the code name of agent Lee Stetson portrayed by Bruce Boxleitner. Mrs. Amanda King (Kate Jackson) was recruited into the agency because she really was a mild-mannered housewife. Mrs. King had to keep her involvement as an "unofficial" spy a secret from her children, Philip and Jamie, and her mother, Dotty West, played by veteran actress Beverly Garland.

3. **(C) Mel Allen.** Allen and his signature exclamation "How 'bout that!" were put to rest with his passing in 1996, ending a 58-year career in broadcasting that included 20 World Series and 24 All-Star Games behind the mike. His career was composed mostly of radio broadcasts and the occasional voiceover as in the case of the long-running "This Week in Baseball." He was known as the "Voice of the Yankees."

4. **(C) The Poppy Family.** The core of the Canadian Poppy Family was Terry Jacks and his wife Susan. Terry went on to solo success with an even bigger hit with a remake of an old Kingston Trio song, "Seasons in the Sun," which stayed at #1 for three weeks in 1974.

5. **(E) British Columbia.** After joining the league as the first expansion club, the British Columbia Lions won their first Grey Cup as CFL champions in 1964 and then competed for over 20 years until they won their next in 1985. In 1995, the B.C. Lions, Winnipeg Blue Bombers, Saskatchewan Roughriders, and the other Canadian teams were joined by the Memphis Mad Dogs, the San Antonio Texans, the Shreveport Pirates, and the Birmingham Barracudas. Even though the Grey Cup was won by the two-year U.S. franchise Baltimore Stallions, alas the southern experiment was a bust, and none of these teams competed in the league again.

6. **(B) The Lion.** An aficionado of stride piano, Willie "the Lion" Smith began as a ragtime performer, but expanded his repertoire to include jazz, blues, and even the roots of rock and roll. He is credited as the piano player on what is considered the first blues record ever recorded, "Crazy Blues" by Mamie Smith in 1920. He played with Eubie Blake, Fats Waller, and Luckey Roberts. He was named by Duke Ellington and Artie Shaw as a major influence and one of their best teachers.

7. **(D) "The Adventures of Ozzie and Harriet".** DeFore played Ozzie's prickly neighbor, Thorny Thornberry. Lyle Talbot was Joe Randolph and Mary Jane Croft was his wife, Clara. Frank Cady, perhaps better known on TV as Sam Drucker on "Petticoat Junction," played Doc Williams. June Blair was featured in later seasons as David's wife, June (the role she also played in real life). The original TV series ran for fifteen years from 1952-1966 on ABC.

8. **(E) The Tornadoes.** The Tornadoes were an instrumental band taking much of their inspiration from the electric string-rock played in the States by such guitar wizards as Dick Dale, Duane Eddy, and Bob Bogle. "Telstar," named for the satellite, was a monster hit that stayed at #1 for three weeks in 1962, nearly two full years before the Beatles had a #1 hit in the United States.

Quiz #119 — **Ships in the Night**

1. What was the name of the ship that carried Phileas Fogg to England in Jules Verne's "Around the World in 80 Days"?
A. Harpoon
B. Henrietta
C. Harpsichord
D. Hispanola
E. Half Moon

2. What ship, launched in 1934, was the first British vessel over 1000 feet long?
A. Valiant
B. Malaya
C. Nelson
D. Princess Royal
E. Queen Mary

3. The USS Constitution is the oldest ship in U.S. government service. What U.S. Coast Guard training vessel is the second oldest?
A. Eagle
B. Tiger
C. Juniper
D. Enterprise
E. Botany Bay

4. What was the destination of the ships Susan Constant, Godspeed, and Discovery?
A. Bermuda
B. India
C. Greenland
D. Jamestown
E. Rio de Janeiro

5. What was the name of the cargo ship on which "Mister Roberts" served?
A. USS Compass Rose
B. USS Sea Tiger
C. USS Macbeth
D. USS Nevada
E. USS Reluctant

6. Sir Francis Chichester sailed around the world in 1966-67 in what 53-foot Bermuda yacht named after an insect?
A. Gypsy Moth
B. Grasshopper
C. Dragonfly
D. Water Beetle
E. Skimmer

7. Field Marshal Lord Kitchener was traveling to Russia aboard what ship when he died in 1916?
A. HMS Bounty
B. HMS Doodlebug
C. HMS Hampshire
D. HMS Nelson
E. HMS Exmoor

8. Which warship saw action as a bombardment vessel in both the Korean War and the Persian Gulf War?
A. USS California
B. USS West Virginia
C. USS Idaho
D. USS Wisconsin
E. USS Sullivan

Answers to Quiz #119 — **Ships in the Night**

1. **(B) Henrietta.** Verne posed for the illustration of Professor Aronnax in the original editions of "Around the World in 80 Days" in 1873. It was Verne's most commercially successful novel, selling more than 500,000 copies in the first year alone.

2. **(E) Queen Mary.** The Queen Mary reigned for more than a decade as the world's fastest ship. She carried Winston Churchill while he signed the Normandy invasion plans, and inspired Hitler to offer his highest bounty to the German U-boat captain who could sink her. She still holds the world's record for the most passengers carried — 16,800 when she served as a troop carrier during World War II. Since 1967, the Queen Mary has been docked in Long Beach, CA as a floating hotel.

3. **(A) Eagle.** The Eagle is the former German naval training vessel Horst Wessel, acquired by the U.S. in 1946 as part of WWII reparations. Three other vessels of this design were built by Germany, and all three remain in service in Portugal, Romania, and Russia.

4. **(D) Jamestown.** The settlers of Jamestown arrived in America on these ships in 1607. Replicas of the three ships are exhibited there.

5. **(E) USS Reluctant.** The Reluctant carried necessities such as dungarees, toothpaste, and toilet paper. According to Mr. Roberts, it made regular runs from Tedium to Apathy and back, an occasional run to Monotony, and once in a while to Ennui. The ship's crew referred to the ship as "the Bucket."

6. **(A) Gypsy Moth.** The 65-year-old Chichester completed his solo circumnavigation on May 28, 1967 by returning to the port of Plymouth 226 days after he left. His only port-of-call on the entire trip was Sydney, Australia. Chichester was knighted in 1967 by Queen Elizabeth II with the same sword used to knight Sir Francis Drake — England's first sailor to travel around the world.

7. **(C) HMS Hampshire.** Kitchener was Britain's most distinguished WWI soldier, appointed as War Minister by the Asquith government in August 1914. He was a rash strategist, sometimes approving missions without thought to organization or adequate reinforcement. Kitchener's official visit to Tsar Nicholas II in 1916 was a relief to the war cabinet, but the trip ended tragically when the HMS Hampshire struck a mine on June 5, 1916 and sank off the Orkney Islands.

8. **(D) USS Wisconsin.** The USS Wisconsin also served during WWII, but was decommissioned following service in the Korean War. The ship was reactivated in 1988 during the Reagan-Lehman naval buildup of the1980s. The USS Missouri and the USS Wisconsin saw action in the Persian Gulf War in 1991, but were immediately mothballed again afterward. The USS Wisconsin fired 324 16-inch rounds at shore targets during Operation Desert Storm.

Quiz #120 — **Railroad Ties**

1. "Engine Engine #9" and "King of the Road" were train-inspired songs that hit the Billboard top 10 in 1965 for what recording artist?
A. Roger Miller
B. Willie Nelson
C. Boxcar Willie
D. Johnny Cash
E. Johnnie Ray

2. In the movie "Throw Momma from the Train," Danny DeVito tried to convince what actor to participate in a scheme to kill DeVito's mother?
A. Peter Sellers
B. Rob Reiner
C. Ron Howard
D. Paul Reiser
E. Billy Crystal

3. "Locomotive Breath" was an FM favorite for what unique and long-lived rock band?
A. Savoy Brown
B. Mott the Hoople
C. Traffic
D. Jethro Tull
E. Jefferson Starship

4. What was the name of the engine of the CF&W Railroad that ran through Hooterville to the Shady Rest Hotel on TV's "Petticoat Junction"?
A. Mother Hubbard
B. Stemwinder
C. Cannonball
D. The Iron Horse
E. The Lightning Express

5. Who pitched the most shutout games in his major league career?
A. Nolan "The Tex Express" Ryan
B. Walter "Big Train" Johnson
C. Christy "Old 86" Mathewson
D. "Railroad" Rube Waddell
E. Grover "Junction" Alexander

6. Whose picture appeared on the 1950 U.S. postage stamp that honored railroad engineers?
A. Walt Disney
B. Casey Jones
C. Smiley Burnette
D. George Pullman
E. George Westinghouse

7. Who is the author of the beloved "Thomas the Tank Engine" series?
A. G.K. Chesterton
B. Rev. W. Audry
C. Hamlin Garland
D. August Derleth
E. Watty Piper

8. What NFL defensive back intercepted a record 14 passes in a season?
A. Dick "Locomotive" Lynch
B. Emlen "The Engine" Tunnell
C. Dick "Night Train" Lane
D. Lionel "Little Train" James
E. Jack "The Track" Christensen

Answers To Quiz #120 — **Railroad Ties**

1. **(A) Roger Miller.** Roger Miller won 11 Grammies in 1965 and 1966, and recorded such top 40 hits as "Dang Me," "Chug-a-Lug," "Do Wacka Do," "England Swings," and "You Can't Roller Skate in a Buffalo Herd." By 1985, he had entered a new stage in his musical career as the composer of the Broadway musical "Big River," based on the writings of Mark Twain.

2. **(E) Billy Crystal.** The movie is essentially a comedic remake of Alfred Hitchcock's "Strangers on a Train" with DeVito as the mama's boy who offers to exchange murders with his writing professor, Billy Crystal. The unforgettable Anne Ramsey had the role of "Momma."

3. **(D) Jethro Tull.** "Locomotive Breath" was a cut on Jethro Tull's classic 1971 album "Aqualung." Jethro Tull, led by one of the only flute-playing rock and rollers, Ian Anderson, has been recording in one form or another since 1968. The band took its name from the 18th-century agronomy pioneer who invented a seed drill.

4. **(C) Cannonball.** The Cannonball was an 1890s steam engine, coal car, and coach car that traveled from Hooterville to Pixley and Crabtree Corners. CF&W Railroad Vice President Homer Bedloe (played by Charles Lane) made occasional appearances as the nemesis of Cannonball lovers, threatening to turn the train into scrap iron.

5. **(B) Walter "Big Train" Johnson.** Walter Johnson recorded 110 shutouts. No other pitcher has ever even come close, before him or after him. Grover Alexander mustered up 90 shutouts and Christy Mathewson managed 80. Nolan Ryan retired with 61.

6. **(B) Casey Jones.** Folk hero Casey Jones was killed in a 1900 train wreck when the Cannonball Express he was running crashed into two freight trains in Vaughn, Mississippi. Jones was immortalized in song in 1909 by Wallace Saunders, T. Laurence Siebert, and Eddie Newton.

7. **(B) Rev. W. Audry.** Audry began the stories back in the late 1940s and had a chance to see their popularity renewed in the 1980s when Thomas and his friends Edward, Gordon, James, Percy, and Henry were featured on the public television series, "Shining Time Station." Ringo Starr and George Carlin have served as narrators for the model-action animated stories in the guise of the tiny Mr. Conductor who is visible only to children.

8. **(C) Dick "Night Train" Lane.** Dick Lane achieved this astounding feat in his rookie year for the Los Angeles Rams in 1952 when NFL teams played only 12 games per season. Lane also played as a receiver during his career, once catching a 98-yard touchdown pass.

Quiz #121 — World Geography

1. In what country do the Tigris and Euphrates rivers join?
A. Iraq
B. Syria
C. Saudi Arabia
D. Iran
E. Turkey

2. Vinson Massif, at just over 16,000 feet tall, is the highest mountain on what continent?
A. South America
B. Asia
C. Australia
D. North America
E. Antarctica

3. What is the northernmost city in Australia?
A. Darwin
B. Perth
C. Brisbane
D. Auckland
E. Sydney

4. What is the largest island found in the Indian Ocean?
A. Grande Comore
B. Hawaii
C. Lipari
D. Madagascar
E. Pentecost

5. The Danube River runs along the northern border of Bulgaria, separating Bulgaria from what neighboring country?
A. Bosnia and Herzegovina
B. Slovakia
C. Germany
D. Romania
E. Greece

6. The Cheviot Hills separate what two countries?
A. Haiti and the Dominican Republic
B. North Korea and South Korea
C. Scotland and England
D. France and Spain
E. United States and Mexico

7. Beginning at the confluence of the Ping and Nan rivers, the Chao Phraya River is the principal river running through what Asian nation?
A. Cambodia
B. Thailand
C. Afghanistan
D. Burma
E. Ceylon

8. The name of what world capital means "elephant trunk" in Arabic?
A. Dar es Salaam
B. Cairo
C. Madrid
D. Khartoum
E. Dakar

1. **(A) Iraq.** The Tigris flows for 881 miles and the Euphrates 753 miles before they meet at Qarmat 'Ali, near Basra, to form the Shatt-al-Arab.

2. **(E) Antarctica.** Vinson Massif is part of the Ellsworth Mountains of western Antarctica. It was discovered in 1935 by American explorer Lincoln Ellsworth.

3. **(A) Darwin.** Port Darwin, a deep inlet of the Timor Sea, was discovered in 1839 by John Stokes, a surveyor aboard the HMS Beagle. He named the site after the Beagle's famous passenger, naturalist Charles Darwin. The city of Darwin was not established until 1869 but was known as Palmerston until renamed in 1911.

4. **(D) Madagascar.** Madagascar, located off the southeast coast of Africa, is the world's fourth-largest island. The island extends 1570 kilometers from north to south and is about 570 kilometers wide at its widest east-west extent.

5. **(D) Romania.** Bulgaria is bordered to the east by the Black Sea, to the south by Greece and Turkey, and to the west by Serbia and Macedonia.

6. **(C) Scotland and England.** There is also a neighborhood area in Los Angeles known as Cheviot Hills.

7. **(B) Thailand.** The Chao Phraya flows for 225 miles to empty into the Gulf of Thailand just past the capital of Bangkok at the Samut Prakan. From its headwaters to the sea, the river falls less than 80 feet.

8. **(D) Khartoum.** Khartoum is the capital of Sudan, and is located just south of the confluence of the Blue and White Nile rivers. Dar es Salaam, the capital of Tanzania, means "house of peace" in Arabic.

Quiz #122 — **Ghost of a Chance**

1. Who played the cursed and cowardly Simon de Canterville in the 1944 movie version of "The Canterville Ghost"?
A. Laurence Olivier
B. Alec Guinness
C. Edward Everett Horton
D. Charles Laughton
E. Orson Welles

2. What 1950s hit song was revived as the love theme for the Patrick Swayze-Demi Moore movie romance "Ghost"?
A. "In the Still of the Night"
B. "Canadian Sunset"
C. "Moonglow"
D. "By the Light of the Silvery Moon"
E. "Unchained Melody"

3. What legend of football was nicknamed "The Galloping Ghost"?
A. Jim Thorpe
B. O.J. Simpson
C. George Blanda
D. Don Hutson
E. Red Grange

4. Who played the spooked reporter who spends a night in a haunted house in the comedy "The Ghost and Mr. Chicken"?
A. Dick Van Dyke
B. Strother Martin
C. Don Knotts
D. George Kennedy
E. William Holden

5. What was the name of the ghost who tormented Shakespeare's "Macbeth"?
A. Banquo
B. Duncan
C. Hamlet
D. Lady Macbeth
E. Rosencrantz

6. Alice Ghostley played the mother of what TV superhero?
A. Captain Nice
B. The Flash
C. Superman
D. Batman
E. Mr. Terrific

7. What was the object of purity used by the Ghostbusters to battle the villainous Vigo the Carpathian in "Ghostbusters II"?
A. Baby bottle
B. Statue of Liberty
C. Space shuttle Enterprise
D. Toilet brush
E. Bar of Ivory soap

8. "The Christmas Ghost" and "The Beech Tree" were children's books written by what Nobel-winning writer?
A. Upton Sinclair
B. Pearl S. Buck
C. F. Scott Fitzgerald
D. Ernest Hemingway
E. Sinclair Lewis

Answers to Quiz #122 — Ghost of a Chance

1. (D) **Charles Laughton.** In this film, Robert Young co-stars as an American WWII soldier who, along with Canterville's young heir (Margaret O'Brien), helps the ghost perform a heroic deed and lift the curse that has left him to wander the earth. The movie has been remade twice with John Gielgud and Patrick Stewart in the translucent title role.

2. (E) **"Unchained Melody".** "Unchained Melody" originally appeared as the theme for the 1955 movie "Unchained," which starred football player Elroy "Crazylegs" Hirsch. The song was a quadruple hit in 1955, hitting #1 for Les Baxter, #3 for Al Hibbler, #6 for Roy Hamilton and #29 for June Valli. The Righteous Brothers's version came out in 1963 and peaked at #4. When "Ghost" was released in 1990, the Righteous Brothers's version returned to the charts, peaking at #13.

3. (E) **Red Grange.** Harold "Red" Grange gained national fame while playing as a runningback for the University of Illinois. Between 1923 and 1925, he rushed for 3,637 yards and scored 31 times. He became the focus of a controversy when he elected to leave college to play professional football for the Chicago Bears. Some have credited that move with turning pro football into a popular spectator sport.

4. (C) **Don Knotts.** Knotts made the nervous twitch an art form. He has appeared as the neurotic "man on the street" on "The Tonight Show" with Steve Allen, the fidgety Ralph Furley on "Three's Company" and the triggerhappy Deputy Barney Fife on "The Andy Griffith Show." As Barney Fife, Knotts won five Emmy Awards for Best Supporting Actor in a Comedy Series between 1961 and 1967.

5. (A) **Banquo.** The entire Macbeth clan is wracked with guilt. Macbeth is tormented by the ghost of his friend, Banquo, who has been murdered by three assassins hired by Macbeth. Lady Macbeth is plagued by sleepwalking, trying to remove imaginary blood spots that will not come clean ("Out, damned spot! Out, I say!") after helping her husband to dispatch the king, Duncan.

6. (A) **Captain Nice.** William Daniels starred as a meek chemist whose potion grants him superpowers transforming him into "Captain Nice," a reluctant hero who fights crime only at the insistence of his pushy mother (Alice Ghostley). The TV series was created by Buck Henry.

7. (B) **Statue of Liberty.** The Statue of Liberty has several other important screen credits on her résumé, including appearances in "Judge Dredd," "Batman Forever," "Splash," "Working Girl," "Saboteur," "Remo Williams...The Adventure Begins," and her most dramatic appearance at the end of "Planet of the Apes."

8. (B) **Pearl S. Buck.** Pearl S. Buck became the third American to receive the Nobel Prize for literature in 1938. She is best remembered for her novels set in China, the country where she once served as a missionary. The first volume of her "House of Earth" trilogy, "The Good Earth," won a 1932 Pulitzer Prize. The trilogy concluded with "Sons" and "A House Divided." She also wrote "Dragon Seed," telling the story of China's struggle with Japan in the 1930s.

Quiz #123 — **Letters of the Alphabet**

1. What letter is entered into baseball scoring books to signify a strikeout?
A. E
B. K
C. S
D. T
E. X

2. What single letter is used in the International Code of Signals to indicate "I require medical assistance"?
A. H
B. L
C. M
D. W
E. X

3. What is the name of the omnipotent race represented to humans in the form of actor John de Lancie who has plagued "Star Trek" captains Picard, Sisko, and Janeway?
A. A
B. J
C. K
D. Q
E. T

4. What is the only Scrabble letter tile with a value unshared by other letter tiles in the game?
A. J
B. K
C. V
D. X
E. Y

5. In the movie "Men in Black," the alien immigration agents are identified by single-letter designations. What letter is assigned to the new agent played by Will Smith?
A. J
B. K
C. O
D. Q
E. Z

6. What alias was used by Robin Scott when he recorded the 1979 #1 hit song "Pop Muzik"?
A. M
B. O
C. Q
D. W
E. Z

7. What Algerian film was nominated for a Best Picture Oscar in 1969, and won a Best Foreign Film Oscar?
A. "B"
B. "C"
C. "D"
D. "O"
E. "Z"

8. How many chemical elements are represented on the periodic table by single-letter abbreviations?
A. 4
B. 9
C. 14
D. 18
E. 23

Answers to Quiz #123 — **Letters of the Alphabet**

1. **(B) K.** Historically, scorers have used single letters to keep baseball scoring simple. The letter S was already used for "sacrifice," so scorers used the last letter of "struck," K, for a strikeout. A normal K is entered if the batter goes down swinging, and a backward K is entered for a called third strike.

2. **(D) W.** The first International Code of Signals was drafted in 1855 by a committee set up by the British Board of Trade. It contained 70,000 signals using 18 flags. It was published in 1857 in two parts; the first contained universal and international signals and the second British signals only. The Code has been revised several times, most recently in 1965.

3. **(D) Q.** Q's first appearance was in the debut episode of "Star Trek: The Next Generation" titled "Encounter at Farpoint." The Q was named by Gene Roddenberry for British "Star Trek" fan Janet Quarton.

4. **(B) K.** The K tile is worth 5 points. Only the J and X, worth 8 points each, and the Q and Z, worth 10 points each, are more valuable.

5. **(A) J.** Tommy Lee Jones, Smith's senior partner, is known as K. Agents named J(ay) and K(ay) also appeared in the "The Private Eye" episode of "The Beverly Hillbillies." They were bank robbers posing as government agents, duping Jethro who wished to become a "double-naught spy."

6. **(A) M.** As Scott was putting the album "New York, London, Paris, Munich" together, he was looking for an alter ego. Working in Paris, he looked out the window and saw a giant "M" for the Paris Metro and decided it was deliberately vague enough to generate some interest. While "Pop Muzik" was M's only American hit, he charted three more times in Britain. He also recorded two albums with Japanese pop star Ryuichi Sakamoto.

7. **(E) "Z".** "Z" lost the Best Picture Oscar to "Midnight Cowboy." It is one of only six foreign pictures that have ever been nominated for a Best Picture Academy Award. The most recent foreign film with that honor was "Life Is Beautiful" in 1998. None have won.

8. **(C) 14.** Alphabetically, they are: B (Boron), C (Carbon), F (Fluorine), H (Hydrogen), I (Iodine), K (Potassium), N (Nitrogen), O (Oxygen), P (Phosphorus), S (Sulfur), U (Uranium) V (Vanadium), W (Tungsten), and Y (Yttrium).

1. What industrialist was worshipped in the future created by Aldous Huxley for his novel "Brave New World"?
A. Andrew Carnegie
B. Albert Speer
C. Cecil Rhodes
D. Henry Ford
E. George Westinghouse

2. In the movie "Running Brave," Robby Benson starred as what American runner who won a gold medal at the 1964 Summer Olympics?
A. Max Truex
B. Billy Mills
C. Frank Shorter
D. Dave Wottle
E. Bruce Jenner

3. According to the theme song of his TV series, what western hero was "brave, courageous, and bold"?
A. Wyatt Earp
B. Bat Masterson
C. Buffalo Bill
D. Matt Dillon
E. Billy the Kid

4. In the 1944 book "Brave Men," what writer described World War II as "a flat black depression without highlights, a revulsion of the mind and an exhaustion of the spirits"?
A. Charles Kuralt
B. Eric Sevareid
C. Edward R. Murrow
D. Ernie Pyle
E. David Wayne

5. What comic book hero was teamed up with others in the long-running DC Comics series "The Brave and the Bold"?
A. Spider-Man
B. Superman
C. Aquaman
D. Hawkman
E. Batman

6. After the Braves baseball team moved from Milwaukee to Atlanta, what team moved into Milwaukee to become the Milwaukee Brewers?
A. Houston Colt .45s
B. Seattle Pilots
C. Texas Rangers
D. Boston Braves
E. Pittsburgh Steagles

7. What was the first U.S. military decoration, instituted by George Washington during the American Revolution as a reward for bravery in action?
A. Washington Ribbon
B. Purple Heart
C. Victoria Cross
D. Organdy Peacock
E. George Cross

8. What was the nickname of the reformed hood played by Bart Braverman who was Dan Tanna's legman on the TV detective series "Vega$"?
A. Bowzer
B. Bozo
C. Beezer
D. Binzer
E. Beaker

Answers to Quiz #124 — Home of the Brave

1. (D) Henry Ford. The book takes place in the year 632 AF (After Ford). Introduced into the cold scientific "brave new world" of Huxley's novel is a "savage" who reads Shakespeare and believes in spirituality. The title of the book, which is highly ironic, comes from Shakespeare's "The Tempest."

2. (B) Billy Mills. Mills had finished second in the American trials, and was largely ignored at the Olympics in Tokyo until he won the 10,000 meters in a dramatic upset over world record holder Ronald Clarke. His winning time in Tokyo was 46 seconds faster than his previous personal best.

3. (A) Wyatt Earp. "The Life and Legend of Wyatt Earp" ran on ABC during 1955-61. The TV series opened with Earp (Hugh O'Brian) becoming the Marshall of Ellsworth, Kansas. During subsequent years, Earp moved to Dodge City and then Tombstone, Arizona. The six-year run of the series ended in Tombstone with a five-part story about the infamous "Gunfight at the OK Corral."

4. (D) Ernie Pyle. Ernie Pyle's sympathetic reports of common young men fighting in battle were immensely popular, appearing in syndication in 366 daily U.S. newspapers. The columns were collected into the books "Ernie Pyle in England," "Here Is Your War," "Brave Men," and "Last Chapter." Pyle won the Pulitzer Prize for distinguished reporting in 1944. Covering the war firsthand proved to be fatal to Pyle who was hit by a sniper's bullet in the South Pacific on April 18, 1945.

5. (E) Batman. "The Brave and the Bold" title started in 1955, but the first Batman team-up issue was #59 with Green Lantern. The series continued with Batman as the main character until issue #200, ending in July 1983. "The Brave and the Bold" #59 in mint condition can fetch $100 from comic book collectors.

6. (B) Seattle Pilots. The Pilots, an expansion team formed in 1969, were the first Major League Baseball team in Seattle, but remained there only one year before moving to Milwaukee. The Pilots were the focus of pitcher Jim Bouton's controversial baseball memoirs, "Ball Four." Just to complete the circle — Bouton ended his career after a short 1978 appearance with the Atlanta Braves.

7. (B) Purple Heart. The Purple Heart disappeared after the American Revolution ended, but was revived as an award on the 200th anniversary of Washington's birth, February 22, 1932. The Purple Heart is now awarded for those wounded or killed in the service of their country. Washington's portrait appears in relief on the medal.

8. (D) Binzer. Binzer's real name was Bobby Borso. Binzer was more enthusiastic about his job than competent. "Vega$" was a popular show setting the dashing Robert Urich, as detective Dan Tanna, in exotic locations around Las Vegas amidst beautiful women.

Quiz #125 — You Can Call Me Al

1. For which movie did Al Pacino win an Oscar for Best Actor?
A. "Dick Tracy"
B. "The Godfather, Part II"
C. "Scent of a Woman"
D. "Dog Day Afternoon"
E. "Scarface"

2. Baseball player Al Kaline, with 399 homers, is the career home run hitting leader for which Major League Baseball team?
A. Oakland A's
B. Detroit Tigers
C. Baltimore Orioles
D. Washington Senators
E. Philadelphia Phillies

3. What actor appeared with Paul Simon in the music video for Simon's hit "You Can Call Me Al"?
A. Dan Aykroyd
B. John Belushi
C. Chevy Chase
D. Bill Murray
E. Eddie Murphy

4. Al McGuire ended his basketball coaching career at what university by winning the 1977 NCAA championship?
A. UCLA
B. Northwestern
C. Georgetown
D. Marquette
E. Kansas

5. What Academy Award-winning actor was the Harvard college roommate of Vice President Al Gore?
A. Jack Lemmon
B. Denzel Washington
C. Tom Hanks
D. Nick Nolte
E. Tommy Lee Jones

6. On the science fiction TV series "Quantum Leap," Dr. Sam Beckett traveled through time changing history for the better. What former child star played his holographic companion, Al Calavicci?
A. Tommy Kirk
B. Jon Provost
C. Will Mumy
D. Roddy MacDowell
E. Dean Stockwell

7. What pop singer had top 10 albums titled "Year of the Cat" and "Time Passages"?
A. Al Stewart
B. Al Hirt
C. Al Jarreau
D. Al Kooper
E. Al Martino

8. Comedy writer Al Franken was a regular on "Saturday Night Live" partnered in a vaudevillian-style act with what other comic?
A. Tom Davis
B. Chevy Chase
C. Dick Ebersol
D. Michael O'Donoghue
E. Larry David

Answers to Quiz #125 — **You Can Call Me Al**

1. (C) "Scent of a Woman". Pacino's acting career started off with a bang when he won a Tony Award in 1969 playing an embittered drug addict in "Does a Tiger Wear a Necktie?" Pacino was nominated for Best Actor Oscars for "Serpico," "The Godfather, Part II," "Dog Day Afternoon," and "...And Justice for All," and for Best Supporting Actor Oscars for "The Godfather," "Dick Tracy," and "Glengarry Glen Ross."

2. (B) Detroit Tigers. Kaline spent his entire 22-year career playing outfield for the Tigers from 1953-1974.

3. (C) Chevy Chase. In the video, Chase lip-synchs with Simon's singing voice, while a silent Simon stands alongside him playing a variety of musical instruments.

4. (D) Marquette. McGuire's Marquette Warriors upset the North Carolina Tar Heels 67-59 to win McGuire's final game as a coach. The usually staid McGuire broke down and cried, later commenting, "We Irish have tear ducts."

5. (E) Tommy Lee Jones. Tommy Lee Jones made his film debut in 1970 in "Love Story" as the Harvard college roommate of Ryan O'Neal.

6. (E) Dean Stockwell. In the 1991 episode, "A Leap for Lisa," Dr. Beckett witnessed the arrest of a much younger Al Calavicci, bringing a change in history that resulted in Beckett and Al never meeting. Sam's new "observer" was Edward St. John, played by another former child star, the ubiquitous Roddy MacDowell.

7. (A) Al Stewart. The Scottish Stewart also had top 10 singles with the title tracks from both albums in 1977 and 1978. The song "Year of the Cat" was written about British comedian Tony Hancock.

8. (A) Tom Davis. Franken and Davis acquired the final apprentice positions as writers for the first season of "Saturday Night Live." Until that point they were so broke, they earned a living playing Santa Claus and Winnie-the-Pooh at Sears during the Christmas season.

Bonus Question #1001

Who saved herself from execution at the hands of the caliph Scahariar by weaving a tale that lasted one thousand and one nights?

A. Scheherazade
B. Pandora
C. Arachne
D. Circe
E. Ariadne

Answer to Bonus Question #1001

(A) Scheherazade. The caliph Scahariar trusted no woman, and killed each of his wives the day after their marriage to avoid any infidelity. Scheherazade married the caliph, and through her lengthy tale, earned the caliph's admiration, ending his campaign against murdering women.